One King, One Law,

Three Faiths

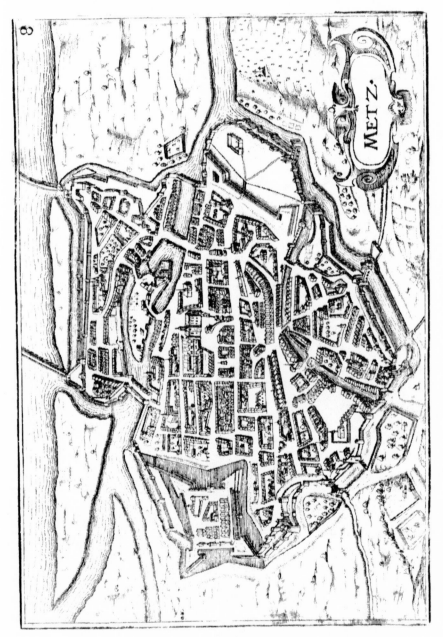

Metz in 1638, according to a map by Nicolas Tassin. The Beinecke Rare Book and Manuscript Library, Yale University.

One King, One Law,

Three Faiths

Religion and the Rise
of Absolutism
in Seventeenth-Century Metz

Patricia Behre Miskimin

Contributions to the Study of World History, Number 90

GREENWOOD PRESS
Westport, Connecticut • London

Library of Congress Cataloging-in-Publication Data

Miskimin, Patricia Behre, 1960–
    One king, one law, three faiths : religion and the rise of absolutism in
    seventeenth-century Metz / Patricia Behre Miskimin.
       p.   cm.—(Contributions to the study of world history, ISSN 0885-9159 ; no. 90)
    Includes bibliographical references and index.
    ISBN 0–313–30728–8 (alk. paper)
      1. Metz (France)—Politics and government—17th century. 2. Metz (France)—Church
history—17th century. 3. Church and state—France. 4. France—Church history—17th
century. 5. France—History—17th century. I. Title. II. Series.
DC801.M65M57   2002
944′.3853033—dc21   2001018025

British Library Cataloguing in Publication Data is available.

Library of Congress Catalog Card Number: 2001018025
ISBN: 0–313–30728–8
ISSN: 0885-9159

First published in 2002

Greenwood Press, 88 Post Road West, Westport, CT 06881
An imprint of Greenwood Publishing Group, Inc.
www.greenwood.com

Printed in the United States of America

Copyright Acknowledgments

The author and publisher gratefully acknowledge permission for use of the following material:

Extracts in Chapter 5, reprinted from *Religion*, Volume 23, No. 1, Patricia E. Behre, "Raphael Levy
. . .' A Criminal in the Mouths of the People," pp. 19–44, 1993, by permission of the publisher Aca-
demic Press London.

Extracts from "Jews and Christians in the Marketplace: The Politics of Kosher Meat in Metz," by P.
Behre Miskimin, *Journal of European Economic History*, Volume 26, Number 1, Spring 1997, pp.
147–56.

In memory of Harry,
of course

Contents

Acknowledgments

It is a keen pleasure to uphold justice, on however small a scale, by discharging one's obligations to friends and associates. Such pleasure is now mine in the opportunity to thank the many individuals and institutions who have aided me during the preparation of this monograph. First and foremost, I am indebted to both Fairfield University and Yale University for institutional support, access to resources, and ongoing help in the research and preparation of the manuscript. Financially, I received important early support from the French government through its Bourse Chateaubriand, and from the Yale Center for International and Area Studies, the Richter Summer Fellowship Program, the John F. Enders Fellowship and the Mrs. Giles Whiting Fellowship Program at Yale.

The Yale History Department provided funds, also in the early stages of the project and much appreciated help in the later stages through its Visiting Fellows Program.

My debts to individuals are perhaps even more pressing, and here I must begin by thanking Peter Gay for scholarly advice, criticism, patience, and friendship at every stage. His constant good will and generous gift of his attention has certainly improved the final product, leaving any remaining deficiencies to be owned solely by the author. David Underdown also assisted as "midwife" to the project and offered important early guidance and advice as to both style and content. My gratitude to both these scholars exceeds the capacity of the space allotted to me for this testimonial. Similarly, Paula Hyman and Jon Butler offered critical early advice, reading drafts of this work in its dissertation stage. Keith Luria and John Merriman provided important suggestions in that same period, as well as support and encouragement since.

In Israel Rivka Duker-Fishman at the Hebrew University in Jerusalem, helped to foster the initial questions that led to this work. The entire staff of the Archives Departementales in Metz deserve my sincerest expression of thanks for their help during the major research period. Other critical research could not have been completed without the assistance of staff members at the Archives Nationales and the Bibliotèque Nationale in Paris.

Among my colleagues, I owe a special debt to fellow members of the History Department at Fairfield University: Drs. William Abbott, Cecelia Bucki, Ralph Coury, Danke Li, David McFadden, and Gavriel Rosenfeld; and Professors Harold Forsythe, Lawrence Kazura, and Walter Petry. Their comments and support, along with those of emeritus colleagues, Dr. Richard DeAngelis and Professor Paul Davis were invaluable. Professor Elizabeth Hohl, also of the Fairfield History Department, deserves special thanks for suggestions at every stage of the project. Her challenging and provocative questions and her critical advice allowed me to improve the content and style of the final manuscript. And though neither she nor any of the others mentioned here should be held responsible for any infelicities which remain, Professor Hohl should be considered among those most guilty of sustaining the author in matters large and small through her steady friendship as well. Evelyn Becker at Fairfield helped in a variety of tasks crucial to the preparation of the manuscript. Special thanks go to Linda White, whose tireless efforts throughout helped bring the project to fruition. Thanks also to Judith Hohl for assistance in the final stages.

Heather Ruland Staines, Marsha Goldstein, and Meg Ferguson at Greenwood Press, deserve credit for suggestions leading to important revisions of the manuscript, for patience in waiting for those revisions to occur, and for guidance throughout the publication process.

There are many others who have encouraged and challenged this work along the way. Among the most important have been: Drs. Philip Eliasoph, Orin Grossman, Catharine Higgs, Mary Frances Malone, John E. Mason, Ellen Umansky, and Meredith Baldwin Weddle. In addition, my thanks to Katherine Davis, Ruth Gay, Kathryn Loomis, and Wesley Pippert.

My daughter, Leah, contributed great stores of patience, in often abiding the less-than-perfect circumstances required for her mother to work.

Finally, it is my bittersweet task to acknowledge two very dear friends who are not here to see this book appear in its final form, though their help was so crucial to its production. The first of these is Stanley J. Kay Jr. who sustained me and my family during the last years of this project, and who, through the intensity of his love and wit, recalled me to life when that possibility seemed most remote.

I close by remembering the courage and constancy of Harry A. Miskimin Jr., a fine and noted scholar in his own right, but an even better husband. Though he is not here to see this project in its culmination, his importance to its beginning and its middle are overshadowed only by the joy and solace which he gave, and somehow still gives, to its author. It is to his memory, then, that I dedicate this work.

Notes on the Text

To make the text as accessible as possible to English-speaking readers, I have translated all French quotations that appear throughout the following pages. My attempt has been to keep as close to the original words as possible, without altering the meaning. Explanations of the method used in particular passages appear in the notes to relevant chapters. In some cases, French terms or titles have been retained, where a literal translation would produce a misleading meaning for modern readers. The title of the official known as the *bailli*, for example, has been left in French, since his function was that of a local magistrate rather than of a modern "bailiff." This has also been done to preserve a French feel in the book. Finally, archival sources that appear repeatedly in the notes often include abbreviations (after the first reference) listed in the bibliography.

Introduction:
The Crown Confronts Three Faiths

To many outsiders, a Messin was a slow, plodding Germanic character, dull of wit and heavy of speech, prone to extreme if slow-burning anger and a rough superstition-laden religion—a thick-headed boob who drank a thin, bitter wine fit only for his own crude palate.[1] To such observers, the stupidity of the Messin was nowhere better expressed than in his weird credulous fancies. In 1632, one writer illustrated his view of Messin ignorance in the tale of a popular uprising. The details are worth recounting.

During an extremely wet season, of incessant rain and constant flooding, peasants from the countryside around Metz began to spread a rumor that the 15 days of rain they had suffered were the result of city dwellers in Metz placing tobacco plants in their ornamental gardens. Everyone knew, they maintained, that tobacco plants attracted storm clouds and rain, in the same manner in which tobacco drew water out of the human body [presumably when smoked]. The fertility of American soil [already planted with the weed publicized by James I of England] was attributed to this property of tobacco: its ability to bring rain. Panicked by the continuous downpour which threatened to wipe out their harvests, the gullible farmers descended on the city and began madly ripping out the gardens of their urban neighbors. They demanded that local authorities order the removal of tobacco plants from the town, and when they failed to get satisfaction on this point they continued their rampage from neighborhood to neighborhood. In this they were assisted by bands of young men from the city, anxious to join the melee, if not also convinced of the power of tobacco to induce precipitation. Widespread injuries resulted, as well as a few deaths, when rioters clashed with municipal militias brought in to contain them.[2]

We cannot be certain of the reliability of the anonymous reporter of this event, and given the absolute lack of reference to it in official records, it is quite possible that the raid on tobacco in Metz never took place at all, or at least not as described. Nevertheless, the story as recounted illustrates the amused scorn with which the Messin was viewed by other Frenchmen. The writer, by the way, made no distinction between Messin peasants and the urban residents of Metz itself. All were crass buffoons.

There were, of course, more objective elements of Messin identity, determined merely by one's residence in the diocese of Metz—an area encompassing the city of Metz and its surrounding countryside, including some 15 Catholic parishes. By 1600 Metz's Protestant population was also significant, and a small but cohesive Jewish community added to the mix. Metz was perhaps the only French city of this era to have this particular formula of religious diversity in clear evidence, for while Protestants still lived in many areas of France under the protection of the Edict of Nantes, the Jewish community of Metz was one of the very few groups living openly as Jews in the kingdom. Jews in the south, most notably in Bordeaux, largely resided as "new Christians," or converts, though they often practiced a semiclandestine Judaism in their homes.[3] And while a few Jews also probably lived in Paris, the lack of official recognition of them makes their lives all but invisible to us. So Metz, in our period, represented one of the only areas of France in which members of these three faiths, so central to the modern Western tradition, coexisted openly, albeit with great friction.

Belonging to Metz, then, meant belonging to this diverse city, with its total population of about 20,000 souls—an enclave then roughly comparable in size to Dijon, Caen, Amiens, or Tours.[4] This concentration of population existed despite Metz's location in the area of France with the lowest population density.[5] Because of its strategic location along the Moselle and Seille rivers, Metz was also a center of commerce and, even during the turbulent war years that dominated the century, an important transport stop for goods (especially textiles) shipped between the Germanic lands and the Low Countries, and towns in the south of France and Italy. It was also, like most of France and Europe at this time, an agricultural area. Because Metz lay in the physical sphere of the Wars of Religion and the Thirty Years War, it also saw a brisk business in those trades such as horse dealing, necessary for the support and provisioning of armies.[6] We will return to Metz's heritage as a war town and the significance of its early history in Chapter 1, after briefly examining the city's general aspect in the years just before 1633, when our own consideration of its political transformation really begins.

As one might expect, the people of seventeenth-century Metz shared many characteristics with other Frenchmen and Europeans of their age. For one, theirs was a society in which the family and its needs lay at the center of existence, and this was true despite the relative precariousness of that unit's survival in a world far more familiar than ours with infant mortality and the obliteration of whole families during times of famine and epidemic.[7] Though modern scholars have raised questions about the role of children within medieval and early modern families, there is no evidence that people in Metz cared less for their children in this period than they do today, or even that they refrained from openly expressing their affection and concern.[8] Individuals apparently mourned the loss of children or of spouses, even as they pragmatically expected to have future children or a second spouse. Consider, for example, the sixteenth-century case of

Jean LeCoullon, a Messin farmer and journal keeper whose family ultimately converted to Protestantism. Jean's grief at the death of his four-year-old son, also named Jean, cannot be denied. As Jean sat at his child's bedside, he wrote, watching the ravages of plague consume the boy, his own suffering became unbearable. Finally, he recounted, "I cried to God to take him from this world." The depth of Jean's anguish, and his willingness to express it—in fact his inability to hide it—are evident and moving.[9]

Similarly, in the seventeenth century Raphael Levy, a Jewish trader whose trial and execution are discussed in Chapter 5, faced his own death sentence with thoughts primarily of his children. As we shall see, one of his last acts was to plead with members of his community to provide for his affianced daughter's dowry.[10] While there is some evidence that Jewish families were considered remarkable in their devotion to children, even by the Catholic majority, we see many signs that children were appreciated by most in this society, even if as idealized innocents.[11] Certainly any perceived attack on children—including allegations by both Catholics and Protestants that members of the other group were kidnapping and forcibly converting their children—created a highly charged public furor. Children were the objects of intense attachment and emotion from adults. If this had not been true, they would not have served so frequently as the flash points for the far-reaching and pervasive hostilities that will concern us at length.

Thus, while the visual and plastic arts might suggest an absence of children as children in this period, more fundamental considerations in Metz point to their importance as critical members of the family—a family that, with all of its extended members, provided the very basis of time in this society. While most individuals had, at best, an imprecise sense of dates and time during this era, family events—births, marriages, and death—served as chronological anchors, perhaps even more critically than they do today.[12] For Jean LeCoullon and later Messin chroniclers, the birth of children and various other family events set the boundaries of life and punctuated their personal histories. Political events in the town, when Jean mentions them at all, were invariably set out in relation to personal events or personally significant agricultural developments. "Fighting began in the year my third son was born" or "warfare in the region forced the wedding date to be changed" were typical allusions to public developments in Jean's journal, along with such references as one to an official's visit occurring "when wine was valued at . . ." The cycle of family, the cycle of the seasons, and for that matter the cycle of the Church as linked to these, defined life in Metz for people of all classes and all trades, whether they were directly dependent on the land or, as with most of the city's denizens, only indirectly so. Let us work through these cycles briefly to make the broadest generalizations about Messin society, contrasting it as appropriate with the rest of France.

To begin: birth. As mentioned, high levels of infant mortality had a profound impact on life in Metz, as elsewhere. Jean's parents, for example, lost 10 of their 13 children in infancy. Other indications of low survival rates in the seventeenth century include the repeated requests of the clergy in Lorraine for additional public cemetery space. specifically for the graves of children.[13] The frequency of such early deaths made the midwife a tremendously important figure in the town, and even more so in rural areas. Among Christians she might be responsible for bringing the newborn to baptism, without which his or her soul was doomed. The choosing of midwives lay in the hands of the curé or parish priest, and midwives in turn elected a *matronne*—a sort of "first midwife"—to assist at all births. Midwives were the first to be blamed for infant deaths, but they were also often the first to be honored (undoubtedly for reasons of expedience), especially by poorer people who frequently chose the delivering midwife or a member of her immediate family as godparent to a newborn.[14] For reasons that are unclear, recently married couples, even if relatively unknown to the parents, were also favorite choices for godparents. A couple married on the day of a child's birth was thought to bring particular luck. Prominent nobles or local officials were also often chosen, a sign of deference or perhaps of hope from the parents for financial rewards.[15] Most often, though, friends, neighbors, and especially relatives from both sides of the family became godparents to a new child. Children were also sometimes given more than one set of godparents, though the proliferation of godparents was ultimately discouraged by the Catholic Church.[16]

It was upon baptism that a child formally received its name, and we can learn much from the first names most Messins gave their children in this period. Among Catholic families the most popular names were traditional family names or (the same thing, really) the names of saints. Jean was the most common name for boys in this region, with Nicolas and Pierre next in popularity, followed by François and Jacques. One should note that of these Nicolas was the only regional or Germanic-sounding name.[17] For girls, Anne and Catherine were the most frequently given names, with Marie and Marguerite the next most popular. Protestants, not surprisingly, often chose names from the so-called Old Testament for their children, and the switch in first names (from names of grandparents, parents, or other relatives to biblical names) may signal a family's conversion to Protestantism when more explicit indications cannot be found. Among the LeCoullons, for example, Jean's own children were named exclusively after relatives or saints. His eldest son, Collignon, was named for Jean's father. His other children were Mangin, Claude, and three sons successively named Jean, the last of whom outlived his journal-keeping father. However, Collignon's children (from two marriages, both to Protestant women) bore names exclusively from the Bible, most from the Old Testament. They were: Sara, Abraham, Suzanne, Elizabeth, Salome, Esther, Paul, and Daniel. Before their birth we hear nothing from Jean (their grandfather) to indicate that his family was Protestant. In fact, he mentions at length his own aborted education with local priests (which accounts in part for his somewhat unusual literacy) and his first marriage "in the Roman Church." However, at some point after his eldest son's marriage, he begins to refer to Catholics as "papists" and to lament the suffering of Protestants in the town. It may be that his son's marriage to a Protestant is the starting point for the conversion of at least part of the extended

LeCoullon family or that marriage may have followed an intellectual journey toward conversion begun by Jean. We cannot be sure. Regardless, the names on the family tree correspond with a religious transformation.[18] Jewish families, of course, also often named their children for biblical figures, although in their case such names were also invariably family names used for centuries.[19]

The surprising fluidity in Catholic-Protestant conversions among individuals over just such issues as marriage is considered in Chapter 4. In fact, the relative willingness of common folk to downplay religious differences (at least between Christians) points to a slowly creeping secularization in Metz—a perfect early laboratory for religious pluralism before the age of the philosophes—which will concern us throughout this study. We will consider secularization not only through the positive evidence of it in this society (argued particularly in Chapters 2, 3, and 4), but also through the somewhat desperate backlash against it represented by a ritual murder trial (Chapter 5) and an anti-Protestant polemic (Chapter 6).

With birth and baptism, Catholic children were immediately initiated into the life of the Church, and this was reinforced through attendance at mass; regular religious rituals like first communion and marriage, which served as rites of passage; and through passive observance of religious processions, feast days, and holidays. Church celebrations were of course often linked to the agricultural calendar. Many children, not only the offspring of the elite, received a rudimentary education through the Church, particularly after efforts at such early schooling were emphasized by Counter-Reformers later in the century. Still, at least until the middle of the seventeenth century, belonging to the Catholic Church was as natural and reflexive as breathing for most Messins. Certainly most families did not offer children an option to choose, even among Christian confessions. Upon the first real opportunity to do so—upon marriage—some Messin Catholics did convert to a spouse's Protestantism, as we shall see, and not always with great fanfare or commotion. Protestants in Metz also showed a certain willingness to marry out of their faith, but this was particularly true once the civil penalties against Protestantism increased later in the seventeenth century, as we will discuss in Chapter 6. By the same token, Messin Catholics remained Catholic if their families had largely done so. The most important influence on most individuals in either case was the family, along with the norms for their neighborhood and their profession, and the Church and religion figured primarily as a reflection of that very personal reality.

True adulthood came for most Messins with marriage, although this phenomenon was not always detached from that of birth or impending birth. Here the Messin seems to have differed from his or her fellow Frenchman. Demographers studying the intervals between marriage and the birth of first children have found a somewhat higher virtue rate, if you will, among Messin couples than among French men and women in general. Allowing for variations in gestation, one such noted scholar has found that 5 percent of the region's children were known to be conceived out of wedlock, whereas just under 10 percent were so conceived in the kingdom at-large. He gives no reason for this disparity, and we can only speculate that family and religious teaching may have held firmer in the northeastern frontier than elsewhere. This might be considered particularly surprising in a region, like Metz, embroiled in warfare and its attending social chaos, where thoughts of imminent mortality might be expected to discourage sexual abstinence. Perhaps greater restraint prevailed among young Protestants and Jews, and this tipped the balance; or perhaps Messins in general were either more pious or more prudish than other Frenchmen.[20]

In other ways we find Messin couples roughly similar to others in France, with most women marrying for the first time at age 18 or 19, and most men marrying for the first time at age 23 or 24.[21] Marriage usually took place between people of similar social or professional rank. Hence a young cobbler might typically marry a cloth maker's daughter or the widow of a cooper.[22] And marriage, even in relatively cosmopolitan Metz, usually involved two members of the community itself. When one spouse did come from outside of the city, that spouse was almost always from a neighboring community or nearby village. There is one noteworthy exception to this rule. In Metz residents were apparently far more likely to take French-speaking spouses from farther away than to take spouses from neighboring Germanic areas.[23] When Messin women married soldiers garrisoned there, they too almost always chose men from the more distant areas of "Old France," such as Picardy, Normandy, Provence, or Burgundy, than from nearer areas in the cultural orbit of the Holy Roman Empire, including Strasbourg. This inclination was notably, or even remarkably, as true for Messin Protestants as for Catholics. The only group it did not hold as true for was Jews, who married coreligionists from Germanic areas with much greater frequency, undoubtedly out of necessity given their small numbers in Metz.[24] Jews were also far less likely to convert or to marry outside of their faith. The propensity of Christians to marry other Messins or Frenchmen, though, suggests fairly effectively that by the mid-seventeenth century, belonging to Metz, for those who lived there, meant belonging (at least culturally) to France as well. Before we end our introduction with this point, however, let us continue our survey of Messin daily life, addressing the intermingling of marriage with our last consideration—death.

Like all areas subject to high mortality (both infant and adult), Metz saw a high rate of remarriage among its residents, with most people remarrying within the first year after a spouse's death. As in all of France, however, women usually spent a longer period in widowhood before remarriage and were also less likely than men to remarry at all. Jean LeCoullon fit this pattern; one year after his first wife, Jeanon, died, he began to bow to friends' and relatives' suggestions that he consider remarrying. Although the date of his second marriage might suggest a pragmatic attitude toward love and mating, upon closer inspection (and with the unusual opportunity to read his own words), we see no lack of feeling for his first wife. Following her death in July of 1553, he himself fell into a fever, exacerbated perhaps by the heartsickness he vividly recalled. "I waited only for death to rescue me from sadness," he wrote, "for I suffered such profound pain from my wife's death that I cannot here describe it. She was among the most virtuous women in this world."[25] Despite his marriage to Martinette Caignard in 1554, Jean maintained close ties throughout his life to his first inlaws, the grandparents of the two surviving children of his first marriage. Though Jean lived in the century before that described by much of our demographic material, his words nonetheless confirm the universality of grief in any age that knows death, hence in any age.

In fact, Messins knew death intimately during the seventeenth century; the area suffered significant depopulation (a 30–50 percent decrease) between 1618 and 1668—the years surrounding the so-called Thirty Years War.[26] This drop in population compares with that suffered by nearby areas of the German Empire in the same period, but diverges from the pattern in southern France, which saw a general, if not uninterrupted, increase in population over those years.[27] Indeed, if not for the demographic crisis in the northeast, France's total population would probably have registered a more robust increase during the century. Further, as we shall see in Chapter 1, Metz's population had already begun to decline in the sixteenth century, making for a longstanding downward trend.

Disease was the single most important factor in the depopulation of northeastern France in this era. Warfare and even famine figured primarily as contributors to the outbreak and spread of illness. The worst single epidemic of the seventeenth century came in the 1635–36 winter, when the most disastrous plague (or possibly flu) of a plague-filled era swept through the region. Boulay, the home of Raphael Levy, and a village of some 900 people located about 20 kilometers from Metz, lost 206 victims in this period, among them its curé.[28] Precise figures of the number of deaths in Metz itself are not readily available, but births there declined dramatically in the years following the epidemic, a good indication of the decrease in the adult population. In 1635 the city recorded 1,163 births (a number somewhat larger than in earlier years, due probably to an influx of war refugees); in 1640 only 786 babies were born. The city's demographic recovery, if judged by its birth rate, took fully 40 years, for it was not until 1675 that as many children were born annually as in the years before 1635.[29] The Protestant community, we should add, seems never to have recovered from the 1635–36 disaster.[30] Losses throughout the region were at least as dramatic, varying between 25 and 50 percent. Survivors' accounts of their symptoms were often vague, but the most common epidemics of the era probably resulted from outbreaks of typhus and scarlet fever (both referred to as purple fever) and bubonic, rather than pneumonic, plague.[31] The authorities, meanwhile, did what they could. In June of 1638 each head of household in Metz was assessed four sols toward garbage collection to prevent contagion. In other instances, town officials struggled to bury the cadavers of plague and war victims, in order to contain infection.[32]

Of course death occurred in other, more mundane ways, as well. Jean recounted the tragic demise of a friend killed by infection to a wound following a minor farming accident. There were always more deaths in the winter than in the summer, and large numbers of women certainly died in childbirth. Still, the death and destruction associated with war and epidemic provided a more pungent element of Messin identity, albeit a negative one. And in this the Messins considered themselves different from other Frenchmen.

This raises the question of whether Messins, in fact, considered themselves French at all. Culturally and religiously, as mentioned, the city was more diverse than much of the kingdom. In some communities such diversity might have produced a relatively cosmopolitan outlook. However by the seventeenth century, we can fairly conclude, most Messins did consider themselves French — loyal, if beleaguered, subjects of the French kings. Historians have dated the political Frenchification of Metz, or rather its realignment with France, from 1552 onward.[33] In addition, developments in the first half of the seventeenth century made the connection more explicit. Among these were a 1614 decree ordering local officials to take an oath of loyalty to Louis XIII, the abolition in 1633 of all appeals to the Court of Spire, and the obvious 1648 Peace of Westphalia, which made nearly a century of French military domination official in an act of formal annexation.[34] By the mid-seventeenth century, we have evidence that even familiarity with the German language was seen as slightly unusual in Metz.[35]

Frenchness lagged in Metz only in terms of enthusiasm for new French organs of government, as opposed to older traditional, locally autonomous institutions. Historical resistance to France will concern us in Chapter 1, while a more critical later development will occupy us in Chapter 2—the replacement in 1633 of the local council of magistrats with a new parlement of Metz. In both cases religious discord destroyed the possibility of real resistance to French takeover. The complex relationship between this discord and new political realities, new social relations, and an ironic underlying diminution of the role of religion itself—in other words, secularization—underlies this study. Chapters 3 and 5 look particularly at the role of the Jews, and of anti-Semitism, in this scenario.

For Messin Christians at least, identification with France came to resemble the identification of most Messins with the Catholic Church—a loosely accepted fact of life, based on family and cultural traditions played out every day. It should not surprise us, then, that in the same period when Catholic leaders sought to reinvigorate Catholicism in the region, and make Catholic allegiance stronger and more durable, the same phenomenon can be seen with regard to "Frenchness" and the acceptance of centralized French authority and forms of government. In many cases the same individuals promoted both movements. In 1612, for example, André Valladier, vicar-general for the diocese, asserted that Metz was thoroughly French, even if it was also the city "the most rotten" with Protestantism in the kingdom.[36] As the Counter-Reformation spread throughout the realm, Catholicism and Frenchness became more closely aligned in Metz as well. This resulted in part from a calculation by Messin clerics that embracing French centralizing institutions would help them eradicate local Protestantism. Their satisfactions and frustrations on this score will be particularly examined in Chapter 4. Chapter 6, meanwhile, explores the political and religious attitudes of one particularly vocal churchman and his and others' attempts to define who, properly, belonged in Metz and who did not. While this one priest was not entirely typical in Metz, his philosophy of exclusion arguably was.

In all, the following chapters attempt several things. They explore Jewish-Christian relations in this one French town during the seventeenth century. And within this, they consider Catholic-Protestant relations as well. They briefly trace the progress of the Counter-Reformation in Metz, both the efforts of the clerical elite and the reception of those efforts by the general population. They provide a picture of how men and women in Metz reacted to their neighbors; how they went about their lives; and how they worked, fought, formed alliances. In addition, they analyze the changes in government that brought Metz finally and unequivocally into the increasingly centralized (and therefore unwittingly more secular) absolutist French state. One could devote volumes to such an effort. But the study here makes no claim to address all aspects of Messin history, even for the years 1633–1700. Instead, the intention throughout is to understand, as completely as possible, the most commanding element of that history—the connection among religious tension, political change, and social reconfiguration.

Specifically, we find a world in which religious diversity (and the resultant discord) changed political relationships, social relationships, and even the intellectual climate. The major political change was a fragmentation in the earlier local coalition that had preserved Metz's autonomy, leaving the city vulnerable to French takeover. In social relations, an almost inevitable interaction took place between adherents of all three faiths. If not always amicable, this interaction nonetheless diluted the influence of Catholic notables in Metz and perhaps even of religion itself. Finally, one sees the slow progress of secularization, certainly in political life, but most evident perhaps in the stinging backlash against it represented by the ritual murder trial of Raphael Levy and the anti-Protestant fulminations of the priest Martin Meurisse.

In this sense, then, religious zeal ironically aided in the diminution of religion in public life. It is in our third area—of intellectual change—that Metz can be seen as a somewhat advanced laboratory for ideas that were percolating throughout France and even Europe. As a city with an almost unique religious mix (certainly for France in this era) it grappled with the logical results of religious pluralism well before other regions in the kingdom had done so.

Let us begin, then, with an overview of Messin history, tracing the sixteenth century's formation of a distinctly early modern link between religion and politics—a link so different, if not wholly divorced, from an earlier medieval combination.

NOTES

1. For a reference to the inferiority of Messin wine, see Fernand Braudel, *The Identity of France*, trans. Sîan Reynolds (New York: Harper and Row, 1988), p. 349. This reference appears in a generally useful section specifically about Metz on pp. 329–50.

2. Bibliotèque Nationale [hereinafter B.N.], *Nouvelles Acquisitions Françaises* [hereinafter N.A.F.], vol. 22669, fol. 21.

3. For a later study of Jews in the South, see Frances Malino, *The Sephardic Jews of Bordeaux* (Tuscaloosa: University of Alabama Press, 1978), and selected sections of Cecil Roth's *A History of the Marranos* (New York: Jewish Publication Society of America, 1959). For information on the Jews of Avignon (who practiced their religion openly and whose residence in medieval times had been protected by the popes living there) see Philippe Prévot, *Histoire du ghetto d'Avignon* (Avignon: Aubanel, 1975); and René Moulinas, *Les juifs du pape en France* (Paris: Commission française des Archives juives, 1981). For other works on the Jews in France, see notes to Chapter 3.

4. Jacques Dupaquier, *La Population Française aux XVIIe et XVIIIe Siècles* (Paris: Presses Universitaires de France, 1979), p. 40. Note also that this figure represents a reduction from our best estimates of the population in 1300 (roughly 30,000); see Chapter 1.

5. Ibid., p.36. Dupaquier estimates the total population of France at about 20 million at the beginning of the seventeenth century, although he acknowledges the difficulty of reaching a precise figure before more systematic record keeping began in 1790.

6. The production of armaments and ammunition was particularly brisk in Strasbourg. Metz may have specialized more in the storage of some military items. See Braudel, pp. 103ff.

7. Guy Cabourdin, *Terre et Hommes en Lorraine* (1550–1635) (Nancy: Université de Nancy, 1977), pp. 103ff.

8. Modern studies of the family that have suggested that parental affection was either rare or rarely expressed in this period include Philippe Ariès's *Centuries of Childhood: A Social History of Family Life*, trans. Robert Baldick (New York: Vintage Books, 1962), and Lawrence Stone's much scrutinized *The Family, Sex, and Marriage in England, 1500–1800* (New York: Harper and Row, 1977). This reduces these two works somewhat unfairly, of course, but the notion they raise—that differences in the early modern world made for different parental attitudes—remains sufficiently provocative to deserve our attention here. For a more recent study, see Steven Ozment's *When Fathers Ruled: Family Life in Reformation Europe* (Cambridge, Mass.: Harvard University Press, 1983), and his more recent work: *Flesh and Spirit: Private Life in Early Modern Germany* (New York: Viking, 1999).

9. E. de Bouteiller, ed., *Journal de Jean LeCoullon* (Paris: Librairie de D. Dumoulin, 1881), p. 21.

10. See Chapter 5.

11. See Steven M. Cohen and Paula R. Hyman, eds., *The Jewish Family: Myths and Reality* (New York: Holmes and Meier, 1986), pp. 3ff. (Hyman's introduction).

12. Cabourdin offers a fascinating example of early modern man's fluid concept of time, in the description of a case in which four men were asked in 1556 to state their age and asked again in 1566. On the second occasion, the individuals added between 15 and 16 years to their ages, even though only one decade had actually passed. See Cabourdin, pp. 112–13.

13. Cabourdin, Ibid., p. 95.

14. Ibid., pp. 171–72.

15. Ibid., p. 176.

16. Jean LeCoullon's children largely had cousins of Jean or his wife as their godparents. In one case their neighbors served as godparents.

17. Jean Houdaille, "La Population de Boulay (Moselle) avant 1850," *Population*, vol.22, no. 6 (November–December 1967), 1061.

18. Jean's family tree is diagramed in Cabourdin, p. 97.

19. Among Jews, records of 1621 suggest that the most popular male names were

Solomon, Abraham, Jacob, and David. In 1637 Solomon, Abraham, and David remained the most popular names for Jewish boys, but a few families also named their sons Bernard, Nicolas, and Alexandre, probably in keeping with local trends in the Christian population. In general, women were not recorded by name in these rolls of Metz's Jewish families; however, widows were named in the later 1637 list. Among the widows were individual women named Rachel, Esther, Rebecca, and Sara, but also three Annes, one Françoise, one Antoinette, one Fremine, three Fleures, and one Magdaleinne. This seems to indicate a greater likelihood for Jewish families to give girls locally popular names, particularly as their links to Metz endured. Boys, on the other hand, continued for the most part, to be given traditional biblical names. See Archives Départementales de la Moselle [hereinafter A.D.M.], 1M: 191 (Bl).

20. Dupaquier, p. 27.

21. Ibid., p. 26. The average age for women on first marriage seems to have risen as the century wore on, so that by the latter part of the century women married, on average, at 23. The age for men, 23–24, held relatively constant. See Cabourdin, p. 118.

22. This was true for Jean LeCoullon and also true for Philippe de Vigneulles, a Messin born in the late sixteenth century. Philippe, the grandson of a textile merchant, married the daughter of an impoverished cloth dealer. See Jean Rigault, "La fortune d'un protestant messin du XVIIe siècle: Philippe de Vigneulles (vers 1560–1634)," *Annales de L'Est*, no. 2 (1951), 81. Also see Dupaquier, p. 26, for more general information on marriage patterns.

23. Jean Rigault, "La population de Metz au XVIIe siècle; Quelques problemes de démographie," *Annales de L'Est*, no. 4 (1951), 312ff. Rigault's figures suggest that Catholic "mixed" marriages (that is, where one spouse did not come directly from Metz) increased as the century wore on. Catholics, he suggests, were more successful at attracting Catholic immigrants later in the century than were Protestants. It was the Protestants' insular tendency, he writes, that prevented them from truly recovering demographically from the harshest years of epidemic. This, he claims, was far more important than Counter-Reformation persecution in weakening the Protestant position, at least up until 1685.

24. Among those German Jews who married Messins during the seventeenth century was Gluckel of Hameln, whose second husband was a wealthy banker in the city. See Book 6 of *The Memoirs of Gluckel of Hameln*, trans. Marvin Lowenthal (New York: Schocken, 1977), pp. 222ff. See also Natalie Zemon Davis, *Women on the Margins: Three Seventeenth-Century Lives* (Cambridge, Mass.: Harvard University Press, 1995).

25. Bouteiller, p. 22.

26. Marie-José Laperche-Fournel, *La Population du Duché de Lorraine de 1580 à 1720* (Nancy: Presses Universitaires de Nancy, 1985), p. 107.

27. Dupaquier, p. 11.

28. Houdaille, p. 1057.

29. Rigault, "La population de Metz," p.309.

30. Ibid., pp. 310–11.

31. Cabourdin, p. 99.

32. B.N., N.A.F., 22669, fol. 122.

33. Among those using the 1552 date for French control of Metz are Henri Tribout de Morembert in *Le Diocèse de Metz* (Paris: Letouzey & Ané, 1970), and Gaston Zeller's *La Réunion de Metz à la France*, vol. 2 (Paris: Société d'Edition: Les Belles Lettres, 1926).

34. Morembert, pp. 113 and 119.

35. See Chapter 5 for information on a witness's knowledge of German, contained in the transcript of the trial of Raphael Levy. Also note that Gluckel of Hameln lamented

that her inability to speak French hindered her communication with her new Jewish neighbors and inlaws in Metz—a sign that Jews in Metz also increasingly spoke French (though also an early form of Yiddish). See her memoirs, pp. 222ff.

36. Morembert, p. 114.

Part I
New Political Realities

Chapter 1
The Oath Outside the Gates

What most people know about the city of Metz, and what most people knew as the sixteenth century neared its midpoint, is that it was a place of coming and going, of passing through, of stopping en route, of moving on. Planted squarely between the arms of the Seille and Moselle rivers, and on the border between modern Germany and modern France, it has long been a crossroads to merchants, traders, refugees, wanderers, and most of all to soldiers, all of whom have viewed it as another step on the road to their larger purposes. Today's network of rail lines and highways, of meandering roads and communication links with Luxembourg to the north, Belgium beyond, to Paris and Berlin, is less a testament to modern invention than an underlining of earlier routes linking Metz to its neighbors while still, oddly, detaching it from them. Today it is, as it was, more often one stop in a traveler's journey, than a final destination—a place to refuel, regroup, restock, or resell. By European standards it remains both peculiar to itself and the place where disparate elements of European society collide or conform to each other.

Small wonder, then, that this city's inhabitants, the Messins, developed an identity at once cosmopolitan and protectionist. Unable to withstand the influence of the strangers passing through, but unwilling to relinquish the rooted traditions that served as their cultural ramparts, the Messins were perpetually out of step with their more powerful "protectors" from east, west, or beyond—too Celtic to be Gallic, too Gallic to be Roman, too Roman to be German, too German to be French. The ancient home of two tribes, the Leuques and the Mediomatrices, Metz was sufficiently isolated by its geography—surrounded by forests and flowing water—to perhaps deserve being called "the fortress of the Gods," or *divodurum* in the language of those who met Caesar's troops as the common era began. However, by the Middle Ages, and certainly by the dawn of the early modern era, this fortress had long since fallen, changing hands and technical allegiances repeatedly from the time of Roman infiltration to that of

Frankish control (after the fifth century) and finally, by the twentieth century, to Imperial protection. Reluctantly or resignedly, Metz knew first hand some of the greatest military leaders of that early age, from Caesar and Attila to Charlemagne, the last of whom admired the city's aspect sufficiently to bury one of his favorite wives there, alongside the tombs of his sisters and assorted other Carolingian relatives. These early conquerors left the city a rich but mottled legacy: fortifications and an aqueduct but also a tradition of warfare and of being on the wrong end of military siege. Perhaps the most successful conqueror of all, the nascent Church, united the region's disparate beliefs under the Christian rubric, infused with the symbols and images that would inspire and oppress successive generations of Messins.

The topography of the Messin countryside, and the strategic location of the city in this fertile grape-growing region, made for prosperity in some seasons and vulnerability in others. As a center of transport, lying along a major north-south axis of Roman Europe, and along the east-west transept from Rheims to the Rhine, Metz and the Messins profited from trade in lumber, livestock, and wine, viticulture, and the exchange of money. A Roman project of 56 C.E. connecting the Moselle to the Saone, and a network of roads for military transport, only heightened the possibilities for Messin merchants. By the Middle Ages, the city was sufficiently famous to be labeled "Metz the rich,"[1] and by 1300 roughly 30,000 souls resided in this northern Gallic outpost.[2]

However, with prosperity also came desirability, a dangerous attribute that continued to lure military men with large ambitions and hosts of disruptive and violent troops. By the mid-sixteenth century, varied warfare in and around Metz had seriously depleted the city's fortunes. Hostilities between the Spanish-born Charles V, elected Holy Roman Emperor in 1519, and the French Valois particularly, brought companies of transient soldiers to the region, who, by their very presence, brought volatility and uncertainty. With their allegiance a mere commodity for sale to the highest bidder, their sustenance largely dependent on thievery and pillage, their subjection to law minimal, and their military discipline an oxymoron, fighting men in the early modern period more often brought chaos to an orderly town than order to a chaotic one. And chaos, or even impending uncertainty, was anathema to merchants, regardless of their places of origin or their destinations. Blocked roads, disrupted fairs, and a reputation for bands of cutpurses abroad in the area sufficed to drive away traders. What was lost in one decade was not easily recovered in the next. Where soldiers lodged, trade declined. Famine and hunger, never far from most Europeans' experience in this age, grew and spread like weeds under such circumstances. Epidemic, at best only semidormant, likewise flourished wherever malnourished people lived close together and made its own contribution to the cycle of poverty and despair. In an age of primitive hygiene, as one scholar has put it, "any concentration of men created a pathogenic zone, and any migration helped to propagate the scourge."[3] Soldiers also brought illnesses directly and distributed them randomly across the countryside they traveled. Thus they took supplies from farmhouses and granaries and left flu or plague behind in return—a grim and unwelcome exchange that most civilians were powerless to re-negotiate.

How profoundly had such ills affected the Messins by 1544? The peril and hardship inherent in daily life appear in the rare but telling chronicles of working people: a woman bears 13 children, surviving somehow the problematic obstetrics of the age, and then sees all but three of her babies die in infancy; a farmer desperate for relief from a summer heat wave, drowns in a stream surrounded by friends powerless to help; flu in the winter or plague in the summer robs parents of their children and neighbors of their kin. In these and other ways the Messins shared the vulnerability of all Europeans of the period.

Still for the Messins, belonging to Metz meant to be disproportionately afflicted by such woes and to suffer other extraordinary travails peculiar to a restive land. Certainly we know that local merchants and magistrates complained repeatedly of a disintegration of order there and of an attending raft of social problems.[4] With commerce on the wane, perhaps since the fifteenth century, brigandage became a steady concern of local leaders in the new century. Some blamed the situation on events in Germany where, after 1517, peasants inspired in part by Luther's message may have tried to hasten the coming of a new economic day by attacking and looting the homes of the wealthy.[5] In fact, powerful families from areas bordering Metz may have been at least as responsible, sponsoring raids on the town by groups of their followers. In 1518 a feudal lord from his chateau in the Palatinate successfully extorted money from the Messins to procure the retreat of armed men he had directed to lay siege to the city.[6] The main road from Metz to Frankfurt had already become quite dangerous for travelers, as the surrounding forest provided cover for thieves. During this period Metz's magistrates counseled merchants not to pass through the area, a devastating handicap since Frankfurt was a major commercial center and an important magnet for Messin merchants. Hoping to reduce their tax assessment from the empire, Messin leaders may have exaggerated their plight somewhat; nonetheless it seems clear that by the mid-sixteenth century the town had lost much of its medieval prominence. At one time a haven for money brokers and exchangers (the chronicler Geoffrey de Villehardouin mortgaged his property with a Messin banker before setting out on the Fourth Crusade), the city was forced to borrow money itself from its wealthier citizens in 1514 to maintain the Hôpital Saint Nicolas, the local poorhouse.[7]

It is a declining city and its worried notables whom we meet in Metz in 1544. One finds them exercising the city's usual response to trouble— desperately maintaining Metz's independence from the German segment of the empire and from France as well. Neutrality in time of war and political independence were seen as the only protection from ruin. By declaring neutrality (if not always practicing it) the Messins hoped to salvage at least some of the ordered detachment preferred by businessmen. As the sixteenth century progressed, however, true neutrality became practically impossible, particularly once loyalties became overlaid with religious controversy. As one Messin put it, the process of offending neither Charles V nor Francis I was like trying "to swim between opposing currents." Of course religious disputes only added to the chop in the water.[8] From 1544 we can trace the beginning of the end of Metz's neutrality and, increasingly, the end of its independence as well.

That neutrality was the casualty not of war—the Messins had somehow survived warfare in and around the city before—but rather of local disintegration, which came foremost in the form of religious division and discord. Susceptible to the same pressures that fueled the Wars of Religion throughout the continent, Metz in the sixteenth century fell to the French, riven by her own internal strife. However, the true success of France's takeover came, we will demonstrate, in the seventeenth century and through an even more extensive religious factionalism in Metz. One of the few French towns in that century with notable Protestant and Jewish communities as well as its Catholic majority, Metz became thoroughly French as much through its own failures as through the French king's abilities. Religious diversity—or rather the Catholic majority's unwillingness to abide it—divided Metz against itself.

The relationship between adherents of these three religions will dominate this study, and our consideration will lead to several conclusions. First, Protestant-Catholic-Jewish relations were complex in this period and determined by often competing religious and secular concerns. Abiding distrust of each group for the other two remained, but alliances were made, increasingly, in response to daily realities. Second, to some degree, secular interests were beginning, slowly, to predominate, certainly in the realm of local and national politics. This was not always good for the Jews—the smallest and most vulnerable of Metz's religious minorities—though usually it was. Secular attitudes grafted onto the Christian past yielded inconsistent results (occasionally a bigotry based vaguely on race rather than faith). Finally, some of the most explosive clashes between members of these groups (such as our 1670 ritual murder trial) emerged in seeming reaction against increasing daily contact and the de facto pluralism engendered by it.

In any case, politically, the central government prevailed. "Centralization," then, came not from the center but from the periphery—encouraged even, in some instances, by those in local government. Absolutism prevailed, in part, because of the failure of the dominated to resist that system's tempting possibilities (i.e., of restoring a quickly evaporating homogeneity). More important, religious division and discord subtly but steadily eroded the foundations of faith itself. Religion, or religious zeal if you will, ironically produced secularization.

This will be our case to prove—that local factionalism, born primarily of religious tension, aided the process of secularization, and within this, the triumph of the French absolutist state in Metz. New political realities, new social realities, and this new intellectual disposition were all nourished by daily events. Of course one sees evidence of secularization throughout France in the seventeenth century, to some degree, and centralizing absolutism is merely one of the first and most obvious signs of it. However, in Metz we see more clearly a pattern in which secularization (and the centralization that served as its herald) resulted in part from religious zeal. For religious zeal provoked discord and division, even among Christians, and this in turn led to pluralism, however unwelcome or begrudged. We begin in the sixteenth century for one obvious reason: it is the period in which a Christian alternative developed in Metz, as in Europe, and in which a new small Jewish community was established there. Specifically, we choose 1544 as a date of departure because it provides a convenient symbolic event that illustrates the traditional autonomy of Metz's local leaders and that also, by its contrast with later events, marks perhaps the last stage of those leaders' control over the city's political fate. Developments of the sixteenth century thus presaged the more extensive disintegration of Metz's autonomy in the seventeenth century.

In June 1544 Holy Roman Emperor Charles V planned to visit Metz, and his impending arrival prompted excitement and also some anxiety, among the city's residents.[9] While shopkeepers and other townspeople may have hung banners, while the clergy readied their best vestments, and as children, perhaps, gathered flowers as potential tributes or reveled in the building carnival atmosphere, local magistrates were at least as busy but with apprehensive and more somber tasks. One imagines these local notables, in clutches of two or three, whispering soberly in the corridors of their *palais*. There, most likely, they conferred among themselves, anticipating the emperor's entourage in the manner of young children awaiting the holiday onslaught of stern scrutinizing relations. Once physically present in Metz, Charles would, by tradition, have supreme authority over all local judicial matters, and all justice during his stay would be administered in his name. He would be able to pardon prisoners according to his whim, for example, or order the return of anyone previously banished by the town officials. In preparation for this interruption in their power, local judges took certain precautions, moving the most dangerous or subversive prisoners from out of the emperor's likely view, leaving only minor offenders in city jails. This, they hoped, would lessen the likelihood that the desperate pleas or pathetic countenances of the incarcerated would melt the emperor's heart and thereby incite his mercy.[10] Reinforcements were ordered to stand watch at all the city gates to anticipate not only the emperor's arrival but also the possibility of civil unrest within Metz from those who might use the occasion to rise up against their local judges. Town-employed bombardiers were ordered to keep the artillery ready, and lookouts were stationed around the clock in several of the highest church towers. To the magistrates, then, a sense of impending danger was perhaps more prominent than one of celebration.

Displaying their traditional independence most vividly, local magistrates would also not allow Charles to enter through the gates until, still standing outside with his attendants, he took an oath swearing to respect the city's privileges and not to allow any violence to come to its magistrates or bourgeoisie, either from within or without. Upon leaving, custom further required that the emperor return the keys to the city and to the precise official from whom he had received them. Moreover, while the emperor was in Metz, residents could not pass through the gates after dark without the express permission and presence of one of the town magistrates.[11] The importance of these strictures cannot be exaggerated in an age in which these symbols of security and civic pride—the city gates and the keys which unlocked them—were also still a major practical component of the town's defenses.[12]

These preparations derived from Metz's peculiar status within, though not entirely within, the aegis of the Hapsburg Empire. Technically Metz in 1544 was a *Reichstadt* or Imperial city like any other in Charles's realm. This meant that Metz and its residents were obligated to pay certain taxes and to offer military support for the emperor in times of war. They were to provide armed men, or better yet money, toward each emperor's coronation in Rome when power changed hands.[13] The Messins were to appeal local disputes to the Imperial tribunal, since 1527 sitting in Spire, and they were to submit themselves to the emperor's direct jurisdiction and obey all Imperial decrees.

In reality, however, Metz was not like other *Reichstadts,* either culturally or politically. It had a complex Celtic-Gallic heritage. Most residents in 1544 spoke French, and the links with France were more than just linguistic. The city generally maintained amicable relations with France. French kings were accustomed to knighting select members of the Messin nobility at their coronations. Men from Metz had fought for the French in the Hundred Years War, and had devotedly traveled across France to be cured by the famous royal touch.[14] The death of French kings, moreover, elicited the same ritual Te Deum in the cathedral in Metz as that accorded the demise of emperors. During the Great Schism, Messin leaders had followed the Avignon popes, just as some of their descendants would harken first to French (rather than German) reformers in the early days of Protestantism. Louis XI was one of the first French kings before 1500 to try to profit from this special relationship, as part of his larger military campaign in Luxembourg.[15] Among other acts, he pensioned the Messin notable Michel de Gournay, who had come to him as part of a delegation pleading Metz's neutrality. On a popular level, Metz also seems to have kept a strong connection to France. In the sixteenth century, Messin pilgrims preferred French holy sites to those in the empire. And in the seventeenth century, as noted, Messin women who married outsiders chose men from far-off French-speaking regions more often than those from neighboring Germanic towns.[16]

In 1526, with war with the Hapsburgs imminent, Francis I seemed well aware of Metz's strange hybrid status. Recognizing Metz as an Imperial city and as neutral (according to the imprecise contemporary understanding of that term), he nonetheless also referred to the city's inhabitants as "our subjects."[17] How different, then, was this city from its neighbor Strasbourg, where German language, money, units of measure, and political administration remained dominant and apparent, and where the more ephemeral aspects of Germanic culture arguably have prevailed even into modern times.

Another key factor separating Metz from other *Reichstadts* was its local political structure—a feature which in 1544 distinguished it as independent from France as well. Even if not fully autonomous, Metz's leaders clung to their own local judiciary, in which members of the town's patriciate held the most powerful posts. And they considered local courts sovereign, in practical terms, and essential as a sign of the town's special status. Members of Metz's ruling families, who traded the most powerful civic posts back and forth among themselves in heavily controlled "elections," routinely spoke of the *république messine* and of the traditional "constitution" that upheld their privileges. In fact the republic had lasted only from roughly the thirteenth until the mid-fourteenth century.[18]

Thus it was this pride in their independence and claims to sovereignty that fueled local leaders' precautions at the time of Charles V's arrival. The emperor's visit, while an honor, also represented a dangerous moment when Messin separateness and political integrity would be put to the test, and had to be maintained and asserted as publicly as possible. The small detail of containing Charles outside of the city gates, making him take an oath before entering Metz, embodied a far more extensive set of assumptions about government there. By making the emperor seem to ask permission to enter, the Messins proclaimed their control over their own government and courts. The oath outside the gates thus carried essential symbolic weight in Metz, with both the visceral power and the fragility implicit in all symbols, for symbols are only as strong as the communal faith that upholds them. Built on belief and mutual acceptance, they crumble if seriously questioned. In 1544 the local leaders vigilantly toiled to quash all doubts. The emperor might come, and then might go, but the same local men would still manage the courts and claims of the Messin populace.

But we have promised a contrast with Charles's 1544 entrance. Picture, then, a comparable moment in April 1552—the arrival of French king, Henri II, in Metz after defeating Hapsburg armies near Luxembourg. While relatively uninterested in Metz itself, the French king nonetheless saw the city as a valuable base from which to conduct other military operations in the region, such as forging a route to the Rhine.[19] Like the warriors and merchants who had used the city before, Henri found in Metz a way station along a wider path—a means to an end rather than an end in itself. And how was Henri received? Arriving at the head of an extensive army, the French king took the usual oath upholding traditional Messin privileges. He vowed to protect its customary independence and autonomy, and agreed not to interfere with its local judiciary. Later that night he even lodged at the same home the emperor had frequented in 1544.[20] But Henri nonetheless arrived in Metz as a conqueror. Or, given Metz's Gallic heritage, he came as a reconqueror. And this was nowhere more apparent than in the initial oath taking, performed now within the city gates, in fact, in front of the cathedral at Metz's very center. Preceded by a constable, holding before him, appropriately enough, an unsheathed sword, Henri controlled the symbols here.[21] No asker of permission, he entered Metz by right and took his oath more as an act of politesse than as one of humility or concession. And though Henri promised to relinquish any involvement in Messin government after the war should end, most in Metz saw French ascendancy there as practically inevitable.[22]

How, in the space of only eight years, had this change occurred? For it was not only France's military power, prodigious though it was, that commanded the difference in these ceremonies.[23] Metz's cultural attachment to France also fails entirely to explain Henri's improved position. There was no pro-French political party per se in the town, and if the Messins spoke French, they also seem not to have relished the prospect of French encroachment on their government or courts. Above all else, the continuing internal disintegration of the Messin government allowed for the change, particularly the increasingly divisive effect of alternative Christian religions. Let us then consider the changes in Metz in this period, in the isolated oaths of these visiting monarchs, as a narrow entry into our scrutiny of Metz's overall transformation into a truly incorporated French city in the next century. Religion was a major source of the fragmentation that allowed Henri II to install the French flag in Metz in 1552. Much deeper and more pervasive religious discord—involving not only the two Christian communities but a Jewish population as well—remained the undercurrent that allowed Henri's successors to expand his encampment there, and to make from it a permanent provincial center. Before we can fully explore this religious division, though, let us describe the reality that allowed for the first glimpse of French power in the few years before Charles's exit and Henri II's arrival.

The basic building blocks of local government in Metz, since the thirteenth century, were six *paraiges*—each one a consortium of local privileged families—which collectively controlled all local offices. Traditionally, wealth alone had determined a family's position in the city and its eligibility for one of the six ruling *paraiges*. But by the time of Charles' visit, these groups had become static and linked to hereditary claims rather than to actual wealth. Each of five *paraiges* furnished two members to a central judicial and administrative body, while the sixth and largest *paraige* furnished three. For obvious reasons, this body of magistrates was known as the Treize or Council of Thirteen, and it influenced most local government decisions. If too many paupers seemed to be making their way into Metz—refugees from war, famine, or personal reversal—the Treize might strengthen the usual controls at the city gates, or banish the unwanted.[24] If special preparations were needed for a monarch's entrance, as they undoubtedly were in both 1544 and 1552, then the Treize would so order. If a cobbler assaulted a baker for infringing on his space at the market square, the case might also end up eventually before the Treize. And if a particular problem arose, such as the outbreak of war in the region, judges of the Treize might appoint the commission (made up of their brethren from the respective *paraiges*) to study and act on the threat. Historically, the members of the Treize could be commoners or nobles (that is, those with titles granted to them by the emperor or the kings of France), but always drawn from among the circle of elite families. From the mid-fourteenth century until the mid-fifteenth century, there were about 150 families in this ruling circle of the *paraiges*. By 1537, according to the most knowledgeable historian in the field, intermarriage and the ravages of time had diminished their number (only 25 families remained) and greatly reduced their personal fortunes. By 1500 so diminished in size was this oligarchy that it lacked enough male bodies to staff the necessary institutions it controlled. The Council of Thirteen, for example, somewhat absurdly had only 8 to

10 members after that year.[25]

In addition to the Treize, and superior in power to it, was a chief magistrate and executive, the *maître-échevin*, and his council of lesser *échevins*. Similar to *échevins* elsewhere in France this official was chosen from among the same group of privileged families (but only from among the nobles within that group). The post of *maître-échevin* rotated annually, and the holder of the post generally acknowledged no authority, secular or episcopal, between himself and the emperor. He operated, almost, as an independent ally of the Imperial overlord. The *maître-échevin*'s council of lesser *échevins* was chosen by him and varied in size. Together these three entities—the *maître-échevin*, his council, and the Treize—initiated legislation in Metz and sat as its courts. In some cases the *maître-échevin* and his council served as the court of first resort—the first court to judge on a given case—but in most others it served as a court of appeal for cases previously tried before the Treize. The actual dispensation of cases between these groups is not entirely clear, and their jurisdictions and duties often overlapped. This is perhaps not surprising given that the various jobs were essentially exchanged between the same group of men in one generation. In special circumstances the *maître-échevin* and Treize might also call an assembly of the Three Orders—clergy, nobility, and bourgeoisie—in order, for example, to approve wartime improvements of the city's defenses. But the deputies assembled from each parish to serve in this body also typically included many of the *échevins* and members of the Treize or their relatives. Lesser officials included three *maires*, or mayors, who served primarily as gatekeepers at the entrances to the city but who did not participate in the judicial decisions controlled by the magistrates.

In this way, a consortium of notable families controlled most local justice in Metz and its dependent countryside. Though technically a city like any other in the empire, these notables nonetheless saw Metz as a *Freireichstadt*, in terms of status if not in terms of any clearly documented rights. Over the years, the act of swearing loyalty to the emperor (like the emperor's right to countermand the local judiciary) had atrophied, so local leaders only made this pledge when the emperor was physically present in the city. The emperor's entrance in 1544, dictated by the outbreak of warfare in nearby Luxembourg the year before, was thus an unusual occurrence, one which, had the emperor been stronger, might have threatened the besieged notables even further. As it was, the precautions mentioned earlier, and measures usually taken after the emperor's departure (essentially reversing any act he might decree contrary to their wishes) preserved the magistrates' power and thereby preserved Metz in its working autonomy. Once the emperor departed, the magistrates simply rescinded his orders. Banished outcasts pardoned by the emperor during his visit, for example, often found their pardons revoked by the local judges as soon as the emperor had left.[26] In addition, the Messin notables had various other means for preventing outside interference in their affairs. Though Messin residents had the right to appeal decisions of their courts to the Imperial Chamber, in reality few did. Perhaps this was because most knew the retribution they would suffer from local magistrates for such impudence. According to one account, a merchant who rashly set out toward Worms in the fifteenth century, hoping to appeal a judgment of the Treize, found himself hotly pursued by agents of the Messin magistrature. The hapless man was hunted down, captured, and hauled back to the city, imprisoned and fined for his hubris. When he attempted to escape, he was banished for six months.[27] Town magistrates continued to insist well into the sixteenth century that Imperial courts had no jurisdiction over the Messins and no power to reverse local court rulings.

In fact, Messin magistrates seem rarely to have failed to rally the requisite energy for declaring their sovereignty and independence. Proclaiming themselves and their city "outside the bounds and boundaries of Germany" (*hors des limites et pays d'Allemagne*), they maintained their own army of mercenaries as well as a local militia, but stoutly refused to send soldiers to fight with Charles V's armies.[28] Their spiny intransigence was particularly apparent at tax time. On several occasions in the sixteenth century the town's magistrates refused to submit to new Imperial taxes, claiming their sovereign freedom from such impositions, only to make "voluntary" contributions of the assessed amounts. This was the frequent tactic of local judges—to loudly assert victory in principle and then quietly capitulate in practice. This method seems at least to have won them delays or even reductions in their assessments, if not true freedom from Imperial taxation.

On other occasions during this century Messin notables maintained that their free and independent status required them only to pay those impositions to which they had expressly consented.[29] In 1521, for example, the Messins bitterly opposed their assessment for Charles V's coronation, pleading poverty and privation as brought on by warfare. In truth, Metz's assigned contribution for that year—40 mounted men, 250 foot soldiers, and 500 gold florins—seemed more commensurate with the city's long-past prosperity than with its current situation.[30] After almost two decades of negotiations they won a one-third reduction in their tax. Five years after Charles's 1544 visit, local magistrates similarly resisted the Diet of Augsbourg's new *Baugeld, a* tax designed to nearly double earlier collections for the maintenance of the Imperial Chamber (the appeals court). So reluctant were the Messins to comply with this new imposition that the city almost came under an Imperial ban for its tardiness.[31]

An aversion to taxes also united the Messin elite, the *corps des métiers*, and the general bourgeoisie. The city's normal revenues consisted of proceeds from a sales tax, or *droit de vente*, tolls taken at the city gates, fees for registration of various acts (deeds, wills, etc.), and judicial fines and confiscations. Hence there was no direct regular city-sponsored tax, and this served to preserve the bonhomie between middle-class shopkeepers and ruling magistrates.[32] This relative unity, in turn, helped Metz's citizens to maintain their civic independence prior to 1552. Unity also upheld the tenuous neutrality of these middle years at the dusk of Imperial control. Given the importance of accord among Metz's leading citizens, and the vulnerability of the city's existence, it is not surprising that with the disintegration of that unity, many other bulwarks of Messin identity similarly crumbled. Among these were the city's famous neutrality, its detachment from active warfare in its vicinity, and its ability to shrug off outside political control, at least in most daily instances. The system of local government, already endangered by the diminution of the *paraiges* as mentioned, grew even more imperiled after 1541, largely due to religious tension among the city's Christians. With that tension came the inflammation of normal disputes between magistrates and their families into full-fledged feuds, in which faith overlaid and intensified the usual issues of money and influence.

Evidence suggests that reformist ideas had been taken up in Metz as early as 1519, with the city's proximity to Germany, and its cosmopolitan trade aiding in the process. By 1525, according to one calculation, roughly 500 Messins openly embraced reform. By 1540, Protestants could be found in the top ranks of local government. And by October of 1543, Charles V felt sufficiently compelled by this threat to ban Protestant preaching and banish all those who spread Protestant ideas to their fellows.[33] The most ardent Catholics in Metz welcomed the emperor's intercession in the fight against heresy, ignoring for the time being the disturbing precedent it set for the city's independence from outside interference. Here we see the small germ that would sprout and grow into a vigorous plant under the French. In such a climate, even the Messin tradesman's yearning for commercial recovery could not prevail. In 1544 the same magistrates who steeled themselves against the emperor's incursions cancelled two fairs allowed by him in Metz, because they feared German merchants would use the market gatherings as a stage for the spread of Lutheran propaganda.[34]

Following the emperor's ban, many Messin Protestants were in fact banished. We have evidence of the Strasbourgeois regularly taking in Protestant refugees from Metz.[35] But as the years passed, other Protestants—the wealthier—managed to remain in Metz and even to practice their religion openly. In some cases they even retained public offices. As in other parts of Europe, Protestantism proved especially attractive to the upper ranks of Messin society, particularly the bourgeoisie, where readers and intellectuals could be found in combination (often within the same individual) with those who saw in Protestantism a new power equation with exciting opportunities for personal advancement. As precarious as the Protestants' existence sometimes was, after 1544, a certain amount of intellectual freedom was nonetheless possible in Metz. The location of the town as a trading center and the nature of its inhabitants allowed for exposure to a variety of ideas within Christianity.[36] The existence of these Protestant Messins and their descendants, by turns secure and critically precarious, will concern us particularly in future chapters. For now we need only note that as greater numbers of Metz's wealthy considered and adopted Protestantism, a fault line opened up within the ruling oligarchy among those who had formerly faced outside pressures together. These first small steps toward division would lead to a longer and more troubled journey toward an apparent loss of political autonomy: new social relations; and a less obvious, but more fundamental, atrophy of religious certainty—in other words, secularization.

Consider the dispute which arose in the sixteenth century between two prominent Messin families—the DeHeus and the Gournays. Like many bitter clan battles, it sprang from an initial closeness and similarity rather than from innate differences. Both families had long wielded influence in the *paraiges* and had therefore regularly furnished members for various posts in the magistrature in the centuries before the sixteenth (Nicholas DeHeu, for example, served as *maître-échevin* in 1485; in 1479, Michel de Gournay was part of a delegation to Louis XI, as mentioned).[37] There had been the predictable social connections between the families, and when Catherine de Gournay married Nicholas DeHeu at the end of the fifteenth century, the ceremony seemed to cement the links between them. However, when Catherine died just two years after the wedding, her relatives insisted that her dowry be returned. Nicolas, who followed the custom of his time and quickly remarried, refused. This dispute made for strained relations between the two extended families, but the whole affair might have remained a garden-variety squabble had it not been for the element of religion, introduced in the following generation. Four of Nicolas DeHeu's five sons (presumably from his second marriage) were attracted to the early Protestant movement. The Gournays remained loyal to Rome. Their enmity deepened by this new area of disagreement, the struggle between the DeHeus and the Gournays quickly became political as well—they bickered over each others' fitness for public office and each family tried to thwart the other's ambitions. Because of these families' prominence, the feud ultimately affected the entire city.[38] Nicolas DeHeu the younger, *maître-échevin* in 1528, tried to uphold Messin neutrality in the wars between France and Spain, begun two years earlier. However, the Gournays quickly accused him and others among the Protestant DeHeus of collaborating with France, then somewhat uncomfortably aligned with the German Protestants. In 1542 Robert DeHeu (Nicolas Jr.'s brother) was deposed from the post of *maître-échevin* on the grounds of his alleged Protestant sympathies. Later, he was also accused on paltry evidence, of conspiring to turn Metz over to the French. Other less prominent Messin Protestants were similarly suspected of pro-French loyalties. Ironically, Metz's Protestants actually had reason to shun the French, since they were far more likely than Catholics to fall victim to French troops' assaults on civilians. In some cases, Catholic Messins may have encouraged soldiers' violence against Protestants. In April of 1542 Messin Protestants wrote to their coreligionists in Strasbourg, pleading for rescue from the advancing French, insisting that "they would rather die than become French."[39]

It should be noted that accusations of pro-French sympathies fell on others as well during this period. In the year of the emperor's entrance, 1544, one observer estimated that at least 400 Messin men had joined the French army. In light of such a scandal, the emperor and his councillors deemed it necessary to execute someone, as a cautionary example to other French-leaning Messins. The original choice for this harsh justice was a Protestant-sympathizing soldier of fortune, the nephew of Guillaume von Furstemberg and a relative of the Landgrave of Hesse.[40] Tried and convicted of recruiting for the French king's army, the lord enlisted a coterie of German princes to plead for his pardon from the sentence—execution by decapitation in the central town square. The emperor reluctantly gave in and granted clemency, but as the scaffold was already built, he insisted that another man, a pauper, be substituted in the nobleman's stead. According to a Venetian ambassador, the poor wretch finally chosen was reported to have lamented his cruel fate saying, "Just my luck! Half of this city is engaged in spying for the king [of France] and it's me alone who has to die for it."[41]

In this tense period of suspicion no Messin was entirely safe from rumor. Those at odds with the powerful Gournays were the most vulnerable. The rancor that developed between the Gournays and their enemies encouraged complex alliances in Metz, alliances that were not always even consistent with religious affiliation. Thus, while religious differences fragmented Messin society, they did so in multilayered and unpredictable ways. And to some extent, these religious feuds, born of zeal, made the whole issue of religious loyalty so complicated that religion was slowly subject to diffusion as a primary force in Messin public life. We can see this process at work even in the sixteenth century. It was not simply that Catholic civic leaders split with Protestant leaders; rather, religious discord produced an entirely new environment in Metz, where new political deals could be made and old ones unmade, and where traditional power equations required recalculation.

For example, in 1551 then *maître-échevin*, Nicholas de Gournay, spread the rumor that the new bishop of Metz, Robert de Lenoncourt (linked, oddly enough, by marriage to the DeHeus) was aiding French efforts in the region. This Gournay denounced Lenoncourt as a potential French agent, and attempted to foment suspicion against him at Charles' court. The Lenoncourts were one of Metz's oldest noble families. Robert's uncle, also Robert de Lenoncourt, had served as archbishop of Rheims and had laid the crown on the head of Francis I.[42] Otherwise, however, there was little real proof of Lenoncourt's affection for France, and he certainly seemed not to have worked for France's military success in Metz. Probably Gournay actually disliked the bishop's attempt to move his residence back to Metz from the nearby town of Vic. Since the thirteenth century, the bishops of Metz had come from the House of Lorraine and city officials, fearing their power, had assiduously discouraged them from living within the city or exercising influence in local government. In fact, when Lenoncourt accepted his high clerical post he became the first bishop allowed entrance to Metz since 1484.[43] This was insupportable to the albeit Catholic Gournays, for a resident bishop would be likely to wrest power away from local leaders. Hence they bitterly opposed Lenoncourt and his efforts.

However, the Gournays' campaign took an odd turn. For without any support from the other *échevins*, the deposed Robert deHeu, ousted as a Protestant, saw an opportunity and seized it. What ensued was a political alliance between the Protestant DeHeus and the bishop of Metz, Lenoncourt. Scrambling to preserve what remained of their influence, the DeHeu family broke its bonds with the other members of the *paraiges* and compromised the city's integrity in the process. Ultimately the bishop of Metz struck his own bargain with the magistrates because above all else he feared French troop incursions into the city. In 1552 he agreed to leave Metz in order to maintain a semblance of Messin unity, but by that time French troops were literally at the gates, and all the regrets of both Catholic and Protestant magistrates could neither gain back the time they had lost to internal division nor resuscitate their defenses against outside forces—defenses that had prevailed for centuries. As religious unity deteriorated among the magistrates, their civic unity similarly evaporated, and the entire structure of autonomy and neutrality began inexorably to implode. What they could not have seen, without omniscient powers of prophecy extending to the eighteenth century, was that the staunch attachment to religious differences that produced this emerging disunity would also sound the death knell for faith in general—at least insofar as faith determined civic power. Notables in Metz made a last ditch effort to counteract the imminent French threat. Some, including the previously vilified Robert DeHeu, tried to raise an army for the city's protection and even debated whether it was worth inviting an Imperial army to help in the effort. Others appealed for aid from their neighbors in Strasbourg, who alas had no troops to spare.[44]

Thus, when Henri II entered Metz in 1552, he made his vow of protection to a magistrature essentially different than the one which had so adamantly required the same of Charles V in 1544. And though the French king promised to relinquish all control on the day his troops should leave, clearly the Messin judges could not approach this monarch as they had the emperor. They could not simply wait for his departure and then reverse French orders—rebanish a pardoned miscreant, invalidate a feudal obligation. First, Henri and his successors made sure that after 1552 their troops were never absent from the vicinity. The French just didn't leave. Secondly, as we are now free to discuss in greater detail, the French program became increasingly comprehensive. It rested on an underlying process of secularization which perhaps none of the actors, not even the king himself, could have foreseen, or understood if they had. In the short term, the French Crown, consciously or not, slowly sought to change the very structure of Messin government, particularly and somewhat ingeniously through changes to the Messin courts.

According to Gaston Zeller, Henri II's occupation of Metz was meant only to prevent an anticipated Imperial military encampment there.[45] This may have been a miscalculation on Henri's part, but the essential fact for us is that initially the French plan does not appear to have included real incorporation of the former Gallic capital. On April 10, the duke of Montmorency, representing the French king whose sons his sons would come to oppose, arrived with a large force of armed men. After a wan show of resistance the magistrates opened the city gates. While exceedingly nervous about the French presence, most Messins simultaneously lacked any real galvanizing enthusiasm for the emperor. It was an uncomfortable moment for both the city's leaders and the general population, given the cultural ties to France previously discussed, and the Messins' political claims to independence from both sides.[46] In the end they chose unavoidable expedience—the French troops were simply too numerous and well armed for much debate.

The exact size of the force which took Metz is not known. Estimates vary between 40,000 and 100,000. By contemporary standards they clearly represented an unanswerable threat. French commissioners to Lorraine, before the takeover of Metz, had demanded substantial provisions for the king's army, including 200,000 loaves of bread, 50 beeves, and 600 sheep per day. The meat was meant for those *lansquenets* who did not observe Lent (probably German Protestants hired to fight with the king against the Counter-Reformation emperor), while fish, eggs, and cheese were ordered for the French Catholics in the force.[47] The commissioners' religious sensitivity represented a wasted effort since, according to one observer, few of the troops, Catholic or Protestant, observed Lenten dietary restrictions, even on Good Friday.[48]

The soldiers encamped in the southern section of Metz, between its two rivers. Initially allowed free entrance to the city, local citizens' pleas eventually convinced commanders to confine the soldiers to their camp. Scavenging troops had apparently lost no time in sacking urban gardens and homes and raiding nearby vineyards. On April 18 Henri II himself entered the city as described, and after three days left a garrison of about 3,500 men in place with a military governor in charge not only of their conduct but also of civic order in Metz in general. Before he left, the king also ordered the local populace disarmed, and required the magistrates to take an oath to support French efforts against the Holy Roman Empire.[49] Despite a later attempt by Charles to reclaim the city, the French held their ground and by early 1553 faced no real threat from the greatly diminished Imperial army.[50]

If the 1552-53 reconquest of Metz by the French was the result of military accident, as Zeller claims, the subsequent transformation of local government was clearly one of intentional (if haphazardly executed) design. French kings and their ministers set out to overpower local institutions and co-opt them into an ever more centralized system. In fact, the installation and growth of the French military in Metz was inextricably linked to the initial changes in the town's judiciary, for almost from their arrival, these military officials and military institutions wielded power over the city's police and courts. By 1554 the French garrison included roughly eight companies of foot soldiers, an equivalent or slightly greater number of light cavalry, 30 *arquebusiers à cheval*, or mounted marksmen, and 50 lancers in the personal service of a newly appointed military governor. In all, the force included some 2,000 men, and while this group varied in size in subsequent years, it did so only as the military presence gained in obvious permanence. The branches atrophied, but only as the roots dug deeper. By the next decade a citadel was added in Metz (in keeping with French practices for recently annexed territory), with permanent quarters for at least 400 men.[51]

The king's military governor and his direct subordinates fairly quickly acquired serious judicial powers as well, and it is partly through them that the French monarchs first infiltrated and then overran the local judiciary.[52] Chosen from among the traditional "sword" nobility in this century, military governors were not, however, always able military men. Most often they came to the post from favored positions in the royal court, where they continued to reside, reveling in political intrigue as much as in the debatable glories of war. Nor were most of these officials regularly seen in the cities they nominally controlled. Jean Louis de Nogaret de la Valette, duke of Epernon, served as the king's military governor for Metz for more than 50 years, from 1583 to 1634, but visited the city only ten times during that period.[53] Instead, the governor's "lieutenant" exercised his powers when the higher official was absent and this post too generally went to a noble, chosen by the governor with the king's approval.

Also in 1554, the king installed a *président royal* to judge cases involving soldiers, but this official later came to preside over general sessions as well, along with members of the traditional magistrature. From 1555 the *président royal* presided over a tribunal that met twice daily to hear complaints, but with a subset of the Treize and *maître-échevin*'s council also in attendance. By 1556 the bishop of Metz was forced to cede further powers to the military governor and this president. Moreover, the very process for selecting local magistrates changed. Parishes continued to offer their candidates for *échevin*, but the military governor and the *président royal* chose the Treize and *maître-échevin* from among that group. The *échevins* were inducted in the usual manner, but now the king's representative administered the oaths of office and these included a pledge to guard "the person, property, honor, and profit" of the king of France and to fully acknowledge "his justice, rights, and authority." [54]

The military governors' influence was further extended by their authority over all "foreigners" in the city—a large group since according to contemporary calculations, it included all those not strictly native to Metz or the *pays messin*, as well as the non-French. A Strasbourgeois may not have seemed quite as foreign a "foreigner" in Metz as a Berliner, but he was a foreigner nonetheless. Other outsiders—and there were many, as mentioned, in this crossroads town—included refugees from fighting in neighboring regions, those with regular business in Metz, young men and women seeking work often as domestic servants, and the large number of foreign-born soldiers, some of whom intermarried with Messin women. By the latter half of the sixteenth century this body of foreigners further included a small community of Jewish traders and merchants and their families, installed in Metz by special royal fiat, despite the centuries-old ban on Jewish residence still technically upheld for the rest of France. These Jews, who will concern us at length in the following chapters (since their presence obviously changed the religious picture in Metz), were not the first of their religion to live in Metz. Zealous Christians killed or drove off a medieval Jewish community in the fiery years surrounding the Crusades or, centuries later, during the first outbreaks of plague. Regardless, the Jews' continuing official status as outsiders—even after they had established a community of several generations' standing, and cultural and educational institutions of great renown—put them under the daily control of the military governors. Thus the sheer number of men and women classed as "foreigners" in Metz, and the number of disputes which involved at least one such non-Messin, gave the governors a significant role in local judicial matters.

In 1592 the governor, his lieutenant, and the *président royal* were joined by yet another lesser royal appointee. The *procureur générale* could also dispense justice in the king's name under certain circumstances. These men served as a constant reminder of the royal claim on Metz, even during periods when they refrained from intervention, for they effectively established a level of administration that was arguably superior to the traditional local magistrates—arguably because the precise jurisdiction of each body or individual remained somewhat murky throughout the sixteenth century. A bourgeois innkeeper accused of brawling with an unruly soldier might find himself examined in the governor's chamber or, more likely, before the *président royal*. Or he might well be tried and sentenced first by the town *échevins* and then try, particularly if he were well connected, to appeal their sentence to royal officials. In serious cases, or if the *président royal* were absent, a Messin convicted by the Treize might follow the example of his predecessor who vainly tried to appeal to Spire, and now attempt to bring his claim before the king's own council in Paris. Sometimes such renegades succeeded in having their cases reheard; sometimes there were sent back to Metz to suffer the fines or punishment previously assessed. The significant element is that they did go to Paris (apparently in ever increasing numbers as the seventeenth century opened) and that local magistrates were losing their strong-arm powers to prevent it.[55] Certainly the magistrates complained, but to whom? To the king himself who, even if he decided in their favor, was of course asserting his place at the top of this still-jumbled pyramid. The base of Metz's judicial structure, then, was more than a little confused well into the first decades of the new century. One might say that only the top was clearly delineated and fully constructed.

In the last years of the sixteenth century and the first of the seventeenth, Metz was still not what we might call "thoroughly French" in outlook or administration. Messin residents had received citizenship in 1559, at least insofar as citizenship meant exemption from the *droit d'aubaine*, or confiscation of goods to which non-Frenchmen were subject in the ancien régime.[56] The Messins were, by their leaders' own admission, the king's "servants;" but they were not yet his "subjects." Even Henri III did not presume to clearly possess the hearts of the Messins. "The" city of Metz was not, from that French king's perspective, "our" city of Metz.[57] Messin magistrates still considered their decisions binding and final, even if all city residents did not. The city did not choose deputies for the Estates General until 1614. But if these symbolic signs of Messin separateness persisted, practical manifestations of independence were rapidly dwindling. The *maître-échevin* and Treize still sat in judgment over the residents of Metz, but the new royal appointees had diffused many of their traditional powers, and local miscreants were increasingly bolder in defying the magistrates' orders. The pretense that royal intervention was a temporary necessity of war was steadily losing credibility, as Henri IV appointed further royal officials to oversee local court matters.[58] Most of all, it may have been this progenitor of the Bourbon kings who first determined to supplant the local magistrates altogether, by establishing two superior royal chambers in Metz itself—the Parlement finally called in 1633, and the *bailliage* founded eight years later. These are the institutions we must next consider. Thus the town's evolution, from frontier outpost to obedient provincial capital, seems already charted by the end of the sixteenth century. Just as religious discord had allowed the French royal armies to enter Metz and encamp there—local magistrates torn by personal religious rivalries had stood helpless to resist first the French troops and then the French functionaries—so religious controversy of a more extreme nature in the seventeenth century was central to the full realization of the royal program. The French kings' campaign of dominance was vigorous, to be sure. If considered in sum over the span of several reigns it was also remarkably systematic. Historians, like Zeller, have appropriately paid homage to the royal campaign by charting its steady progress in Metz and other outlying areas of absolutist France. However, if, for a moment, one looks beyond the intense artificial light of royal efforts—the designs of Richelieu and his king, the craft of Louis XIV and his bureaucrat-warriors—one sees a world of far more interesting mixed shadows and complex optical effects. The wranglings of local politics and piety actually allowed the royal program, vigorous though it may have been, to succeed. Religion and religious controversies, especially the Catholic-Protestant struggle, had already begun to erode traditional alliances in the sixteenth century—inserting new and more potent discord into the privileged class which had previously stood as the bulwark against all incursions on Metz's independence. This erosion, ultimately an erosion of the foundation of faith itself, is what allowed for the establishment of the Parlement, and the *bailliage* in the first half of the seventeenth century. Later in the seventeenth century the breakdown of local alliances became vastly more apparent, and inspired dynamic action actually aiding and promoting the French takeover of Metz. The city's Catholics actually tried to enlist royal help in local religious struggles, a favor the French king was only too willing to grant, seeing in his involvement the full implication of a change in the status of Metz itself. Secularization, and indeed "centralization" in this sense, reveal themselves as less the products of simple addition or subtraction than of subtler and more complicated processes: namely, multiplication and division.

To understand this more fully, let us begin by observing the more obvious phenomenon—centralization—at work. As this represented indeed the first and most visible expression of secularization, it is appropriate to introduce it at once, even if more substantial shifts in social relations (the full promise of secularization) will occupy us in subsequent chapters. For now we must outline the basic changes to Messin government in the seventeenth century, beginning with the establishment in 1633 of the Parlement of Metz.

NOTES

1. Gaston Zeller, *La Réunion de Metz à la France, 1552–1648*, vol. 1 (Paris: Société d'Edition: Les Belles Lettres, 1926), p. 191. In this first chapter of historical background I depend heavily on the work of Gaston Zeller, particularly on material reviewed in the two-volume study cited above. Other useful histories are cited in the following notes.

2. Francois-Yves Le Moigne, ed., *Histoire de Metz* (Toulouse: Editions Privat, 1986), p. 139.

3. Jacques Dupaquier, *La Population Française aux XVIIe et XVIIIe Siècles* (Paris: Presses Universitaires de France, 1979), p. 20.

4. Public documents of this period are rife with the complaints and pleas of local residents or their agents for relief from the ravages of war and the taxes needed to sustain it. In 1636 local magistrates begged the king to discontinue or decrease his impositions on the Messin bourgeois, and they complained bitterly of the disruption of commerce resulting from fighting in the region. See B.N., N.A.F. 22669, fol. 81 (September 19, 1639); see also vol.. 22670, fols. 85, 88 and 90.

A variety of orders by the city's military governors attests to the intransigence of soldiers, repeatedly threatened with corporal punishment for chopping down or raiding the woods, fields, and orchards around the city. See B.N., N.A.F., 22669, fols. 125, 127, and 133. In addition, young men were pressed into *corvées* to help fortify the city against attack and residents' carts and wagons were periodically requisitioned for the army's use. For a typical order regarding service on the *corvée* see B.N., N.A.F., 22669, fol. 159 (June 1639); for an order requisitioning carts see B.N., N.A.F., 22669, fol. 14 (April 1639).

5. Zeller, vol. 1, p. 192.

6. Ibid., pp. 192–93.

7. Ibid., p. 195.

8. Ibid., p. 255. According to Zeller, the writer's exact words were that negotiating the tricky diplomacy was like trying to *"naiger entre deux eaues."*

9. Ibid., p. 213.

10. Ibid.

11. Ibid.

12. The significance of symbolism at public festivals has long interested social historians. For two excellent French studies highlighting such material see Barbara B. Diefendorf, *Beneath the Cross, Catholics and Huguenots in Sixteenth-Century Paris* (New York: Oxford University Press, 1991), and the less recent work of Sharon Kettering, *Judicial Politics and Urban Revolt in Seventeenth-Century France* (Princeton, N.J.: Princeton University Press, 1978). For an English analogue covering roughly the same period, see David Underdown, *Revel, Riot and Rebellion, Popular Politics and Culture in England 1603–1660* (Oxford: Clarendon Press, 1985).

13. According to Zeller, Imperial taxation was traditionally based on two impositions, the *denier commune* or *Gemeine Pfennig*—a permanent money tax only irregularly collected and enforced in Metz—and the *contribution matriculaire* or *Matrikularbeitrag*, sometimes called the *aide* or *Hilfe*—a requisition of men and equip-ment primarily for military purposes. This second imposition, he writes, generally occurred to support an elected emperor's journey to Rome for coronation, or to protect the empire against external enemies, though contingencies were often loosely interpreted to fit into these categories. For more specific numbers imposed on Metz in various years see Zeller, vol. 1 pp. 218–35.

14. Marc Bloch, *Les Rois Thaumaturges* (Strasbourg: 1924), p. 108; reprinted in English as *The Royal Touch, Monarchy and Miracles in France and England,* trans. J. E. Anderson (New York: Dorset Press, 1961); cited by Zeller, vol. 1, p. 243, note 3.

15. Zeller, vol. 1, pp. 242–43.

16. See Introduction, p. xviii

17 Zeller, vol. 1, p. 253; see note 2.

18. See Alain Girardot: "La République messine," chapter 6 in Le Moigne, *Histoire de Metz,* pp. 137–67

19. Peter Sahlins, "Natural Frontiers Revisited: France's Boundaries since the Seventeenth Century." *American Historical Review,* vol. 95, no. 5 (1990) 1423–51.

20. Zeller, vol. 1, pp. 361–62.

21. Ibid., p. 361.

22. According to Zeller, though no Messin notable sought to hasten the French takeover, no one could deny the likely ascendance of the French, "an event which undoubtedly must toll the knell of Messin independence." See ibid., p. 248.

23. Zeller particularly emphasized Imperial weakness in describing the "accident" or series of accidents that led to French domination. See ibid., pp. 415–16.

24. Among acts promulgated by the Treize was one in 1625, imposing quarantines and other regulations during an outbreak of epidemic; B.N., N.A.F. 22668, fols. 1 and 3.

25. Zeller, vol. 1, p. 183.

26. Ibid., p. 213.

27. Cited by Zeller (vol. 1, p. 237) from the Chronicle of Philippe de Vigneulles.

28. In the early sixteenth century, the city had a permanent mounted mercenary force, varying in size from 40 soldiers (1520–30) to 27 men (1551–52). These mounted soldiers were generally brought from Germany. In the same period the Messins also employed roughly 11 foot soldiers; 41 *couleuvriniers,* or musketeers; and 48 sentries. These last three groups were generally recruited from city and area residents. See Zeller, vol. 1, p. 215.

29. The term "notable" is a general one, used here to indicate those prominent Messins of some wealth and standing who dominated civic affairs.

30. Ibid., p. 221.

31. Ibid., p. 235.

32. Ibid., p. 184.

33. Ibid., p. 189. For further information on Protestants in Metz, see the work of Henri Tribout de Morembert, particularly his two-volume work, *La Réforme à Metz* (Nancy: Université de Nancy, 1969–71), as well as that of M. Thirion, *Étude sur l'Histoire du Protestantisme à Metz et dans le pays messin* (Nancy: Imprimerie F. Colllin, 1884).

34. Zeller, vol. 1, p. 276.

35. Ibid., pp. 189ff.

36. Morembert, in his rather nationalistic but still seminal work cited above (see note 33), ascribed the success of Protestantism in Metz during the sixteenth century to religious trends first, and political trends only secondarily. Hence he saw the first wave of Protestant sympathizers arising from among the Messin clergy itself, with pivotal members of the laity later following suit. According to Morembert, writings by Luther were first brought to Metz in 1519, most probably transported by merchants from Strasbourg and Switzerland. In addition, Messin theologians were influenced by many standard pre-Reformation tracts, including Erasmus's *March of Folly,* Thomas More's *Utopia,* Johannes Reuchlin's *Mirror of the Eyes,* and Ulrich von Hutten's *Letters of Obscure Men.* See Morembert, vol. 1, *Le Lutheranisme,* pp. 21ff.

37. Zeller, vol. 1, pp. 245–46; see also note 2 on p. 246.

38. Perhaps this case is most useful in pointing up the difficulty of trying to classify the precise source of discord. The war between the DeHeus and the Gournays was simultaneously economic (though they were of the same socioeconomic class), religious, and political. One might compare the feud most effectively to the complex Italian vendetta in which issues of family loyalty often influenced successive generations.

39. Zeller vol. 1, p. 265.

40. The precise name of this individual is unknown; see Zeller, vol.1, p. 275, note 1.

41. Ibid., p. 275.

42. Ibid., p. 286.

43. For more information on the problematic relationship between the bishops of Metz and secular municipal authorities, see Zeller, vol. 1, pp. 195–200.

44. Ibid., p. 342.

45. Ibid., p. 315.

46. According to a contemporary legend (which Zeller rejects) the magistrates had in fact betrayed the city, and succumbed to the French without a struggle and without local merchant and tradesmen's knowledge. See Zeller, vol. 1, pp. 354–55.

47. *Lansquenets* are mercenary foot soldiers armed with pikes or lances. For other information on provisioning the troops stationed in Metz see Zeller, vol. 1, pp. 326–27.

48. Zeller, vol. 1, p. 357, note 3; cited from J.-F. Huguenin, *Les chroniques de la ville de Metz, recueillies, mises enor dre [sic.] et publiées pour la premiere Fois (900–1552)* (Metz:1838), p. 866.

49. Zeller, vol. 1, p. 362.

50. There is some indication that the Spanish troops were particularly vulnerable to the cold, damp Messin winter. See Zeller, vol. 1, p. 415.

51. Zeller, vol. 2, p. 80.

52. Ibid., pp. 87–89.

53. Ibid.

54. Ibid., p. 17.

55. For an interesting related study, charting the later cases of several Jews who also went to Paris (in direct disobedience to local Jewish leaders' rulings) see Frances Malino, "Resistance and Rebellion in Eighteenth-Century France," *Transactions of the Jewish Historical Society of England*, vol. 25, (1987–88). A version of the same research appears under Malino's name in Bernhard Blumenkranz (ed.) *Les Juifs en France au 18e siècle* (Paris: Commission française des Archives juives, 1994).

56. Zeller, Vol. 2, p. 257.

57. Ibid., p. 259.

58. The first *procureur général*, we should note, appointed by Henri IV in 1592, was a Protestant. See Zeller, vol. 2, p. 202.

Chapter 2
Frenchification, Centralization, and the Parlement of Metz

Upon its establishment in 1633, the Parlement of Metz faced a barrage of hostile opinion from varied quarters. Local magistrates, their judicial preeminence in Metz jeopardized, fought zealously to protect their authority, or at least to limit its erosion. Popular opinion of the new court was mixed. And even the royal military governor and his lieutenant, who had controlled local government in fact for two decades, displayed suspicion of the new court, undoubtedly concerned that their own power would now be eclipsed by that of this tribe of Parisian lawyers, courtiers, and actual or soon-to-be robe nobles.[1] Why then, despite the real local opposition to Parlement, did that institution not only endure, but succeed in capturing the dominant place the Crown sought for it? Or, more specifically, what engine was driving the triumph of Parlement in Metz? Was it, as has traditionally been supposed, the juggernaut of "centralization," emerging entirely from Paris and the royal court? Even recent studies of the consolidation of France under the Bourbon monarchy might promote this view. For scholars looking at other parts of the country at this time, the takeover of local institutions—be it on a governmental level or one involving only the suppression of "popular culture" by an "elite" one—came from outside, from an alien power imposing itself an unwilling local population. The contemporary trend in historiography, set in motion by the work of Robert Muchembled, is vastly less appreciative of either the royal or "elite" presence than traditional studies, but it actually fits quite well in some ways with older views of centralization.[2] Consider, for example, the observation of Emmanuel Michel, whose nineteenth-century work remains the most thorough treatment of the early days of Metz's high court.

Thus, from the first years of its institution, the Parlement of Metz maintained a difficult position: the people resisted its authority; plague and war ravaged its territory. Beyond this, it had to fight with lower judicial bodies which had to be subordinated to it and which misunderstood its powers, and it also had to struggle with the military authority.

Nothing, however, could conquer the vigor of the Parlement; one sees it march with a firm step, toward the goal of its institution, which was to re-attach the Three Bishoprics (Metz, Toul, and Verdun) to France forever, and to strengthen, through the sovereign exercise of justice, the flag which Henri II had planted in the capital of this beautiful province. [3]

In both cases, Michel's and a more general modern view of French transformation such as Muchembled's, an external force primarily is responsible for changes wrought in a distinct community. Michel reduces that force to the royal will, or some nebulous Crown-centered imperative moving the various regions of France toward unification and relative uniformity. And he applauds the transformation. Contemporary scholars observe a more complex and nefarious assault, from forces political, economic, religious and cultural in nature, but still largely foreign and incompatible with the popular society they moved to co-opt.

For our study it remains convenient to use the word *centralization* to describe the process by which local institutions were re-formed and recast as national ones, deriving their powers from a central authority (on which they were thus wholly dependent), but it must be continually questioned whether that process was one entirely, or even primarily initiated from the center. As noted, the success of centralization in Metz owed as much to local forces, local prejudices, and local circumstances, as it did to any royal or central government agenda. For while the impetus to create the Parlement and to suppress the local magistracy came from Paris, the plan would not have succeeded if it had not seemed at several points along the way to satisfy various local interests. Additionally, political centralization in Metz appears as part of a larger social trend and of more substantial (if subterranean) social shifts. These are the changes which we are particularly interested in charting here and in later chapters.

With regard to early political changes, there are three main reasons that local magistrates failed to mount or sustain an effective campaign against central government intrusion into their lives. First, the very nature of Parlement as an appellate court proved alluring to locals. Litigants became unwittingly complicitous in the Crown's scheme. Second, judges of the Parlement, along with other royal officials, embarked on a steady program of rhetorical sabotage, all the more potent for being symbolic. Controlling the language of power led inexorably to power itself. Finally (our most crucial finding) the king's new courts prospered by capitalizing on local instability, particularly religious tension.

To begin with our first point: Parlement, as a court of last resort, had an inherent appeal to a certain section of the populace of Metz. That is, the Crown established the Parlement above local courts, not initially in replacement of them. As a result, any recent appellants who had lost cases before the local magistrates, or who would lose them after 1633, saw in the Parlement a new opportunity for vindication. In fact, one of the first pleas by local magistrates to the king after Parlement's creation was that the validity of their own earlier judgments be reaffirmed. Apparently many in Metz who had lost cases were fully ready to try their luck again before the new high court. The Parlement thus had a natural group of supporters simply because it served as an appeals court. Even the local magistrates themselves, as we shall see here and in subsequent chapters, could not resist the temptation to go to Parlement with their grievances.

It is not clear if the Crown realized that judicial reforms would automatically prove more attractive to local communities than other centralizing moves. Certainly much of the royal program in Metz and throughout the kingdom involved changes to local courts and the establishment of provincial parlements to stand above them.[4] In fact, reform (specifically consolidation) of France's multitudinous courts, some feudal, some episcopal, and some royal in origin, and the rationalizing of different concepts of law, even, was a venerable if haphazard process, begun as far back as the reign of Philip Augustus, and arguably not completed until that of Napoleon. The road to the political consolidation of the kingdom, then, or one of the principle byways at least, had long been thought to lie through the courts. In a more immediate way as well, France's society was a litigious one, so reform of the courts promised in many ways to reform the whole structure of official relationships. More simply, the aim of centralization was also to standardize the judiciary and local government in all of France, for logic's sake, as well as to bind those lower institutions more firmly to the absolute monarchy. For now it is enough to note that Parlement came to Metz with a ready-made, if constantly shifting, constituency, as well as with natural enemies.

Having mentioned this precondition disposing the Messins to accept the Parlement, then, we must now consider the two areas that were less static in 1633 and more subject to debate. Namely, the manipulation of language by local notables and the Crown, and the importance of religious divisions within Messin society. The first of these is worth examining in some depth as we trace the Parlement's history chronologically. The exploration reminds us that this was a society that used and understood two kinds of language: direct and indirect or symbolic language. The ability to control the two was critical to political success. The absolutist monarchy—with its clearer, stronger pyramidical structure—was more effective at this control than was the local government.

Local opposition to the establishment of a *parlement* began in Metz even before the king had officially ordered that high court into being. In the first months of 1632, as rumors spread of Louis XIII and Richelieu's plan to install the court, local representatives of the Three Orders petitioned the monarch and first minister in a fairly obsequious tone, asking them to curtail the program. Reminding the king of their loyalty, the notables emphasized that the population of Metz was already overburdened by having to support and lodge large numbers of troops fighting nearby, in the continuing battles of the Thirty Years War. A *parlement*, and the necessary local charges needed to maintain it, would simply ruin the city.[5] The situation was so dire, they claimed, that "the greater part of the inhabitants (of Metz) have been forced to abandon their homes and flee, having nothing at all with which to feed themselves or their families."[6] They also reminded royal officials, in a less docile tone, that the imposition of a new sovereign royal court in Metz would abridge their ancient and accustomed privileges.[7] And they attempted, with some success, to enlist the help of the royal military governor, as well as influential clerics and nobles, in their cause.[8] The king's response was vague and noncommittal, undoubtedly calculated to be so. He wrote to the inhabitants of Metz simply that he held them entirely in his affection and would protect their best interests.[9] Through such watery assurances, Louis XIII apparently kept the disgruntled at bay, at least until the following January, when a *parlement* was officially created for the frontier province and a date for its installation chosen.[10]

In announcing the establishment, the king and his first minister, the cardinal, used diplomatic language meant to soothe. The *maître-échevin*, his council of *échevins*, and the Treize would continue to meet. The king asked only that they abide the presence of the Parlement in the *palais* used as the Hôtel de Ville until a more convenient assembly space for Parlement could be built. Jurisdictional questions—who would rule in which cases?—were not laid out here. But even the formulas of the Crown's communications on the topic made the overall policy quietly clear. In announcing the imminent arrival in Metz of Antoine de Bretagne, the prospective first president of the court, royal letters acknowledged the event as a project, "to introduce the signs of his (Majesty's) authority in Metz."[11] Local notables, even if they did not outwardly balk at the announcement of Bretagne's arrival, did vehemently protest when that official required an office in the Hôtel de Ville and sent around an architect to seize and redesign it.[12] Throughout the conflict with the Parlement, in fact, local officials particu-larly bristled about issues involving physical space. Repeatedly during the Parle-ment's first years, conflicts arose with the local magistrates over office space, assembly space, and general control of the city's municipal buildings. It was as if local leaders, unable to retain the more potent elements of their sovereignty, felt most acutely the Parlement's growing hold on their real estate. To some extent, in this society the forms of power equaled power—a fact both local leaders and royal officials recognized. The proportion of physical space occu-pied by either group—local courts or the Parlement—thus held great sway in seventeenth-century Metz. The tension between local leaders and the Parlement became a contest for control of the symbols of power, be they tangible symbols (like office space) or a subtler rhetorical advantage.

The importance of symbolic forms is nowhere more apparent than in the induction of Parlement, and the ceremonies surrounding that event in August of 1633. Even beyond the obvious pomp, both local and royal officials employed specific language to further their respective claims to authority. In an elaborate ritual, the new members of the high court (drawn from the king's councils in Paris, or from other regional *parlements* such as those in Dijon, Burgundy or Rouen), sat in the most coveted seats in the cathedral—on either side of the choir stalls. The color and length of their robes was carefully prescribed according to rank. The bishop of Madaure, dressed in his pontifical robes, performed a high mass in their honor.[13] The members then proceeded to the Hôtel de Ville where the edict of their establishment was publicly read and the doors of the building opened to them. Speeches by various local dignitaries, and responses by the new judges, took place throughout the day.

In reality, the scene resembled a confrontation between two separate packs of animals, each group slowly circling the other, carefully attempting to protect its own turf. Local clerics for example, hailed the establishment of the court, but in language laden with implied admonitions. Often they stated as fact that which they wished would be true. The dean of the cathedral, for example, praised the arrival of the king's appointees to the court, "which can have no other object than that of the public welfare and the administration of justice, and to protect the property, tranquility and dignity of all the orders."[14] And, he added, "as nothing is so dear to the king as the preservation of the rights of the church," he was sure that, "the said Parlement will always invoke His Majesty's authority with care and affection." The bishop expressed his certainty that the Parlement would dispense justice fairly, and he used words such as "integrity," "equity," and "sweet influence" to describe what he expected from the court.

Bretagne, for his part, used a similar approach in his address to the audience, which included the body of local magistrates as well as influential members of the nobility. He thanked the bishop for performing the mass, but insisted that the honor fell not on them, as individual members of the new court, but on the king who had sent them. He added that he and the other judges of the Parlement, "do not doubt at all that he [the bishop, acting as a representative of the Church] has a very great joy in seeing the authority of His Royal Majesty appear so happily in all the land." A special royal appointee for the event followed with an even more elaborate speech, reminding the listeners of the divine right of the monarch and the potency of his *gloire*. "It appears," this speaker said, "by history and by general repute, that [France's] kings have been particularly favored and chosen by heaven to provide an example of remarkable piety, justice, and magnanimity to all other princes. For which nations, nay what regions on earth, have not experienced their justice and their power."[15] This speaker's harangue included a lengthy discussion of the nature and benefits of justice, a claim that the poor administration of justice always resulted in corruption and chaos in civil states, and an interpretation of the thought of Plato and Aristotle meant to confirm that justice was a product of divine ordering as administered by the only legitimate earthly arbiter—the prince. This last point represented a recasting of the Thomist philosophy of the origins of law (drawn in part form Aquinas's reading of Aristotle of course), by combining it with the theories of divine right one would most closely associate with James I of England, or later in France, Jacques Benigne Bossuet.[16] The intention here, among royal representatives, was clear: to remind or even warn the Messin populace, and especially local leaders, that henceforth the only legitimate power would be royal power, or that directly emanating from the central state. An original medieval French presence in Metz was repeatedly proclaimed as the true authority, with the implied dismissal of all other forms of governance—such as those developed or upheld during the later

Imperial era—as illegitimate and worthy of suppression. All of these ideas, expressed either directly or indirectly in the Parlement's induction ceremonies, would surface again and fuel very real changes in the dispensing of justice in Metz during the next half century.

Local magistrates also delved into philosophy to protest, if not the Parlement's establishment, then at least its growing jurisdiction during its first years. In February 1634 representatives of the Three Orders asked the king to restore the Treize's right to hear appeals and to judge in the last resort, claiming that only the magistrates of that local institution could serve as the Messins' "natural judges."[17] In a more detailed case three years later, the same body of notables complained that one of the few powers left to local judges—the right to decide small constabulary matters—had been rendered superfluous by the Parlement's ability to hear appeals of their convictions in such matters. The controversy arose when the Treize issued a police ordinance forbidding local sellers of roasted meat and poultry to open their stalls in the marketplace before 10 A.M. The sellers apparently appealed this rule before Parlement, and while the case was pending Parlement ordered the local magistrates to desist in their enforcement of the ordinance. Ultimately, the Parlement upheld the Treize's order, insisting, however, that the words "*De par le roi*" be added to the public placards announcing the rule. But this did little to appease the ruffled magistrates. If Parlement could reverse a police ordinance on appeal, they argued, then the magistrates' power over police matters was entirely ephemeral—only the illusion of power—while real power would rest with the Parlement.

This was, of course, a keen and perceptive statement, one of real insight, by the local judges. They recognized well that the ability to control justice, not simply the existence of certain laws or judgments, was crucial to real authority, and they felt it slipping steadily from their grasp. Their protests to the king, in this case and in others, represented a canny awareness of the important balance between symbolic forms and ultimate authority. However, their grasp of symbolism and its uses was still flawed, and perhaps this explains why their protests fizzled in the end. For in this one case, for example, while local notables began with the fierce proclamation that control over police matters had always belonged to the *maître-échevin* and Treize, as part of custom and tradition, they also looked to the king's edict establishing Parlement as a support for their claim. And once they resorted less to arguments based on ancient rights and privileges, and more on claims springing from royal promises, their case in some sense was lost. From this early date, the magistrates ceded their strongest claim to autonomy in favor of claims which inadvertently bolstered royal preeminence. It was not that local leaders ceased to protest Parlement's growing judicial authority, or the waning of their own. Their complaints—some of which were temporarily successful—fill public records well into the 1670s. But during the 1640s, 1650s, and 1660s, the tone of their complaints changed steadily. They appear less as petitioners refusing to suffer an affront, than as supplicants, pleading for favors. And the desperation of their circumstances led them, ironically, to the very institution they were trying to restrain—the Parlement.

The catalyst for this change was the establishment of a second, related royal court in Metz—a *bailliage*. Designed in 1634 as the king's court of first resort, the *bailliage* was to further diminish the number of cases to be decided in the local magistrates' court, the Treize. For the *bailliage* would hear a significant subset of just those cases supposedly reserved to the magistrates in the edict establishing Parlement. The king claimed to be moved by magnanimity. "In order to favorably treat the *maître-échevin* and Treize of Metz . . ." he would allow them to continue as the final judges of civil cases involving less than 100 livres, and in other cases which resulted in fines less than 60 sols. Other cases would presumably originate in the *bailliage*, and all would be appealable to the Parlement.[18]

Local judges and officials did not welcome this new division of authority. As with the establishment of Parlement, the king's order to create a *bailliage* in Metz (as well as other lower courts in nearby towns) elicited fervent objections from notables. The complaints even outstripped those against the Parlement, perhaps because the erosion of local judges' jurisdiction was at last made explicit and detailed. And again, a dominant issue for the complainants was, not surprisingly, the cost. "The establishment of a *bailliage* in his city of Metz can be of absolutely no benefit to the service of His Majesty," wrote one group of local officials in September of 1634. "Furthermore, it will bring about the ruin and devastation of the said city, by the surcharges of court officers, court costs and trial fees, during a time of such calamity and so full of war." Until this time, they argued, justice had been dispensed freely to the inhabitants of Metz by local judges, and they added defiantly that the administration of the courts was a patrimonial right of the nobility, clergy, and urban patriciate and that it was therefore their right to collect any appropriate court fees.[19] The writers ended by insisting that the king at least postpone the establishment of the *bailliage*. For whatever reason—because the region remained too unstable, because he sincerely sympathized with their cries of impoverishment or because he feared a more volatile or violent resistance—Louis acceded to this last demand and put off this most overt assault on the magistrates' authority for almost seven years. But when in early 1641 he decided to implement the plan, his patience for diplomacy with local judges was greatly depleted, undoubtedly because he no longer feared their disapproval.

The order enacting the earlier creation of a *bailliage* now included a direct and stated "suppression" of the Treize. The Treize were no longer to hold any authority; they were to cease immediately from judging any matters at all in Metz, and even the general populace was forbidden to accord them recognition as judicial officers. Lawyers and clerks for the former Treize were to report now to the royal court, which (in perhaps the cruelest affront) was to occupy the same chamber in which the local magistrates had formerly met.[20] In all, the Treize were to be replaced entirely, and the *maître-échevin* and his councillors would remain, but only as strictly controlled by the Crown. In June, the king would set his own rules for the election of the *échevins*, in a move meant to remind local officials of the source of their authority (and of the king's ultimate right to constrain it) as much as one to change particular procedures.[21]

Members of the Treize, and other local leaders, did not accept their suppression calmly. In April 1641, even before the Crown's plans for new elections of the *échevins* had been announced, the Treize lashed out against the *bailliage*, if not against royal authority in general. One member of the local court, Jean Potet, apparently whipped his colleagues' fury into action. After supposedly uttering "insolent words against the service of his majesty," Potet threatened the commisisoners sent to install the *bailliage*, and he convinced others, including M. de Lambert, the royal military governor, actually to bar the door and seize the keys to the *palais*, refusing entrance to the new *bailliage* judges.[22] The exact outcome of this act of rebellion is not detailed in official records. The Conseil d'Etat, we do know, ordered Potet and his cronies to appear before them in Paris. Lambert apparently escaped with a wrist slapping, being ordered merely to desist in his help to the Treize and to enforce the establishment of the *bailliage*, which he duly did. Again, the local officials backed down and, if grudgingly, accepted the royal order.

In June of 1641, as mentioned, the king ordered a new election of *échevins*, and local notables may have optimistically viewed this as an indication that at least that local body was to be preserved. As it was, this election strengthened the king's claim to be the creator (and thus the rightful destroyer if need be) of local institutions. References to the chief *échevin* appeared in the royal order alternately as *maître-échevin* (the traditional term) and as *maire* (the term more analagous to local officers in other parts of France and to the mere gatekeepers of sixteenth-century Metz).[23] Little distinction between the terms was made, and it seems that this was intentional—an attempt to mollify local leaders and to make the transition from relative autonomy to dependence appear part of a continuum and thus less explosively apparent. The issue of semantics would, however, resurface later. Officers of the *bailliage*, in the meantime, were less inclined to coddle local sensibilities. Making the case for their own authority, and for royal authority in general, they chastised the Treize and *échevins* for claiming any traditional right to exist. The power to create local judicial bodies had always belonged to the French kings, they argued, and this despite the fact that under the empire, Metz's bishops had controlled some aspects of the judiciary and the election of *échevins*.[24]

The *bailliage*, as newly appointed replacement of the Treize, claimed all rights over the *justice ordinaire* of the city, including the administration and regulation of police or constabulary matters. Among the remaining local officials—the *échevins*—the *bailliage* officers acknowledged little remaining power.

It is true that in the declaration of December 12, 1640 his majesty, in order to favor the city of Metz, wanted there to be a *maire* and ten *conseiller échevins* who would have authority over the case and conduct of the common affairs of the city. But their power is so clearly limited and reduced by that same declaration—following the example, the same functions, honors and authority as that of the Provost of Merchants and *échevins* of the Hôtel de Ville in Paris—that it is impossible to think otherwise."[25]

The *bailliage* then issued its own order on June 13, restricting the *échevins* of Metz, and it posted this decree prominently in the public squares and crossroads. The local magistrates then appealed to Parlement to affirm their authority.

The Parlement, supposedly acting in the king's name, supported the *bailliage* when, in July, it expressly prohibited officers of the Hôtel de Ville from exercising any jurisdiction over police matters. Further, the high court also chastised the local magistrates for conspiring to regain powers which, the court decreed, it had no enduring right to possess. Among these were not only the power to issue police ordinances but also the power to regulate trades and tradesmen in the city (and to collect all fees connected with these functions). According to Parlement, these powers now belonged to the officers of the *bailliage*. The court scolded the magistrates as well for using public funds, "in the vain pursuit of their futile claims, by sending messages and dispatching deputies to the [king's] council in Paris, all of which promotes the [financial] ruin of the city, and upsets the public tranquility." Parlement ordered that the local judges desist in their efforts or face steep fines.[26] But despite this order, city notables did succeed in reaching Louis XIII with a new protest of their situation, and they gained his assurances—again only in vague terms—that their powers would be protected. The king was careful not to reveal any details or promise anything specific, and he consistently emphasized that any concession to the *échevins* represented a special royal favor.[27] Daily confrontations between the *bailliage* and local judges therefore persisted throughout the summer and into the fall. The most explosive issues remained the control of public funds and jurisdictional conflicts, but with control of city buildings and placement in public processions also in contention.[28]

By December of 1641, feuding and confusion over just who had jurisdiction over what in Metz had reached such a pitch that the king and his ministers stepped in directly, and a settlement was worked out in his Conseil Privé. The *maire* and *échevins* would continue to control all public funds "belonging to the city" (whatever this meant). They would continue to arrange for the repair and maintenance of public works, city walls, bridges, dikes and the like. They would maintain control over the administration and revenues of the Hôpital Saint Nicolas, but subject to the review of the lieutenant general of the *bailliage* and the king's *procureur*. And they would be in charge of maintaining order in public places and streets, with the power to regulate the shipment of goods along the city's rivers. The magistrates were also allowed to assess taxes on coal, oil, straw, tiles, hay, and wood used for fuel, carried along the Seille or Moselle, and they could issue orders as to such goods' sale or distribution, "according to what they deem necessary for the common good of the city."[29] They were to hold responsibility for the lodging and support of troops in Metz, with the reminder that officers of the *bailliage* (as well as they) were to be exempt from having to lodge troops in their own homes. The officers of the *bailliage*, however, were to have complete jurisdiction over all civil and criminal matters involving the inhabitants of Metz and its surrounding region, over all disputes between soldiers and bourgeois of the city, and over all ordinary police matters. They were to act as judges in the last resort for cases involving up to 60 sols in fines; they were to set all rules concerning innkeepers, cabarets, vagabonds, gambling, and any gatherings which were "il-licit and contrary to good morals." They were also to have charge of the setting of weights and measures, adjudicate disputes between tradesmen and artisans, and administer oaths to newly received tradesmen. Moreover, the *bailliage* was to be entitled to all other jurisdictions, rights and, most important, remuneration, previously belonging to the Treize and *échevins*. It was to render its judgments from the Hôtel de Ville until a more convenient meeting place could be arranged. The local magistrates thus lost on almost all of the most essential points of their complaints.

In subsequent years, members of the local magistracy continued to lodge protests against the *bailliage*, but on a case-by-case basis rather than, as earlier, through general attacks. And increasingly they brought their complaints to royal officials in Metz or (as in the June 1641 petition) to the Parlement, hoping that the high court could act to constrain the lower one. Thus in October of 1642, a petition to Parlement from "the inhabitants of Metz" asked for relief from excessive charges being levied by the *bailliage*, apparently for their own support and for administrative costs. The signatures on the document reveal it as largely the work of local magistrates.[30] In September of 1643 the magistrates claimed that the officers of the *bailliage* were also seizing fees which belonged to the city; at the same time they called for an assembly of the Three Orders to bolster their case.[31] They also contacted the Parlement's first president, now Claude de Bretagne,[32] and asked for his help against the *bailliage*. At the end of the month they persuaded their old friend Lambert to intervene, but the governor did so this time only provisionally. He made clear that his actions were binding only until the king should order otherwise.[33]

In all, these and later cases mark a true sea change in the local notables' dealings with the Parlement and with royal government in general. In early local protests against Parlement and the *bailliage*, notables had often used traditional legal phrases such as "from time immemorial" to describe their respective rights to govern and to decide legal cases in Metz. They continued, as the century wore on, to employ such phrases, but without much potency. Their claim to express an ancient collective memory was proven almost ludicrous by the fact that those who less than a decade earlier had fiercely opposed Parlement were now, in 1642 and 1643, going to that Parlement for help with the *bailliage*. As noted, from its beginning Parlement was always accepted, or used, by those who felt they might profit from it. Appellants who saw in the establishment of the Parlement a new opportunity for redress of old grievances thus did not quibble over the philosophical legitimacy of the new court. They embraced it. And in so doing they accepted the court, de facto, and affirmed its decisions. What we see, however, in the period after 1640, is that the zealous petitioners to Parlement came to include the local magistracy—the very corporate body that had tried to oppose the Parlement, ironically on much the same grounds as they now opposed the *bailliage*, namely, the financial burden of a new court and its offense to custom.

One is tempted to characterize this sea change, as we have called it, as simply a matter of priorities. In other words, Metz's local judges perceived the Parlement as the major threat to their authority until the more immediate competitor—the *bailliage*—arrived on the scene, at which time the *bailliage* became the more proximate foe. Of course this view of institutional motivations is too simple. If the collective memory was not very long, it was also not instantly mutable. Local leaders did not replace their hostility toward Parlement with fear of the *bailliage*. They continued to oppose any action by either body that they felt as an affront to their albeit waning power. However, they seem at least to have been willing to suspend their protests against the Parlement during the *bailliage*'s first years: and they were also willing, perhaps too much so, to attempt to use the high court in their fight against the *bailliage*. As it stood, their efforts contributed to their loss on both fronts. Let us continue to follow these developments in the rest of our period.

In August 1644, during the minority of Louis XIV, the magistrates brought complaints about the *bailliage* to the duke of Schomberg, the new military governor. Once again, they asked for the right to preside over all general assemblies (for example, of the Three Orders) and public ceremonies, the reduction of court fees at the *bailliage*, a reassertion of their control of public funds, and the moving of the *bailliage* out of the city *palais*. Schomberg gently rebuffed their requests. He asked for time to consider their claims (as in those relating to court charges at the *bailliage*), reiterated Crown policies (that the *échevins* must share the *palais* until further notice), or reminded the judges of the limits to their prestige. For instance, he wrote that in all general assemblies, "called by the king's authority or by ours," the clergy would preside and hold first rank, as was done elsewhere in the kingdom.[34]

The magistrates and the officers of the *bailliage* continued to squabble over particulars relating to police matters and fees. By 1647 the royal judges even suggested a compromise, offering to relinquish some police control in exchange for an annual payment of 6,762 livres from the Hôtel de Ville. They refused, however, to cede their authority over the trades or tradesmen's oaths. The local magistrates showed no sign of seriously considering this offer.[35] In 1649 a specific dispute over rank erupted when a councillor to the *bailliage* and an *échevin* who was also a former member of the Treize each tried to precede the other up the aisle of the church in St. Victor parish during the offertory. Though the resolution of this argument is unclear, we do know that the magistrates rushed to the defense of their colleague using many of their old debating points —asserting ancient rights now on a miniature stage. If the *bailliage*'s officer, a M. Marsal, were to claim that he was a royal judge in perpetuity, the *échevin*'s supporters said, then the *échevin*, M. Pied, could counter that the Treize had been created 500 years before the *bailliage* and had enjoyed autonomy unhindered throughout that long period.[36]

In addition to the most apparent shift in the magistrates' dealings with royal institutions (the fact that they began to petition Parlement itself for help against the *bailliage*), a subtler change, in tone, also took place in their protests as the century wore on. They became humbler, more clearly pleading, with royal authorities in general. A good example of this dual change appears in an incident of February 1663, when the magistrates again undertook to limit the *bailliage*'s physical occupation of part of the local *palais*. After years of asserting that the royal court was encroaching on its territory, the magistrates had gained little from royal authorities, either from Lambert and Schomberg, or from the king and his councils. To every protest, royal representatives had given the same reply: royal and local courts must share the space until new quarters could be built. But by 1663 there was still no sign of progress toward erecting a new building. The magistrates went to Parlement or, specifically, to the first president, to state their case yet another time. In this instance, though, rather than asking that the *bailliage* be moved out, they merely asked that their own place be preserved. The *bailliage* and Parlement, and the bureaucracies attached to them, had apparently expanded over the years, to take over an ever greater share of the local Hôtel de Ville, so that now there was almost no space left to the *échevins*—a visible and potent reminder of the jurisdictional triumph of the royal courts. However, rather than voicing their outrage that the royal courts should occupy any space at all in their *palais*, the local magistrates now implored that some space be reserved for them. The local judges, who had begun by begrudging royal courts any portion of their loaf, as it were, now begged themselves for a few remaining crumbs, and they asked this of the very institution whose legitimacy they had previously denied. Significantly enough, Parlement decided in this case that the magistrates would move from their remaining quarters into those occupied by the *palais*'s concierge.[37]

Two years later another dispute between the magistrates and the *bailliage* ended up before Parlement, and this case was one of the few in which the high court unequivocally sided with the magistrates. A group of foreign workers— masons, carpenters, and the like—came to work in the village of St. Julien, near Metz.[38] Their presence greatly troubled Metz's own master masons, who claimed that the foreigners were not paying the appropriate local taxes. Their real fear, of course, was that the newcomers would present competition should they make their way into the city. The *bailliage*, which we recall had jurisdiction over the trades in Metz, gave verbal permission to the Messin masons to seize the foreign workers' tools and thereby prevent their plying their trade in St. Julien. Local magistrates then intervened on behalf of the foreign workers, claiming that the *bailliage* had no right to decide matters in St. Julien. The magistrates, one might add, seemed more concerned about the jurisdictional question than the actual plight of these "foreign" artisans. Eventually the case degenerated into a civil suit between the Messin masons' guild and the foreign workers, with the *bailliage* and the *échevins* lined up accordingly on either side as intervening parties. It fell to the Parlement to decide the matter. On July 1, 1665, the high court sided with the foreign workers—and thus indirectly with the local magistrates—determining that indeed the *bailliage* could not authorize seizure of the foreigners' tools, thereby preventing them from working in St. Julien or even in Metz. The city masons who had confiscated their competitors' tools were fined, thus granting the magistrates a small victory in their struggle with the *bailliage*. But this victory was doubly a Pyrrhic one. For this small concession to foreign workers did little in the long run truly to constrain the *bailliage* or limit its reach in Metz. And again, this case and the others like it solidified the Parlement's own claim to authority in Metz, and to an authority as recognized by the magistrates. Once they had accepted such judgments from the high court—and obviously they had little inclination to reject a decision in their favor—local magistrates could never rescind their tacit acceptance of the Parlement. What remained, then (in a situation reminiscent of the Shavian retort to a compromised "lady"), was only a process of haggling over the details of the Parlement's authority in Metz, not a dispute over the fact of that authority.

Not that the magistrates ceased to try to challenge Parlement's role. But the inherent weakness of their position after 1665 is apparent. In December of that year, for example, the Parlement attempted to regulate just how and when the deputies of the Three Orders could assemble. This enraged the *échevins* and the deputies, who brought their protest to the king in August of 1666. In their complaint the local notables stressed both that their right to call assemblies had long been upheld by the Parlement itself, and that now, "it is very surprising to see the same court deciding matters (about assemblies) without considering that in doing so it is exceeding the bounds of its authority, since it belongs only to His Majesty to dictate to a region the form of its administration."[39] Their argument against Parlement's authority was crippled by their bow to its earlier decisions supporting them. Further, as a challenge to infringement on their traditional autonomy, the protest is also virtually negated by its closing paean to the Crown. The king took advantage of the magistrates' invitation, issuing his own guidelines for the assembly of the Three Orders. He included the proviso that the deputies could not meet in the future without permission from his *procureur* to the *bailliage*.

Finally, in a case from the following decade, we again see the confluence of Parlement, *bailliage*, and Crown interests, and the impotence of the local magistrates confirmed. The issue in this instance involved paupers, and how they were to be treated in Metz. The *bailliage*, as noted, had been given control over vagabonds and the restrictions governing them in December 1641. But the Hôtel de Ville had retained control, with some limitations, over the internal administration of the Hôpital Saint Nicolas. On July 8, 1676, the Three Orders issued an ordinance that all paupers from Metz and its surrounding countryside be imprisoned in the *hôpital*. All other "foreign" beggars were to be given alms and then banished. And while Protestant beggars were not included in these strictures, the city consistory was charged with preventing any begging by members of that sect. Jewish beggars were considered wholly the responsibility of their own community. In addition, a fine of 500 livres was set for any Messin inhabitant caught protecting beggars from the decree.[40]

The local deputies acted out of their assumed power over purely communal affairs. The officers of the *bailliage*, however, saw the order differently, interpreting it as a direct attack on their jurisdiction in police matters. Immediately they lodged a complaint with the Parlement. Parlement considered the matter on July 10 and revoked the deputies' ordinance as illegitimate and an affront to the king and Parlement's authority. The Three orders, it proclaimed, had no right to issue general police ordinances, especially one involving such a large fine.[41] As a result, on July 11 city magistrates issued an order under their own name (not under the auspices of the Three Orders), reiterating their first antibeggar ordinance and ordering even greater restrictions on mendicancy and vagabondage in Metz.[42] The next move was Parlement's, and two days later the court disputed the *échevins*' order, which it called a continuation of the outrage against Parlement's authority, merely disguised under a new title. Again, Parlement revoked the order and forbade the *échevins* from assessing fines against any bourgeois of the city who might aid beggars. The court also forbade the magistrates from placing the words "*De par le roi*" on their published and posted decisions, implying that they were sanctioned by the king. The *bailliage*, meanwhile, also joined the dispute when on July 13 it commissioned the local militia to come to the aid of any inhabitant being subjected to the *échevins*' order.[43]

The entire argument was summarized and argued, at last, by the *procureur*, who had printed a *mémoire* against the Three Orders in particular, and against the local magistracy and its claims to power in general. In this document (whose date is uncertain, but probably from not long after the controversy began) the *procureur* argued the case for royal dominance expansively. At this point, many of the seemingly minor symbolic disputes of the previous years came into sharp focus and revealed themselves as highly significant. For among other things, the *procureur* stressed that the king, in his election order of 1640, had created a new style of Hôtel de Ville, on the model of the Hôtel de Ville of Paris and that it lay within the king's ancient role to do so. As such, the local *échevins* and deputies of the Three Orders should maintain no claim to traditional powers, he said, only to those granted by the king. He added:

If the *maire* of the city of Metz has retained the ancient name of *maître-échevin*, it is an abuse, contrary and prejudicial to the king's declaration, which established the office under the name of "*maire.*" And it has been used only to advance—through a specious name which previously was revered by the general populace—his continual enterprises, and to advance an absolute authority which he still strives to usurp and exercise over the deluded bourgeois. But it is time to disabuse the ignorant people and to inform them that he whom they recognize today under the title of "*maître-échevin*" has none of the attributes of the *maître-échevin* who governed in the days before the Lily had reflowered along the banks of the Moselle, and that he is nothing more than a simple *maire* of a good city, and created according to the example of the *Prévot des Marchands* of Paris.[44]

Echoing the very ideas voiced so long ago at the induction of the Parlement in 1633, the *procureur* used this opportunity to reaffirm Louis's divine right to shape and determine local government in his city of Metz and the king's claim to be the source of all secular power. All pretense of suffering local institutions in their autonomy was abandoned, as the *procureur* urged the king to absolutely cancel the Three Orders, which he described as "useless to the government of the city." In fact, he stressed, the local notables were downright dangerous. In their traditional assemblies they were "always preoccupied with this old idea of democracy which impels them to continually scheme against the authority of those judges (of the *bailliage* and Parlement) who have received their power and form from the monarch."[45]

The magistrates, predictably, reacted hostilely to the *procureur*'s pamphlet. They defended their right to set rules governing local affairs, and they pointed up the impossible dilemma of being at once prohibited by Parlement from issuing orders using the words "*De par le roi*," and at the same time required to place those words at the head of all their written decisions.[46] But despite the anger the magistrates professed toward the *procureur* and his charges, their emphasis here is more telling, and it shows their abject defeat in the rhetorical battle with central institutions. Much of their argument referred to the workings and authority of the Hôtel de Ville of Paris, not to their own ancient rights. And the most vehement sections of their reply involved not the dispute over local authority, but rather the *procureur*'s suggestion that they were somehow disloyal to the king or opposed to monarchy. Their response was thus far less a claim to traditional power and rights, than a defense against charges of *lèse-majesté*—far less an attempt to maintain sovereignty, than an avowal of devotion to the monarch and a claim to belong, absolutely, to the French state.

The key to political viability, one might argue, is to attain at least the illusion of cohesion and unity in a given society, and successfully to use and manipulate symbols and language to animate that society. Within France in our general period, many proofs arise immediately. Certainly those forces promoting revolution at the end of the next century achieved a sporadic cohesion, along with a fairly effective control of the symbols and language of power. Consider, for example, the refashioning of religious icons as republican ones or the replacement—at least in Paris—of an economic and social elite with a political one, based on claims to humble origins and intellectual devotion to the principles of the new state.[47] By the same token, the protagonists in the Vendée uprising in that same period also achieved a degree of unity, while simultaneously capturing the imagination of their local following by capturing its symbols.[48] Our purpose here is not to embark on a fullscale comparison of the struggle between Metz's magistrates and the Parlement and the more notorious political struggles of the early modern era. Rather, we have explored one of the reasons why the Messin magistrates could not even stall Crown policy, despite an obvious depth of feeling. Taking up the second criterion first, we see that Metz's magistrates and local notables failed miserably in controlling the symbols or language of power. They denounced Parlement and the *bailliage* vociferously, it is true; but they also beseeched the Parlement for help, and in so doing they accepted its authority. And they abandoned arguments based on traditional rights and the primacy of custom, in favor of ones that implicitly buttressed royal claims to dominion. These points have been illustrated repeatedly in this chapter. Of course some observers might also note that the lack of control of the military proved a greater handicap to local leaders than their lack of control over language. Nonetheless, a consistent policy and an ability to use rhetoric to move the populace to enact it would have been absolutely necessary to any attempt to truly impede the royal takeover. Local leaders, alas for them, had no such policy and no such ability.

The first criterion — that of cohesion or unity — or in this case the lack of it, provides an even more significant explanation for the failure of the local agenda. And the full consideration of this issue remains to occupy the following chapters. Metz, quite simply, was severely factionalized in the seventeenth century, for in addition to the various competing loyalties that existed in other French cities of the time, and in addition to the problems one might expect in a newly annexed region, Metz had a far greater degree of religious diversity and thus religious bickering on a daily basis, than other towns of its size. The mere fact of this diversity did not weaken local government in the seventeenth century (as it arguably had in the sixteenth). Rather, it was the attempt by notables— the magistrates and the clergy in particular—to end this diversity which crippled their efforts. In attempting to eradicate or restrain religious minorities, local officials further empowered central institutions like the Parlement. Thus, ironically, in trying to achieve our first condition—cohesion as they perceived it —local officials ensured their failure in the second: they did not control the symbols or language of power. Perhaps their biggest misstep was, in fact, to equate cohesion with uniformity and to fruitlessly pursue the latter in an attempt to gain the former. In this they may be excused as men of their times.[49] Regardless, the separation of the various religions in Metz, or in some cases the local authorities' attempt to preserve a separation, proved local government's undoing. For it unleashed the most irrational and often inconsistent impulses in the society. And once those impulses began to dictate local policy, the chance for a concerted resistance to the centralizing, absolutist state, if it ever existed, was lost.

Additionally (and here we return to the most fundamental assertion of our multipart thesis), religious bickering ironically reflects an underlying process of secularization well under way by the seventeenth century, for religious friction represents, in a sense, a last desperate effort to arrest that trend. More than that, though, religious feuding also furthered secularization, because it demanded the redefinition of religious minorities and of their role in an increasingly pluralistic Metz. Let us begin our consideration of this social reordering by examining the place and fortunes of the smaller of our two minorities—the Jews of Metz.

NOTES

1.   For brief biographical portraits of the judges of the Parlement see Emmanuel

Michel's *Biographie du Parlement de Metz* (Metz: Chez Nouvian, 1853). Personal histories of the local magistrates are quite scarce. It is worth noting that members of the Parlement would be ennobled (as a result of sitting on the Parlement), while members of the magistracy were generally men of lesser rank and prestige, and this may have added to the friction between them. Ennoblement in France also generally carried with it exemption from most taxes. For a good general discussion of social class among provincial government officials see Robert Harding's *Anatomy of a Power Elite* (New Haven, Conn.: Yale University Press, 1978). For a thorough treatment of local government and centralization in Languedoc see William Beik, *Absolutism and Society in Seventeenth-Century France* (Cambridge: Cambridge University Press, 1985). See also John Miller, ed., *Absolutism in Seventeenth-Century Europe* (London: Macmillan, 1990), and Richard Bonney, *L'absolutisme* (Paris: Presses Universitaires Françaises, 1989).

2. The basic notion behind discussions of "popular" and "elite" cultures is that two spheres—one that of the economic and educational elite, the other of the poorer masses in society—existed in France in the early modern period, with different customs, ideas, values, and even sensibilities. The Counter-Reformation, according to an admittedly crude reduction of the theory, was largely a process of "elite" culture (the clergy, the wealthy, and literate—the politically powerful) attempting to impose a more standard and orthodox Catholicism, eradicating belief in witches and magic, promoting hard work and virtue among the poor, harshly punishing mendicancy, vagabondage, and so on. See Robert Muchembled's "Lay Judges and the Acculturation of the Masses," in Kaspar von Greyertz, ed., *Religion and Society in Early Modern Europe, 1500–1800* (London: George Allen and Unwin, 1984), for the original statement of the theory of a tension between popular and elite cultures. The same idea is explored in Muchembled's *Popular Culture and Elite Culture in France 1400–1750*, trans. Lydia Cochrane (Baton Rouge: Louisiana State University Press, 1985). For a brief but cogent rebuttal of Muchembled, see Jean Wirth's "Against the Acculturation Thesis," in von Greyertz, pp. 66–78.

3. Emmanuel Michel, *Histoire du Parlement de Metz* (Paris: J. Techener, 1845), p. 37.

4. Of the provincial parlements, four were created during the fifteenth century, three during the sixteenth, and two (Metz and Pau) during the seventeenth. See Michel Antoine et al., *Guide des Recherches dans les Fonds Judiciaires de L'Ancien Régime* (Paris: Imprimerie Nationale, 1958), p. 79.

5. B.N., N.A.F., 22668, fol. 116.

6. Ibid., fol. 146 (April 26, 1632).

7. Ibid., fol. 110, from February 1632. Fol. 146 (see note 6 above) included the same claim of a violation of local privileges.

8. These included the duc d'Epernon and the cardinal de la Valette.

9. B.N., N.A.F., 22668, fol. 147 (May 4, 1632).

10. Ibid., fol. 180.

11. Ibid., fol. 182 (July 16,1633).

12. Ibid., fol. 187.

13. B.N., N.A.F., 22669, fol. 35. This printed account of the first session of Parlement was printed on August 26, 1633.

14. Ibid.

15. The speaker in this instance was Sieur de Remefort de la Greliere, the king's appointed commissioner for the establishment of the Parlement, and *avocat général* to the Grand Conseil in Paris.

16. B.N., N.A.F., 22669, fol. 35. For James I of England's view on the divine right of kings, see James I, King of England, *The true lawe of free monarchies...* (London: printed

and are to be sold by T.P., 1642). [available as microfilm, SZ663, Sterling Memorial Library, Yale University]. For a secondary source, Caroline Bingham, *James I of England* (London: Weidenfeld and Nicolson, 1981). For Bossuet see Patrick Riley, trans. and ed., *Politics Drawn from the Very Words of Holy Scripture* (Cambridge: Cambridge University Press, 1990).

17. B.N., N.A.F., 22668, fol. 218.

18. Ibid., fol. 249.

19. Ibid., fol. 263.

20. B.N., N.A.F., 22670, fol. 2.

21. Ibid., fol. 14.

22. Ibid., fol. 4. Potet, it should be noted, had a history of run-ins with Paris. In November of the previous year he had been arrested in the capital for refusing to pay a tax on foreigners traveling in the city. He had been released, but only after the *maître-échevin* sent written proof verifying his identity.

23. See Roland Mousnier, *The Institutions of France under the Absolute Monarchy 1598–1789*, trans. Brian Pearce (Chicago:University of Chicago Press, 1979), pp. 567–71(on Bordeaux), and pp. 595–600 (on Beauvais).

24. In 1556 the cardinal of Lorraine, who then had a large say in the election of *échevins*, ceded his rights to choose the *échevins* to the king. For this fact and other information relating to the election of the *échevins* see Gaston Zeller, *La Réunion de Metz à la France 1552–1648*, vol. 2 (Paris: Sociéte d'Edition: Les Belles Lettres), pp. 5ff.

25. B.N., N.A.F., 22670, fol. 17.

26. Ibid., fol. 25; fines of 10,000 livres were levied against those involved in deputizing others to go to Paris to lodge protests with the king or his council, with an identical fine on any who accepted such an assignment. In addition, the Parlement set fines on any city clerks who might turn over public funds to the *maire* or *échevins* for this purpose.

27. Ibid., fol. 32.

28. Ibid., fol. 64 and fol. 69 (relating to complaints made in September 1641); see also fol. 49 (relating to a complaint from October 1641).

29. Ibid., fol. 49.

30. The signatures included that of de Gournay, the *maître-échevin*, and Lebachelé, whose name appears in earlier records as an *échevin* sent as a deputy to the royal court in September 1641; from B.N., N.A.F., 22670, fol. 98.

31. Ibid., fol. 116.

32. The son of Antoine de Bretagne.

33. Ibid., fol. 119. Lambert may have been marginally more sympathetic to the local magistrates than was the next governor, the duke of Schomberg. See Schomberg's rebuff of local protests later in this chapter.

34. Ibid., fol. 159.

35. Ibid., fol. 216.

36. Ibid., fol. 279.

37. B.N., N.A.F., 22671, fol. 44.

38. Ibid., fol. 57. The native country of these workers was not given, and the term *foreign* could have been used to describe anyone from outside of the immediate region, but the workers' names suggest that their origins might have been in Germany or the Netherlands.

39. Ibid., fol. 79.

40. Ibid., fol. 128.

41. Ibid., fol. 129.

42. Ibid., fol. 131.

43. Ibid., fol. 133.

44. Ibid., fol. 122 (pp. 3–4 within that document). The "Lily" referred to here is the fleur de lys, symbol of the French Crown.

45. Ibid. (p. 14 within the document).

46. Ibid., fol. 146.

47. There are countless studies devoted to the French Revolution and its many aspects. For a recent synthesis (including an extensive bibliography) see Simon Schama, *Citizens* (New York: Vintage Books, 1989). Many other works, timed to appear for the bicentennial of the Declaration of the Rights of Man are also available but too numerous to list here.

48. For information on the Vendée uprising see C.-L. Chassin, *La Preparation de la Guerre de Vendée 1789–1793* (Paris: P. Dupont, 1892). Also, Charles Tilly's *The Vendée* (Cambridge, Mass.: Harvard University Press, 1964), and the more recent work by Jean-Clement Martin, *La Vendée et la France* (Paris: 1987).

49. We explore this idea again in Chapter 6, in considering the ideas of Martin Meurisse, the bishop of Madaure and a prominent Counter-Reformation Messin cleric.

Part II
Changing Social Relations

Chapter 3
An Illusory Stasis:
The Jewish Community

In midwinter the city of Metz is often gray. It stands austerely, somewhat stiffly, on the banks of its rivers, grimly reconciled to the penetrating cold and generally cloaked in a chill fog. The season there is one of weak but recurrent rain and odd sudden mists—a time when even the cathedral spire, rising above the neighboring buildings, seems unable to pierce the flat pewter sky that covers the city like a pot lid.

Let us consider Metz during this season, in the year 1669, by which time Parlement had become an established, if not universally appreciated, institution. The city's Catholic majority had chipped away at Protestant holdings and was busy harvesting the most vulnerable Protestant souls for conversion; and Christian squeamishness about the city's Jewish population persisted in the complaints of tradesmen and clerics against the Jews and their commerce. It was in this season, and this year, that the authorities hauled Raphael Levy, a Jewish peddler from the nearby village of Boulay, to the local jail.[1] We find him there in December, in his cell, perhaps looking out from the small window which faced the prison courtyard, perhaps lying listlessly on his straw mattress considering the charge against him.[2] Of his actual thoughts during this period we know nothing. Levy, a small-time dealer in assorted goods who traveled frequently to Metz, stood accused of snatching a three-year-old Christian boy from the roadside near Glatigny (less than 10 kilometers from Metz), of spiriting off the child, wrapped in his coat, and of viciously murdering him, moved by a hatred it was assumed Levy felt for Christians, and by the supposed nefarious ritual needs of his coreligionists. The charge was brought without evidence. In fact, as Levy sat in his cell no witnesses had seen a murder take place, much less a Jewish ceremony involving the child or his corpse. There was only a missing toddler, a Jewish man seen riding in the woods on the day of his disappearance, the assumptions and assertions of various local citizens and, most important, more than five centuries of potent and persistent superstition.[3]

The details of the ritual murder accusation against Raphael Levy, as revealed in the records of his trial and appeal before Parlement, will occupy Chapter 5, including how his case contributes to the tradition of such allegations against Jews in Europe. For now, however, it will suffice to consider some of the other factors fostering anti-Semitism in Metz, and some of its less dramatic manifestations there. Subtler currents worked in this society to nourish Gentile prejudices—currents specific to this city in this period. To explore the broader picture of Jew hatred in Metz, then, one must leave Levy in his cell temporarily and consider the city's Jewish community as a whole. For in a way, all of Metz's Jews were, like Levy, locked in a precarious judicial limbo—vaguely accused of unsubstantiated shadowy crimes, hemmed in and suspected, their lives and commerce restricted, but nonetheless changing. Oddly enough, regulations sought to shut the Jews out of mainstream society, while simultaneously ensuring that they be closely watched. As with Raphael Levy, the Jews' jailor also served, ironically, as their protector, shielding them from the worst persecution and potential violence of the crowd beyond their walls. For the Jews of Metz at large, that jailor and that protector was the king. And the pressing desire of Metz's bourgeois tradesmen and local notables (including members of the waning magistracy) to constrain or expel the Jews sent them repeatedly to that king. Anti-Semitism thus played directly into the king's hand. It fueled appeals to Parlement, and to royal officials, which helped to ensure the success of French centralization in Metz. The most violent expressions of Messin anti-Semitism, we shall see, also seem part of an increasingly desperate effort to forestall secularizing trends (of which political centralization was only the most immediate sign).

From the beginning, this particular Jewish settlement in Metz (local citizens fired with plague hysteria had largely wiped out or dispersed the medieval Jewish community of Metz) lived with its fortunes firmly soldered to those of the French Crown.[4] And the extent to which the king controlled local institutions often determined the extent to which he could protect the Jews, as his unofficial wards, from popular hostility. Beginning with Henri II, French monarchs allowed Jewish families to settle (but not to own real estate) in the frontier area in and around Metz, even as they forbade Jewish establishment elsewhere in the kingdom.[5] From an initial four families allowed into the city in 1564, Jewish numbers increased throughout the seventeenth century, in tandem with the burgeoning power and control of France over the city's government.

The relationship between the Crown and the Jews, it should be noted, turned on money, and the monarch's need to infuse specie into a region ravaged by warfare and pleading for relief from taxes imposed to maintain troops garrisoned there.[6] Jewish moneylenders—the first Jews allowed into the region—could serve the Crown's interests in two ways. First, they could bring liquid capital back into the local economy by lending sums to individuals in exchange for material pledges. In this way they indirectly aided the king's tax collection as well (providing local tradesmen, artisans, and others with cash which such citizens then paid over to royal agents and tax farmers). Second, Jewish merchants could encourage trade and commerce, thereby bringing money into France, particularly from foreign markets. Interest in attracting specie into France, and in keeping it there, endured throughout the later sixteenth and seventeenth centuries, promoted particularly by the powerful royal ministers of this age—Richelieu, Mazarin, and especially Jean Baptiste Colbert—as they strained to find ways of financing royal military adventures. Though the Crown's economic policies did not always include encouragement of the Jews (e.g., Richelieu and Louis XIII used the premercantilist ideas of Montchrétien to support their 1615 reiteration of the Jews' expulsion from France), the prevailing fixation with luring cash into depleted regions, and with promoting French mercantilism in general, seems to have worked to the Jews' advantage in Metz.[7]

Perhaps most important, though, the Jews could be, and were, made to pay stiff head taxes for the right to reside in the city and for permission to lend money at interest. From their first entrance into the city, Metz's Jews also paid annual fees or taxes to both central and local government, a portion of which served as poor relief for the city's Christians.[8] With their greater number of international contacts (ironically the result of centuries of itinerancy caused by persecution and expulsion from most of the countries of Europe), Jewish merchants also helped to supply the troops in Metz, especially with arms, horses, and other livestock.[9]

The Jews, for their part, knew full well that their payment of money into government coffers, either directly or indirectly, stood as the sine qua non of their existence in Metz, and they used this fact to influence officials when possible. In October 1633, under fire from local critics, the Jews produced various pieces of evidence to show that they were fulfilling the terms of their *lettres-patentes*. Among these were receipts for the year showing their payment of annual fees, their provisions for the lodging and maintenance of troops of the garrison, and their payment of 300 francs[10] per year to the local *hôpital*.[11] Similarly, in 1647 the Jews justified a request for simplifying lending procedures by referring to the hardships created for poor people by the war, thereby reminding officials of the need for their moneylending in Metz.[12] Moreover, near the middle of the century, Jewish leaders beseeched a local noble to ask the king to reassert their right to travel between Metz and Paris. Such travel was essential, they claimed, "to procure the means of acquitting themselves of their taxes."[13]

This situation of monarchs allowing Jews to settle in a region in order to encourage their commercial activity and channel it to the state's advantage had many precedents in Europe dating back to the medieval period. The charter accorded to the Jews of Austria in 1244 by Frederick the Belligerent had rested on such a motive, as had permissions granted by rulers in Germany and England before that time.[14] The relationship between the Jews of England and that country's medieval kings had rested so clearly on the Crown's craven interests, that the historian Cecil Roth dubbed the Jews of England, the "Royal Milch Cow" and argued effectively that the expulsion of Jews from England in 1290 resulted not from an awakening of piety on the part of Christian rulers but rather from the utter depletion (after many years) of Jewish resources.[15] Less grim examples also abound to show government officials' enthusiasm for fleecing the Jews. In a humorous anecdote from Metz (probably from the middle of the seventeenth century) a military official newly arrived is alleged to have refused to allow the city's Jews to call on him. A contemporary account of that incident ran as follows:

The official was alerted to the fact that they were in his antechamber, but he answered, "I do not want to see those [Jewish] merchants, for they were the ones who killed our Lord." So someone told the Jews that the *maréchal* could not speak to them. "But we are very angry," they replied. "We desire so greatly to offer him our respects, along with a small present of 4,000 pistoles." One hurried to carry their response to the *maréchal* who, as soon as he heard it said, "Let the poor devils enter; they didn't recognize Him when they crucified Him."[16]

In Metz too, then, money stood behind the Crown's general, if not constant acceptance of a steady increase in Jewish population over the seventeenth century, both through natural population growth and through sporadic immigration (occasionally restricted, but to little apparent effect) from Germany and the surrounding wartorn areas of Europe. From the first four families mentioned, Metz's Jewish population grew to just under 70 households by 1624, about 85 households at the time of the Parlement's founding, 119 households in the years just after Raphael Levy's trial, and 294 households by the end of the seventeenth century. By the second decade of the next century, 400 Jewish households existed in Metz, or some 3,000 individuals out of a total population of more than 25,000, with smaller scattered Jewish communities in the surrounding rural villages.[17]

Metz's Jewish population did not grow continuously, however, or without periodic setbacks. And using numbers of households to gauge population trends can conceal important changes which seem to have occurred. Though records are incomplete, rolls of Jewish families compiled for the Gentile authorities in 1621 and 1637, respectively, reveal several interesting points. In 1621 Metz's 69 Jewish households made for a total of 388 individuals (among whom were 144 children, 42 servants, and 68 poor students living in the homes of charitable families). In 1637 the city's 85 households sheltered only 342 individuals, including 159 children, 33 servants, and no students mentioned.[18] The total disappearance of students from the later roll suggests (since we know of no official expulsion of such students from Metz) that the authorities did not ask householders to declare students as their dependents for the 1637 list.[19] However, even subtracting the students mentioned in 1621 (so that the rolls can be compared more fairly), average Jewish household size decreased in Metz between these two periods by about 13 percent. The number of children per household dropped by about 10 percent, and though the number of servants per home (among those who kept servants) remained roughly constant, far fewer families kept servants in 1637 than had done so in 1621. Specifically, in 1621, according to these records, 52 percent of Metz's Jewish families kept at least one servant. By 1637 only 33 percent did so. This indicates that while the number of households increased, the wealth of Metz's Jewish families was quite possibly declining during the period, and either they were having fewer children or fewer children were surviving.[20]

Admittedly these two rolls are too limited in themselves, and span too few years, to offer firm conclusions of the precise changes taking place among Metz's Jewish inhabitants. The drop in household size, for example, might indicate a relative decline in immigration of new Jewish families into Metz, and the resulting division of the existing families into smaller groups as children grew, married, and established their own homes.[21] And comparative population and household figures for the general population during these years are not available. But these two Jewish rolls do show that the city's Jewish community was subject to population pressures and that within a steady increase in the number of households, inconsistencies did occur. They also suggest that taxes and special charges assessed on the Jews may well have resulted in lower personal holdings for the city's individual families. In the early 1630s (as documented in a list probably requested by the newly formed Parlement), the average Jewish family lived in a home of approximately two rooms with a stove. A very small number (less than 15 percent) had space outside to stable horses; and a smaller number (about 11.5 percent) had separate kitchens. About one-third of all the Jewish homes had space set aside for lodging soldiers; about one in five such homes had soldiers actually occupying these spaces at that time. There is some indication that the burden of lodging French troops in Metz fell even heavier on the Jewish community than it did on the general population.[22]

It has been noted that the king of France served throughout the later sixteenth and entire seventeenth centuries as the Jews' patron, of sorts, and that the king's directions (or those of his first minister) ensured that the Jews could continue to live in Metz, albeit under restrictions. Not all of the French monarchs of this period, however, were equally comfortable protecting the Jews. Louis XIII, as mentioned, ordered all Jews to leave the country in April, 1615, giving them 30 days to depart or face the death penalty. In this, Louis was responding to critics who complained of "Jewish usury" ruining the country. There is no evidence that this order was truly imposed in Metz, though the Jews' enemies would periodically invoke it later in the century and call for its enforcement.[23] Louis XIV, for his part, became the only French monarch until that time to visit a synagogue when, in 1657, he attended the celebration of Succoth, the feast of tabernacles, in Metz. This Louis, perhaps encouraged by Colbert who, as noted, often exhibited leniency toward Jews in other parts of the country for the sake of promoting their commerce, generally shielded the Jews with greater zeal than his father had shown. The Jews in Metz reportedly impressed him so greatly, with their display of obeisance and homage during his Succoth visit, that he immediately issued a new set of *lettres-patentes* extending

Jewish rights to import cloth and other goods.[24]

The royally appointed military governors of Metz, following the monarch's lead, also tended to shelter the Jews from local attacks and to protect their commerce and moneylending; but inconsistencies occurred here, in this extension of the royal prerogative, as well. In August of 1644, for example, the duke of Schomberg countermanded an order of the Hôtel de Ville, which required the Jews to provide furnishings for the home of the newly arrived lieutenant, M. de Serignan. The Jews had complained to Schomberg that the order imposed an extraordinary and unjust charge on their community, exceeding as it did the 150 *livres messins* they already had to pay to the local government each month. Schomberg agreed and forbade anyone to exact such extra fees from the Jews.[25] His order, however, apparently had little effect. Taking advantage of the governor's absence not long afterward, local officials seized the property of several Jews in order to outfit Serignan's home. The Jews, in turn, who finally succeeded in contacting Schomberg in Languedoc, denounced the seizures as unjust and cruel and, perhaps even more persuasively, they reminded Schomberg that such neglect of his orders defied his authority, and by extension royal authority as well. Schomberg, writing from Narbonne, reiterated his decree against the imposition on the Jews, condemned the seizures, demanded return of the Jewish property, and threatened fines, including damages and interest, for any who continued to rob the Jews in this way.[26] And yet despite this initially tough stance, the governor eventually bowed to local pressure when (at least two years later) he reversed himself and agreed that the Jews must supply the lieutenant's furniture, linen, and kitchen utensils.[27]

To claim that the kings of France and their agents in Metz served as the Jews' champions, then, is to ignore many necessary qualifications. Too often the royal government slouched its way toward fights with the Jews' enemies, content to make a halfhearted pass, its lance pointed at the ground. Certainly the central government did not profess enthusiasm for Jewish society or extol Jewish virtues. And the role of Parlement remains somewhat unclear. As a branch of royal government, or at least as one of the most visible manifestations of central authority, Parlement might have been expected to follow the king's lead with regard to protecting the Jews from local hostility. By and large Parlement did this but not without exception. The historian and archivist Gilbert Cahen has argued that Parlement was no friend to the Jews of Metz, qualifying almost every action it took in their favor.[28] Other scholars have generally seen the Parlement as an advocate, if a lackadaisical one, of Jewish interests. As we will show, this latter view is more thoroughly justified by the sources, but even here the results are not easily categorized.

Perhaps Metz's Parlement offers us such a mixed bag because of the timing of its establishment. On the one hand, the judges were devout Christians, accustomed to a traditional posture toward the Jews (i.e., to reject them on religious grounds), while on the other, they were part of a society developing, however reluctantly, a more secular position (i.e., to expect and then to insist on Jewish assimilation). Metz, in this way, lay on a major fault line of the early modern era—the fissure between religious identity and a national one. Both, of course, had their problems for the Jews. For if the first trafficked heavily in the deicide charge, either directly or indirectly, the latter could veer perilously close to modern racial theories. This problem will be explored more thoroughly in Chapter 6.

For now, we may begin by asking: how did the Jews of seventeenth-century Metz view the Parlement? Initially at least, they seem to have accepted that institution as an arm of the royal government which had generally protected them in Metz. Later, this sanguine attitude toward the high court would change, as the Jews' long experience of finding greater success dealing with individual leaders than with groups, proved true in Metz as well. But in 1633 their hopes for the new court, as a foil to the local Treize and Hôtel de Ville, ran high. Praising the founding of the Parlement as "an act of good fortune," the Jews petitioned for the registration of their rights and optimistically described the new court as "the protector and guardian of the privileges accorded by the kings of France to their subjects, the Jews."[29] Such language, though formulaic, nonetheless reflects an unspoken understanding among the Jews that royal government, not local institutions, provided their only shield from attack, and their only source of security, however uncertain. Because the Jews themselves initially embraced Parlement as a protector, and because the Parlement grew directly from royal government, it seems fair to consider that court (at least as opposed to local bodies) as aligned with forces that generally aided the Jews. And surely, as compared to most of the Messin notables, Parlement did help the minority and protect its residence in the city. Instances in which the high court digressed from this pattern will be examined later, particularly with regard to Raphael Levy and other related cases occurring at the end of the century. For now, though, one can say that among central government officials (including members of the Parlement) there was a certain acceptance of the Jews of Metz, an occasional concession to their needs, and a tacit resolution that the Crown's interests, both economic and political, were served by the Jews enjoying some security.[30] If unenthusiastic about protecting the Jews themselves, the central government was at least committed to protecting its own *right* to protect whomever it pleased, and any affront to this expression of the royal will invited swift correction.[31] In a largely hostile environment, the king and his representatives thus stood as the Jews' only advocates.

The observation that royal officials wanly supported the Jews in Metz implies the corollary that local officials generally opposed them. This, in fact, was the case. For where royal interests were often served by the Jews' presence in the city, many thought that local ones were not, and town notables—usually more responsive to local complaints against the Jews—made few attempts to hide their resentment of that minority community.[32] Their resentment, it should be noted, was sometimes touched off by economic considerations but more often by religious ones.[33] In addition, Metz's attachment to Catholic orthodoxy (which would also promote institutional anti-Protestantism) certainly contributed to anti-Judaism. Even before Parlement's establishment in Metz, local magistrates had voted whenever possible to restrict Jewish freedom, for example by imposing a rule not included in Henri II's 1602 *lettres-patentes* that the Jews of Metz wear yellow hats to distinguish them from Gentiles, a requirement clearly reminiscent of the medieval Jewish badge first imposed by Pope Innocent III in 1215.[34] In 1627 the magistrates of the Treize prohibited Jewish moneylenders from selling pledges given by one spouse without the consent of the other, only to have Parlement in 1634 give the Jews the right to sell certain pledges without scrutiny from town officials.[35] Complaints of the Jewish community to Parlement in 1633, 1647, and about 1650, further indicate that local authorities repeatedly tried to reduce the interest rate Jews could charge on loans. In at least two of those cases, Parlement supported the Jews.[36] Local officials may also have prompted the order restricting Jewish travel between Metz and Paris, just before the middle of the century.[37] And the Hôtel de Ville (as it had in the 1644 Serignan case) forced the Jews in 1675 to equip the home of the visiting Marquis de Rochefort.[38] The result of this treatment by local officials, not surprisingly, was that in the years before Parlement, and sometimes after, the Jews generally addressed their complaints and requests to individual royal officials, rather than to the local courts or *maître-échevin*.[39] The Jews in Metz clearly came to see local government as their enemy.

As for individual citizens in Metz, it is less clear that the Jews' main detractors were those who owed them money—as scholars have found in many cases of medieval rioting or violence directed against Jews—than that they competed with them in some fashion in the marketplace. This signals the emerging more complex integration of Jews into Messin society, and the secularization slowly taking hold (despite reactions against it) during this century. Specifically, it heralds an economic assimilation which would become more pronounced as time went on. Two particular instances of such competition spanned the century—one involving the city's Christian cloth merchants, and another involving the butchers' guild. In 1633 both of these groups joined tanners, cobblers, and other tradesmen in bitterly opposing Parlement's registration of the Jews' *lettres-patentes*. But disputes that pitted the Jews against the cloth merchants and the butchers, respectively, have left more complete and provocative records than those of other trade groups. Let us, then, consider the problems between the Jews and these two professions separately, as an entrée into the society in which all haphazardly, and often violently, coexisted.

These disputes further support our main thesis—that internal divisions in Metz allowed for French centralization to triumph, and further, that social relations were changing against a backdrop of intellectual change. For though the Jews were still exploitable and exploited in places like Metz, Gentiles were beginning to use them in more complicated ways. This represents a peculiar kind of progress, it must be admitted, but a form of progress nonetheless. It reflects an increasing Jewish utility to Christian Europe, and it was this foundation of utility which won Jews civil emancipation in France at the end of the eighteenth century. At that time, France led Europe in its extension of full citizenship to Jews. Could it be, in part, because of increasingly complex daily business dealings between Jews and Christians in places like Metz—an early laboratory for such de facto pluralism? Let us consider the details.

Cloth merchants were among the most persistent opponents of the Jews in Metz during the seventeenth century, and their hostility brought them on several occasions before local courts and Parlement. As mentioned, they had tried to block Parlement's 1633–34 registration of the Jews' *lettres-patentes*, and while they were frustrated in that effort, they did win certain concessions, such as restrictions on Jews dealing in new goods fabricated in the city or its surrounding region. It is unclear what impact this ruling had on Jewish commerce. Jewish trading sprang directly from the Jews' moneylending, and even after 1634 they could accept both new and old pledges, and sell those worth less than 15 livres after one year.[40] Still, the cloth merchants, or *merciers,* seemed appeased by the 1634 modifications, content that the city's small but growing Jewish population could not infringe directly on their business.

In 1656 the situation began to change, as Parlement relaxed some of its constraints and extended to Jews the right to buy new as well as old clothes locally, and to resell them (the Jews apparently took advantage of this permission, as we will see below). This decision of Parlement only presaged new *lettres-patentes* which Louis XIV issued in the following year (the year of his Succoth visit), giving the Jews of Metz the freedom to buy, sell, and trade all sorts of merchandise, "according to their ancient and accustomed franchises and liberties," as long as they paid the *droits de la ville* on such items.[41] The town *merciers* contested these orders and (again joined by other tradespeople) they brought a civil suit against the Jews, seeking to have the new letters rescinded or at least modified by Parlement. Steeping their complaints in quotations from the Christian Bible, they argued that if registered, the new letters would contradict the 1634 letters as registered by Parlement, and prove detrimental to both traders and producers, among them the *drapiers drapants,* or cloth makers of the city.[42] The Parlement yielded to these arguments, at least insofar as members sustained the ban on Jews buying and reselling locally produced goods.[43] But the *lettres-patentes* otherwise stood.

Before one can dismiss this case, or consign it to the already lengthy list of local tradespeople's actions against the Jews, one should consider the involvement of the third group mentioned, the *drapiers.* In a written statement stemming from the same controversy, Nicholas Gaillard and a group of the Messin cloth makers countered the *merciers'* claim that the Jews' business was hurting the *drapiers'* profession, and they defended the Jews' right to deal in local merchandise.[44] Denouncing the *merciers'* monopoly over retail sales of cloth, the *drapiers* insisted that, "the Jews, from time immemorial, have always possessed the right to traffic in all sorts of merchandise." They explained that the Jews had developed a business of buying wool from Germany and other countries and selling it to them on credit. The Jewish merchants then bought back the finished cloth from the *drapiers* "at a reasonable price," the cloth makers wrote, and resold it, resulting in a greater profit for the *drapiers* than when they dealt with the *merciers.* The Jews also occasionally advanced money to the *drapiers*, "something that not one of the merchant *merciers* has ever done." Through these arrangements, the *drapiers* declared, they had received "great economic relief" from the Jews.[45] The business transacted between the Jews and the *drapiers* thus scuttled the *merciers'* plan to remain the sole provider of wool to the *drapiers* and of cloth to the retail market. Prohibiting the Jews from dealing in local goods, the *drapiers* added, threatened to effect "the ruin and detriment of the undersigned (*drapiers*), who will not be able to support themselves, and who will be obliged to abandon the city if the said prohibitions are not lifted by the court." A variety of individuals signed or put their mark to this statement, which included the final attestation: "I the undersigned hereby declare that it is of great benefit to the *drapiers* that the Jews buy their cloth and that this has never been the cause of complaint."[46]

The declaration of these *drapiers*, while it failed in its main objective—to encourage the Parlement to reverse the ban on Jews dealing in local cloth goods —nonetheless effectively points out that the Jews' relationship with Messin tradespeople was more complex and variegated than one might conclude from the most obvious documents on the topic, such as the continuing opposition of bourgeois citizens to the Jews' *lettres-patentes*. The Jewish community and Jewish individuals had, in fact, become notable, if not powerful, players in the local economy, competitors to many, but also allies to a few. On occasion, some elements in Messin society were willing to defend the Jews, if it suited their own economic interests. As importers and moneylenders—and as businessmen accustomed to making ad hoc arrangements in which they often combined these functions—the Jews of Metz carved out a niche of sorts for themselves. As they did this, and as various Gentile citizens increased their business dealings with them, the Jews became less and less expendable, in that they had become useful to certain people in the city, if not always appreciated. Further, note the centrality of Parlement to these proceedings. The *merciers* and other tradespeople are freely arguing their case before Parlement, and using Parlement's earlier judgments (in this case its 1634 registration of the *lettres-patentes*) as their basis for precedent. This a mere 24 years after the high court's controversial creation.

The complexity of the Jews' position in Metz, as well as the Parlement's growing role in Messin daily life, becomes even more apparent when one considers the case of the town's Jewish and Gentile butchers. Here town magistrates showed their willingness to use the Jews, or even to aid them temporarily, to further their own ends.

The feud between the Gentile butchers and their Jewish counterparts was of long standing, and it endured throughout the seventeenth century, revealing itself in surprising places. There is a vague suggestion, for example, that Metz's Gentile butchers brought the first complaints against Raphael Levy and encouraged the missing child's parents to charge him with murder, thus initiating the proceedings which led to Levy's imprisonment and trial.[47] But long before the events on the road to Glatigny, Gentile butchers, like the *merciers*, had placed themselves in the vanguard of those pleading for further restrictions on Jewish business and, ultimately, for the Jews' expulsion from Metz. Their reasons appear, in the first instance, entirely straightforward. Kosher laws followed by Jewish butchers included rules for the method of slaughtering animals (a single cut across the throat was the method of killing the beast; the blood was drained from the carcass as completely as possible prefatory to other preparations, in keeping with biblical proscriptions found primarily in Leviticus).[48] In addition, certain cuts of meat were forbidden to Jews (portions from the hind quarter when the sciatic nerve had not been removed, as well as certain organs) and the Jewish butchers of Metz could therefore sell these to Gentiles at a lower price than that charged by Gentile butchers. The Gentile butchers thus had economic reasons, in addition to any general distrust of Jews likely among Christians of this era, for disliking the Jewish slaughterers.

One should note that the Jews of Metz had been allowed since at least 1602 to kill a limited number of animals for their own use. It may be that even before 1633, when we first hear of the Gentile butchers' complaints against Jews before the new Parlement, such Jewish slaughterers were quietly selling some of their cast-off cuts of meat to Gentiles.

Regardless, local officials formalized a new arrangement for Jewish slaughtering in May of 1636, after the Jews complained to the *maître-échevin* and Treize.[49] It is unclear why the Jews needed this reiteration of their right to slaughter their own animals if the 1602 permission remained in effect. Records of the period provide no clear explanation, and it may be that the Gentile butchers had found casual means of harassing their Jewish counterparts and preventing them from carrying out their function. Roger Clément suggests that while Jews were allowed to slaughter their own animals virtually from the time of their entrance into Metz, during the early seventeenth century Gentile butchers retained control over where this work might be carried out, and thereby prevented much rival butchering in Metz.[50]

Nevertheless, in a 1636 *ordonnance de police* local officials did reiterate the permission for Jews to kill their own animals, as well as formally allowing Jewish butchers to sell to the Gentile public those parts of the animal forbidden to their own community. The local judges imposed several restrictions: Jewish slaughterers could only kill their animals in places designated by the city; Jewish butchers could not physically impede the business of Gentile butchers; Jewish butchers must promptly and scrupulously pay the *maltôte*, or tax, on the sale of meat; and they must also pay a yearly fee to the city.[51] We do not know the immediate response of Gentile butchers to this action, but they apparently opposed the permission hotly and tenaciously enough, to prompt the *bailliage* in 1646 to demand that they desist in their attempts to block Jewish privileges.[52] In March of the following year, the Gentile butchers appealed to the Parlement to reverse the local order. They argued that the Jews enjoyed other privileges in the city (such as permission to charge interest on loans) and thus should not also reap the profits of selling their unused cuts of meat to Gentiles. Beyond this, they continued, "the Jewish nation is abominable, and their hands contaminate the meat."[53]

In reviewing this complaint, one notes not only the jealousy expressed by the Gentile butchers but also their absolute identification of Jews, even Jewish butchers, with moneylending. They also clearly saw the Jews as a single unified mass, not as a community made up, like the Christian community, of various groups holding different jobs and having different functions. Further, in contesting the validity of the Jews' 1602 *lettres-patentes*, the butchers called that document a "political regulation," in other words one not based on ancient tradition and custom, and therefore not permanently binding.[54] Allowing the Jews to handle meat meant for Gentile consumption, they added, represented an affront to the "liberty and belief of Christians."[55]

In 1647, the *maître-échevin* and judges of the Treize, for their part, defended the Jews' right to slaughter meat, and they attempted through various arguments to justify their own 1636 order to that effect. Their statement before Parlement helps to explain why these local officials, whom we have pictured as so traditionally opposed to Jewish business interests, did a turnabout on this issue. And consequently the affair serves to reiterate one of our main observations—that even hostile groups occasionally helped the Jews, when it served their own interests to do so. In this it is fair to see some degree of secular commercialism at work, supplanting, however incompletely, traditional religious segregation.

The magistrates declared to the high court that they had granted permission for Jewish slaughtering and sale of meat in order to break the Gentile butchers' monopoly in Metz. That monopoly, they claimed, had allowed these butchers to overcharge the general Christian population. Therefore, to relieve the Jews' oppression and to aid the public welfare, the magistrates wrote, they cautiously opened the meat market to Jewish butchers. To justify their action, the judges cited precedents, including the practice of allowing Jewish slaughtering in Italy, as well as the earlier permission for Jews to do so in Metz.[56] No guardians, as a rule, of the Jews' privileges, they nonetheless argued that the high prices charged by Gentile butchers, and their harassment of the Jews, amounted to an abridgment of those privileges. As true men of their complicated times they were careful, however, not to align themselves too closely with the Jewish community, or to advocate mixing between Jews and Christians, contending that granting the permission to Jewish butchers did not change the fundamental status of the minority, "which one has always held as a group separate from the rest of the people, and which has always had its own particular regulations."[57] The magistrates presumably included this point to refute the Gentile butchers' claim that allowing Jews to sell meat would unfairly elevate that community above the low caste deemed appropriate in a Christian society. As for the charge of Jewish uncleanness, the magistrates ignored the religious implications of the issue and insisted at length that Jewish slaughtering practices equaled Gentile hygiene standards. In addition, they pointed out that Jewish butchers never killed infected or sick animals, as this was contrary to their law.[58]

The local officials countered Gentile butchers' complaints of an attack on their Christian "liberty," by stating that liberty is "given" not unconditionally to all to ply their trade, but rather to those who charge reasonable prices in the marketplace. The Gentile butchers, according to the magistrates, had relinquished their right to unchallenged control of the market by overcharging their customers. The judges also accused the Gentile butchers of not complying with local taxes on the sale of meat.[59] This evasion, along with the butchers' uncontrolled raising of prices, justified allowing Jewish butchers to compete. It seems that in 1647 local authorities, frustrated in their attempts to exact taxes from the Gentile butchers, found a fervor heretofore absent for defending the Jews and their own *ordonnance de police*.

Several observations are now worth reviewing. Taken in sum, the magistrates' defense of the Jews in this case reveals itself as less a move to protect that minority than as first and foremost a means of punishing the Gentile butchers' guild for price increases before 1636 and for tax evasion after that date. The magistrates used the Jews to control that Christian trade group and to encourage its members to adopt more moderate prices. The Jewish butchers were a manipulatable group which could, from the magistrates' point of view, serve as a blunt weapon against an intractable body of local businessmen. Thus we see again that the Jews held an odd, but still integral place in Metz's economy at this time. Because they lived under complex restrictions, and because they remained so vulnerable to new and extraordinary regulations, these Jewish butchers (and by extension the Jewish community as a whole) constituted an entity in this city's economy that various officials, from the king to the local leaders, could exploit to their own advantage.

Whether the magistrates succeeded in this instance—in controlling the Gentile butchers by using the Jews against them—is uncertain. We have no written indication that the Gentile butchers lowered their prices or paid their taxes more assiduously after the Parlement upheld the magistrates' permission to the Jews in the 1647 case. We do know, however, that in 1658 the butchers of Metz still felt angry enough to complain against the king's new *lettres-patentes*, which continued to allow the Jews to slaughter their own animals, and they again appealed the registration of those letters by Parlement.[60] By March of 1673, the ardor of local officials for defending Jewish butchering had cooled (perhaps an indication that the Gentile butchers had become more compliant and less in need of discipline), and they imposed further restrictions on Jewish slaughtering, in the form of more explicit limits on the number of animals that could be killed and closer monitoring of butchering practices among Jews.[61] We must remember that whatever flashes of secular commercialism we see in the actions of the local magistrates, they were also still sporadically compelled by a time-honored orientation favoring Jewish segregation. They were torn between two impulses—one secular (and assimilationist) and the other traditional (and exclusionary). Therefore they serve as fitting representatives of the times in which they lived. In fact, when local leaders or trade groups sought comfort in traditional postures barring Jewish integration, one can see a reaction against their own unwitting progression toward closer, more frequent, and occasionally even positive contact with Jews. The Raphael Levy case, which we examine in Chapter 5, can best be understood in this light.

Looking at the butchers' and cloth makers' disputes together, we also see the growing entrenchment of the Parlement in Metz. By the midpoint of the seventeenth century, even the town magistrates were appealing matters before the high court and accepting, to some extent, its decisions. Disputes between the local judges and local businessmen routinely ended up before the high court. It was a fixture of life in Metz, and the rhetorical challenges to its legitimacy had been eviscerated by the ebb and flow of daily passions.

Note the similarity between the argument used by the Gentile butchers against the Jews and that used by town notables against the Parlement when it was first established. In both cases, the claim was made that custom had been abridged and tradition violated such that now the people were robbed of their "liberty." Most interesting, when faced with the Gentile butchers' claims that they had abridged custom, the magistrates hurled back the same counter-arguments that Parlement and royal officials had used against them in 1633— that liberty was given, not inherent and that the public welfare justified a reversal of traditional arrangements. On the most apparent level this similarity of argument suggests the involvement of similar groups in both complaints. The legal and clerical classes undoubtedly had a hand in both controversies and they played on persistent and popular philosophies to frame their complaints. The *drapiers*, one remembers, had also pointed to tradition to justify their claims. But beyond this, and more important, the similarity of these charges and justifications reflects the splintering of groups that might together have fought royal centralization with one unified voice. The magistrates' hold on the moral high ground, as it were, with regard to the establishment of Parlement, becomes tenuous when one considers their adoption of the Parlement's own arguments in dealing with the butchers. And the butchers' professed opposition to innovation at the same time remains entirely limited to this one small issue (and thus less potent) when one remembers that the controversy with the Jewish butchers brought all of the parties involved before the very body—Parlement—that itself had been pictured by local leaders as an innovation. In this the butchers were joined by the other tradespeople already mentioned (cloth dealers as well as goldsmiths, potters, cobblers, and others) who continually petitioned Parlement to constrain or eject the Jews.

In Metz, then, hatred of the Jews (or in the magistrates' case a desire to use them) helped the French Crown establish its own higher courts above local institutions and thus proclaim central authority as the font from which all other government bodies must draw their own power, arranging themselves in descending order. Groups which might have united in the city under one consistent policy, opposing innovation of any kind in government, did not. The Gentile butchers and those who may have advised them, as well as other tradespeople with similar anti-Jewish agendas, were too tempted by the possibility of having the Jews further restricted, or even expelled altogether, to stay away from Parlement. The magistrates were too eager to control the Gentile butchers, in this case, to forswear arguments about the nature of liberty and government which mirrored, and thus enhanced, Parlement's claims to legitimacy. Hatred of the Jews thus contributed (as hatred of Protestants would also do, if in a somewhat different manner) to keeping various local interests off-balance and in slight disarray, and therefore powerless, first against a secular impulse already gaining ground, and second against the Crown's generally cohesive and far more efficient plan of centralization. In the end, one might ask whether the local Catholic majority, even if it had been entirely united under one philosophy, would have been able to reverse these interconnected trends—secularism and absolutism. The answer to this remains unclear. But what is clear is that anti-Semitism on the local level, and the sputtering feuds which grew from it, indirectly but significantly weakened religion as a political force, because they aided the French kings' program. The most glaring example of Parlement's true establishment, and an illustration of the further complexities of anti-Semitism in Metz, await us later, in the trial of Raphael Levy. Before we encounter him again, however, let us consider Metz's other minority: its Protestants.

NOTES

1. The details of the case of Raphael Levy will occupy Chapter 5. For a brief printed account of his arrest, imprisonment and trial see the contemporary work, *Abrégé du Procès Fait aux Juifs de Metz*, author unknown (Paris: Frédéric Leonhard, 1670). For the complete trial records see documents collected at the A.D.M. (Metz), B 2144. For a brief recent treatment see Pierre-André Meyer, "Un cas d'accusation de meurtre rituel à Metz au XVIIe siècle," *Archives Juives*, vol.25, nos. 3–4 (1989), 62–64.

2. We know from the sources cited in note 1 that Levy's cell had a window that opened onto the prison courtyard and that he slept on a straw mattress.

3. See Chapter 5 for a complete discussion of the ritual murder accusation in Europe and references to secondary works examining it. Note that here and in the following chapters I have used "anti-Semitism" as a general term for hatred of the Jews, even though, strictly speaking, the term is most appropriate only in a modern context. I have used Gentile to refer to all non-Jews, when their religion is secondary to their non-Jewishness, even though non-Jews in Metz would more often have referred to themselves as "Christians" or by terms describing their individual confessions.

4. Roger Clément, *La Condition des Juifs de Metz dans L'Ancien Régime* (Paris: Imprimerie Henri Jouve, 1903) pp. 10–17, gives a brief account of the persecution faced by Metz's medieval Jewish community, including the burning of many Jewish homes in 1322 by townspeople anxious to blame the Jews for poisoning wells and bringing on epidemics. Clément cites an eighteenth-century study, *Histoire Générale de Metz* by the Benedictines, Nicolas Tabouillot and Jean François, 6 vols. (Metz: C. Lamort, 1767–90), and its claim that the Jewish community of Metz disappeared without a trace during the fourteenth century; but he has found isolated references that indicate that there may have been a few Jews in the city during the fifteenth century, (pp. 14ff.). For a recent treatment of the community during the eighteenth century, see Pierre-André Meyer's *La communauté juive de Metz au XVIIIe siècle, histoire et démographie* (Nancy: Presses Universitaires de Nancy, 1993).

5. Charles VI ordered the Jews expelled from France in 1394 and in principle this order remained in effect throughout our period. There were, however, scattered Jewish communities in France, in areas not covered by that order, or as allowed by express royal permission. A small community of Marranos, or Jews baptized as Catholics but often still

62

Changing Social Relations

practicing Judaism in their homes, existed in Bordeaux. Another Jewish community centered in and around the town of Avignon. By and large, though, these communities were very small and, outside of Avignon, theoretically living as Christians. The Jews of Metz represented the largest community living openly as Jews in France at this time. The 1394 expulsion did not apply to them because Metz had only recently been annexed. See Clemént, pp. 1–2. For a more general survey of Jewish settlement in France see Bernhard Blumenkranz, dir., *Histoire des Juifs en France* (Toulouse: E. Privat, 1972).

6. For a further description of the miseries brought on by war see Mgr. Charles Aimond, *Histoire des Lorrains* (Bar-le-Duc: Syndicat d'Initiative, 1960), pp. 262–68.

7. Charles Woolsey Cole, *Colbert and a Century of French Mercantilism* (Hamden, Conn.: Archon Books, 1964; reprint of 1939 Columbia University Press edition); for the ideas of Montchrétien see particularly p. 84. For Richelieu's theories about the prince's need to bring money into France, see pp. 138ff. For Colbert's ideas, see pp. 351ff. Colbert, Cole writes, "urged the intendants to pay special attention to anything which tended to 'attract money into the provinces' and thus put the people 'in a position to aid the king by paying their taxes well.'" (from Colbert's letters, cited by Cole, p. 353). Colbert's interest in bringing specie into France, and his related leniency toward the Jews of Bordeaux as well as toward Protestants engaged in trade and commerce is discussed on pp. 351–52.

8. For a general discussion of taxes and fees paid by the Jews of Metz, see L. Vanson, "Imposition sur les juifs en Lorraine dans L'Ancien Régime," *Revue juive de Lorraine*, [vol. And issue nos. unavailable], (1933), 195–207 and 229–41. See also Clément, pp. 118–19.

9. The royal intendant, Turgot, described the industry and ingenuity of the Jews of Metz, particularly in trading in livestock and providing French troops with horses during the war in his *Mémoire de la généralité de Metz, Toul et Verdun*, 1698, A.D.M., 8213.

10. A.D.M., 17J,4 (Lap 4) fol. 20–21.

11. Ibid. For other restrictions on Jewish residents of Metz (including that they rent houses only in the St. Ferroy Quarter) see B.N., N.A.F., 22705, fol. 10.

12. A.D.M., 17J,8 (Ap 6).

13. The precise date of this document is unknown, but its placement and content suggest a date near the middle of the century; A.D.M., 17J,4 (Lap 12).

14. Jacob R. Marcus, *The Jew in the Medieval World* (New York: Atheneum, 1983), pp. 28ff. For another useful sourcebook in English, see Robert Chazan, ed., *Church, State, and Jew in the Middle Ages* (New York: Behrman House, 1980).

15. Cecil Roth, *A History of the Jews in England*, 3d ed. (Oxford: Clarendon Press, 1964). Roth's work follows that of P. Elman, "The Economic Causes of the Expulsion of the Jews in 1290," *Economic History Review*, vol.7, (1936–37), 145–54.

16. B.N., N.A.F., 22671, fol. 164, 1st series.

17. Gilbert Cahen, "La Région Lorraine" in Blumenkranz, p. 80. These figures for the number of Jewish households and individuals may reflect extended households, that is including student lodgers and servants in some cases.

19. If there had merely been a decline in the number of students, even a dramatic one, we might conclude that this too indicated declining wealth among Messin Jews. As it is, the total disappearance of students from the later roll can only imply a difference in the information collected or some other external reason for the exclusion of students from the later communal roster.

20. The latter possibility—that fewer children were surviving—seems more likely, given that these years saw a great deal of illness and intermittent famine in Metz. The year 1636, as noted, was disastrous for the general population of all of the northeast, and

Metz suffered accordingly. See Aimond, pp.265ff.

21. Immigrants marrying into the Messin Jewish community were allowed into the city throughout this period, sometimes for a fee.

22. Figures for average house size are taken from A.D.M., 1 Mi 191 (B1–6), *"Etat des logements (vers 1630)."* While these records suggest that the Jews in Metz were indeed heavily burdened through taxation and other measures, the overall poverty of the community should not be exaggerated. Certain Jews in Metz clearly did amass some wealth, such as Gluckel of Hameln's second husband, the banker Cerf Levy (see Introduction, note 24). We should add that Gluckel, at least, saw Metz's Jews as relatively well-off, at least for sporadic periods of the later seventeenth century. She also writes of the Messin Jews as very learned and pious, and though her memoirs are not objective, the picture she provides of Jews in Metz at least casts doubt on the sweeping generalization of Roland Mousnier that Jews in the northeast were "lower class people of no great education." See Roland Mousnier, *The Institutions of France under the Absolute Monarchy*, trans. Brian Pearce (Chicago: University of Chicago Press, 1979), p. 417.

23. Clément discusses this 1615 expulsion on p. 33 but makes clear in the preceding pages that the Jews of Metz were not forced to leave the city. In 1632, Louis XIII even confirmed the Jews of Metz in their privileges, moved, according to Clément, by the necessity of keeping Jewish moneylenders in the region.

24. Clément, pp. 34–37.

25. A.D.M., 17J, 4, (Lap 6b). Note that with regard to units of money, livres, unless otherwise noted, can be taken to mean *livres tournois*.

26. Schomberg's condemnation of the seizures is dated February 8, 1645; see A.D.M., 17J, 4, (Lap 6b). The Jews initially complained of the seizures to the *bailliage* (Schomberg being absent from Metz), which in turn referred the case to the Parlement, then sitting at Toul. This act in itself, the Jews argued, represented a challenge to Schomberg's authority. It is not clear what the Parlement ruled in this case, or even if the case ever actually received an audience before that body. However, note the Jewish community's preference here for dealing with an individual who had proven sympathetic rather than with an institution of many members. It may also be that by this time the Parlement had proven itself a less dependable protector as far as the Jews were concerned, than the governor.

27. Ibid. This reversal came without any explanation.

28. Cahen, in Blumenkranz..

29. A.D.M., 17J, 4, (Lap 4).

30. In addition to allowing the Jews free religious worship, self-education and other ritual needs, royal appointees allowed the Jews to try their own civil cases without interference from local secular courts. See the ruling of the Duc de la Valette in 1627–28, A.D.M., 17J, 23, (Jur 6 and Jur 8), which stipulated that Jews who did not abide by the decisions of the Jewish court (elected by the community) should be turned out from the city. This order came in support of Jewish leaders' right to punish members of their community. In contrast to this, early in the next century the Parlement would overthrow a ruling by the Jewish leaders; see A.D.M., 17J, 23, (Jur 20 and Jur 21). In that case, Jewish leaders voted to ostracize Saloman Cahen and a group of Jews who had created a disturbance in the synagogue during the 1714 Succoth services. Among other problems, Cahen and his associates had threatened to strangle other members of the congregation. At the end of the month, Parlement supported an appeal by Cahen and overturned the Jewish court's judgment—an act which the Jewish leaders then bitterly denounced as infringing on their traditional privileges. Those who did not understand the full corpus of religious restrictions observed in Judaism, they contended (numbering them at 613

different strictures), could not act as judges of internal Jewish affairs. There is no indication that the Parlement gave in to these arguments.

31. See the aftermath of the Raphael Levy affair in Chapter 5.

32. The following case involving butchers is an exception to this generalization. Much of the information regarding these butchers, as well as the *drapiers*, appeared initially in print in my article "Jews and Christians in the Marketplace: The Politics of Kosher Meat in Metz," *Journal of European Economic History*, vol. 26 (Spring 1997), 1147-155.

33. For an extended discussion of the difficulty of distinguishing between "religious" and other motives, see Gavin Langmuir's complementary works: *History, Religion and Antisemitism* (Berkeley: University of California Press, 1990), and *Toward a Definition of Antisemitism* (Berkeley: University of California Press, 1990).

34. The Jews' complaints against the yellow hats can be found in A.D.M., 17J, 4, (Lap 1). That local regulation was an obvious carry-over from medieval western European laws imposing distinctive clothing or ignominious badges on Jews. See Marcus, p. 138, for Pope Innocent III's decree that Jews be made to wear distinguishing garb. The same notion can be traced through Ferdinand of Austria's sixteenth-century requirement that the Jews of Alsace wear yellow circles and of course into modern times with the Nazis' infamous yellow star. In Metz the yellow hat rule seems to have been imposed on the Jews with varying degrees of stringency. And its enforcement or non-enforcement serve as a barometer of the general climate for Jews in Metz. In 1657 when, as mentioned, Louis XIV relaxed several restrictions on Jews, he also issued an order allowing the Jewish community's rabbi and seven communal leaders to wear more inconspicuous black hats when they traveled in the city. He further allowed all the Jews of Metz to relinquish the yellow hats when outside of the city walls (cited by Clément, pp. 129–30, from Emmanuel Michel, *Histoire du Parlement de Metz*, [Metz: J. Techner, 1845] p.513). Conversely, in 1694 the leaders of the Jewish community complained to the royal intendant that Jean Basse, farmer of the toll at the Porte Serpenoise, was requiring all Jews to wear the yellow hats when passing through the gate and that he was using this easy means of identification to overcharge Jews. See A.D.M., 17J, 4 (Lap 3la–31g).

35. Clément, pp. 147–48.

36. A.D.M., 17J, 8 (Ap).

37. Our knowledge of this order comes from the Jews' request that it be rescinded. Therefore the exact source of this move to restrict the Jews is unknown, though local forces seem the most likely; A.D.M., 17J, 4 (Lap 12).

38. A.D.M., 17J, 15 (Cc246). Included in this document is a receipt for six dozen napkins, one tablecloth, and three additional tablecloths of lesser quality furnished by the Jewish community.

39. Several examples of this have already been mentioned, either in the text or notes to this chapter. For another instance of Jewish leaders addressing their complaints to an individual official, see A.D.M., 17J, 4 (Lap 2), regarding a request by the Jews concerning the goldsmiths, sent to M. de Serignan.

40. See Clément pp. 147–48, as well as preceding pages for a discussion of the history of Jewish trading and rules governing it in Metz. Before 1633, Clément writes, the vast majority of Jewish trading was directly related to moneylending, and the Jewish community was too small numerically to pose a real threat to non-Jewish merchants in the city.

41. Ibid., p. 148.

42. We know from the report of the *drapiers* (A.D.K., 17J, 4 [Lap 16b]) that the

merciers had claimed that free commerce for Jews was "very prejudicial to the *métier,* and particularly to that of the *drapiers.*"

43. Clément, p. 149.

44. A.D.M., 17J, 4 (Lap 16b).

45. Ibid. (final reference is to *grand soulagement);* presumably this trade between Jewish dealers and the *drapiers* had only been carried out legally after 1656.

46. Ibid.

47. See *Abrégé du Procés* for information regarding the butchers' involvement in the Levy case. For a view of butchers in the medieval period, see William C. Jordan, "Problems of the Meat Market of Beziers, 1240–1247," *Revue des études juives*, vol. 135 (1976), 31–49.

48. For a good basic discussion of Kosher laws, including the appropriate Biblical reference see Hayim Halevy Donin, *To Be a Jew* (New York: Basic Books, 1972), pp. 97–120.

49. A.D.M., 17J, 9, (Cc4).

50. Clément, pp. 159–63.

51. A.D.M., 17J, 9 (Cc4); the amount of this tax is not given.

52. A.D.M., 17J, 25 (Pr3).

53. A.D.M., 17J, 3 (Col).

54. A.D.M., 17J, 4 (Lap 7), fol. 20.

55. Ibid.

56. Ibid., fol. 16.

57. Ibid., fol. 19.

58. Ibid., fols. 22–23.

59. This probably refers to a tax imposed in 1642 on all butchers, assessing them for each animal they killed. See A.D.M., 17J, 8 (Ap4b).

60. A.D.M., 17J, 3 (Co4).

61. A.D.M., 17J, 3 (Co 5 and Co 5b).

Chapter 4
A Limited Kinship:
The Protestant Community

If hatred of the Jews in Metz sent bourgeois notables, magistrates, and trades-men to the king and his courts, local fear of Protestantism also strengthened the sovereign's position and took the teeth out of local claims to autonomy. Al-though rank-and-file Catholics often got along with their Protestant neighbors, as we will see, Catholic clerics (still an important component of the city's elite) saw Protestants and Protestantism as impossible to countenance—far more threatening than a handful of perennially degraded Jews. A fuller comparison of clerical attitudes toward Protestants and Jews awaits us in Chapter 6, with the consideration of the polemic of a particularly influential Messin church official. For now we need only explore how Catholic officials' ardent desire to rid their town of Protestants eviscerated their resistance to the French Crown's absorption of Metz, produced even more obvious social realignments than in the sixteenth century, and contributed to the secularizing trend of this era. As with the transformed complaints against the Parlement and *bailliage*, clerics came to depend on arguments laced with paeans to the king, to bolster their attacks on Protestants. They inveighed against those of the *religion prétendue réformée* by questioning Protestant loyalty and obedience to France and her kings—a philosophical position that could only simultaneously support and promote absolutism.

The central government, for its part, capitalized on the opportunity afforded by this approach. Asked in, as it were, to contain the Protestant threat, royal officials accepted the invitation. Innumerable scholars have documented the Crown's role in the Counter-Reformation—its systematic and often brutal method of gnawing away at Protestant freedoms in France in the years before the revocation of the Edict of Nantes in 1685. Such strictures applied to Protestants in Metz as well. Still, the campaign against the Protestants proceed-ed in a somewhat different manner here than elsewhere. Royal suppression of Protestants in Metz took shape in an uneven, almost haphazard, way. Prohibitions were imposed later and enforced more laxly. Early constraints were invariably played off against ongoing protections. While the sustained cohesion of Metz's Protestant community, and the king's foreign policy needs in this unstable region partially explain why this was so, another reason also presents itself.

Royal officials' ambiguous treatment of Protestants in Metz before 1685 proved as effective at controlling the local Catholic leaders and populace, as it did at hemming in and oppressing the minority. It was, in fact, the very inconsistency of the king's program in this century that proved his greatest strength vis à vis local communities like Metz. Inconsistency, in short, produced leverage. Local clerics repeatedly solicited royal officials' help, with the not always justifiable expectation that the king's men shared their goals. Given the persistence of clandestine Protestant worship in Metz, even after the revocation, one might well argue that the most durable result of royal policy toward Protestants in Metz was this neutralizing of local clerical opposition to state centralization. If this result was accidental—a debatable point—it was nonetheless a highly fortuitous outcome for the Crown.

In terms of social shifts, we find that local Catholic laymen increasingly resisted official policy regarding Protestants. Many of the Catholics we meet here consorted with Protestants and appear comparatively unruffled by their presence in the town. Abjuration records of the Protestants themselves, from the final decades of forced conversion, further indicate that religion was becoming somewhat fluid, at least among Christians, and receding in its primacy for the popular classes. The clerical reaction to this, which represents perhaps the strongest indication of a secularizing trend, appears both here and, more directly, in the final chapter.

At one-third of the population in 1633, or some 7,500 souls, Metz's Protestants were both more numerous and more prominent than were its Jews. Their ranks included a number of so-called robe nobles, holding offices from *conseiller* to the Parlement to notary and commissioner of war. They operated freely as bankers, doctors, merchants, and bureaucrats, and members of the cult were well represented among the city's cloth makers, goldsmiths, tanners and tailors. Nearly 70 percent of the urban Protestants were middle-class tradesmen; roughly the same percentage of Protestants living in the villages near Metz were landowning grape farmers rather than petty laborers.[1] Within the city, Protestants lived in the prestigious central parishes: Saint-Jacques, Saint-Simplice, Saint-Croix, and Saint-Gorgon. Judging by the inventories of their estates, these Protestants were also (like their coreligionists elsewhere) highly literate, at least as compared with the city's Catholics. Following the work of Roger Chartier, Philip Benedict has found that 70 percent of all Messin Protestants who left wills possessed at least one book upon their death, while only 23 percent of all such Catholics did. Among the books typically owned by Messin Protestants were the writings of Calvin, tracts by other French theologians, varied works on prayer and personal piety, histories of the Protestant

Church, and inexpensive books on meditation, especially relating to the Eucharist.[2]

This last group of works is not surprising, of course, given the centrality of the Eucharist to Christian belief, and the centrality of controversy surrounding it to the Catholic-Protestant theological debate raging in this period. Between Jews and Christians, the most potent image of fancy, myth, and conflict remained the crucifixion of Jesus (this will command our attention when we return to the case of Raphael Levy). For Catholics and Protestants, it was the argument over transubstantiation and the related debate it actually represented about the role of priest or minister in the lives of the faithful.

In many instances Metz's Protestants behaved as their libraries exhorted them to. They were even less inclined to have illegitimate children than were the relatively virtuous Messin Catholics. The overall rate of illegitimate conceptions for the town, we should recall, was about 5 percent. Among Protestants it was even lower—just over 4 percent before midcentury. When war with the Spanish Hapsburgs was finally ended in 1659, Protestant ministers in Metz eschewed the wanton display of joy and the reckless fireworks-filled celebration promoted by the Crown. Instead, they urged their flock to mark the occasion with fasting, humble prayers of thanksgiving, and a more seemly reserve.[3] Perhaps it was such sobriety that made Messin Protestants seem somewhat dour to Catholics—kill-joys at best, and anti-French at worst. Still they managed, by and large, to avoid the reputation of their English puritan brethren for unreasonable discipline or fanatical moralism. Protestants had a great deal of contact with Catholics in Metz. Their chief pastor, Paul Ferry, was even friendly with Jacques Benigne Bossuet, the famous bishop and preacher of divine right, with whom he engaged in regular but congenial theological debate.[4]

The above details, however, should not depict the Messin Protestant community as politically secure or at peace with the larger society. In fact, several assaults on that community were well under way by the early seventeenth century, and they would contribute to an extreme decline in Protestant numbers and influence in Metz in the years leading to the revocation of the Edict of Nantes. One such assault was purely demographic, and has already been noted—the epidemic of 1635 to 1636. While Catholics in Metz were certainly devastated by illness in that winter, Protestants lost a significant portion of their community which would never be replaced. Records indicate that one of the elements that allowed Messin Protestants to resist mounting pressure to convert—their cohesion and tight-knittedness as a community—also ultimately weakened them in this critical area. They simply did not inter-marry with nonlocal Protestants in large numbers, and so they failed to attract the immigrants which would have been needed to recover from 1635 to 1636. Metz's Catholic and Jewish populations meanwhile, did attract such immigrants through intermarriage, and they therefore ultimately overcame the demographic crises of the 1630s.[5] It was this inability or unwillingness of Metz's Protestants to marry non-Messins, which led Jean Rigault to characterize their community as one "living in seclusion in the interior of the city, cut off from the rest of the world."[6]

In Metz, as elsewhere, the Jesuits stood as the Protestants' most energetic critics. First established in the city in 1622 Jesuit priests began almost immediately to attack Protestant individuals and members of the cult en masse, ostensibly as part of a benevolent effort to convert them, but with all the zeal and dispatch of a hostile army. In February 1642 Louis XIII, perhaps encouraged by his pious queen, Anne of Austria, ceded to the Jesuits the Protestant temple on the rue de la Chèvre, in order that they might there expand their college and base of activities. He also granted them the right, in that same year, to attend Protestant services and dispute any anti-Catholic sentiments expressed there.[7] The combination of physical concessions to the Jesuits along with concessions of access enraged Protestant clerics and fueled a series of charges and countercharges between the two groups which would continue well after Louis XIII's death.[8]

The issue involved more than just physical space. The Protestants had deserted the temple on the rue de la Chèvre in 1597, to move to a much larger building on the rue de Chambière. And the Jesuits, in gaining possession of the building, were ordered to pay the Protestant consistory a substantial sum in compensation.[9] So the transfer of the temple itself should have posed little hardship. But the symbolic message was clear. And in addition, the homes of two ministers lay on the same property, in nearby or adjacent buildings. One of these houses belonged to Paul Ferry, the city's most prominent Protestant, pastor of the community, and a highly influential figure in French Protestant circles in qeneral.[10] Both he and his colleague De la Cloche, the other minister, remained in their homes, steadfastly insisting that the king's order referred only to the abandoned temple and not to any auxiliary buildings.[11]

In April 1642 the wife of minister De la Cloche went so far as to bar the door of her home, refusing entrance to royal agents attempting to deliver an order that she and her family vacate the premises. She held her ground until January of 1643, in part by stubbornly insisting that her house belonged to the Protestant consistory and not to the Jesuits, and in part by taking the more pragmatic step of plastering over the door between her home and the former temple.[12] Ultimately however, though Ferry retained his home and garden (he may have proved that his house lay on a technically separate parcel), the De la Cloches were successfully evicted and the Jesuits installed.

The affair did not end here. In 1644 members of the consistory complained to the new king's military governor, Schomberg, that the Jesuits had yet to pay them for the main temple building.[13] The Crown, unable to deny the validity of their claim, ordered in October of 1644 that 6,000 livres be given the Jesuits from the royal coffers, to pay off the Protestants—a move as sympathetic to the Catholic society as to the Protestant consistory.[14] Even so, the Jesuits did not turn over the sum promptly or completely. Records indicate that the dispute continued well into the next decade. In July 1654 Schomberg ordered the Jesuits to pay the Protestants 3,000 livres for the temple—an order with which they at last grudgingly complied at the end of 1655.[15] During the time that the Protestants waited for compensation, Pastor Ferry added the complaint that the Jesuits had pierced holes or archways[16] in the wall separating the now Jesuit-controlled building from his garden. The case came before the *bailliage*, where Ferry argued that the Catholic priests, under law, had no right to carve windows in their wall and thereby spy on his activities. The Jesuits, for their part, successfully demanded that the four Protestant judges then sitting on the *bailliage* abstain from judging the matter. They then angrily reported that Ferry, without authorization, had taken matters into his own hands and blocked up the windows in question with poles and planks which shut out their light and view.[17] The judges of the *bailliage* ordered Ferry to remove his homemade barriers. And in the following month they settled the case by requiring the minister to pay just over 33 livres, as well as court costs, in exchange for the Jesuits erecting their own screens or trellises over their windows.[18]

What is notable here is not the nature of the fight itself—a dispute over property rights such as any two neighbors might have—but rather the intensity of the arguments and the forum in which they were presented. Clearly the Jesuits wanted to assert their right to the building itself. Metaphorically, if not literally, they were also fighting for a free and unhindered view into the Protestant world—to anoint themselves as the witnesses of Protestant activity in Metz. The Protestants, in this affair of the old temple and Ferry's garden, frantically tried meanwhile to protect their privacy.

Another Catholic-Protestant feud involving bricks and mortar arose in the mid-1650s and occupied nearly a decade, as Protestants struggled to construct a new temple on the *retranchement*, or outer ramparts, of the city. In a lettre de cachet, Louis XIV granted Metz's Protestants the right to construct a new church in an "appropriate spot" on the *retranchement*, with "free passage" to that new building guaranteed to them.[19] But even before ground was broken, local Catholic leaders recommended that the king impose additional limits on the temple.[20] The building should have only one room for the consistory, they held, and its total size should not exceed that of the earlier in-town temple (presumably the one on the rue de Chambière that the king had ordered torn down). They wanted it built of materials no more permanent than those used before, and they wanted access limited in such a way that Protestants going there from the city would have to pass, significantly enough, by way of the rue des Juifs, or other secluded streets, rather than through more central Messin neighborhoods.[21] After construction began, the same clerics complained bitterly that the Protestants had expanded their original building plan, that they had widened roads and knocked out sections of the walls protecting the city from siege, that they had damaged public works, and that they planned to enclose their temple inside a fortified wall which would render it a fortress, capable of sustaining a force of 2,000 armed men. These Protestant "enterprises" were beyond disobedience, according to the critics. They were outrages against the authority of the sovereign and the public security.[22] "Catholics are now in tears," one written protest observed, "not from the fact of the temple itself, since the king has ordered it [to be constructed], but because of the notable enterprises recounted here, which are contrary to His Majesty's intentions."

The Crown's policy in this controversy, as in others between Protestants and Catholics in Metz, seems ambiguous, and certainly more lax than in other parts of France at this time.[23] On the one hand, Louis XIII had allowed the Jesuits to take over the temple on the rue de la Chèvre, and Louis XIV had authorized the demolition of the Protestant building on the rue de Chambière. But by the same token, the young Sun King (or his regents) upheld the Protestants' claim for payment from the Jesuits and allowed his Protestant subjects to build a new edifice to replace earlier more central temples. There is no indication that the arguments of Catholic clerics persuaded Louis to further limit that building's size or the access to it. In 1651 the king (possibly shaken by the Fronde) upheld the rights of Protestant nobles to enjoy benefices to which their land holdings entitled them, and six years later he ruled that an adjunct Protestant judge must sit on all criminal proceedings involving Protestants. However, in 1660 the same Louis ordered that when the *maître-échevin* was absent from Metz, his role should be filled by a Catholic *échevin*, even before a more senior Protestant magistrate.[24] This inconsistent royal program directed at Protestants was often exacerbated, as mentioned, by local sympathies. Let us consider how such attitudes—alternately tolerant and intolerant of the Protestants—played themselves out in additional daily disputes.

A fecund period of complaints against Protestants, and resulting pleas by the minority for protection from their local critics, occurred between 1655 and roughly 1670. Catholic clergy maintained that the Protestants had overrun several villages near Metz and chased away the Catholic citizens, that they had invited in groups of German immigrants who threatened the region's security,[25] and that the number of Protestant schools and teachers had multiplied dramatically since Louis XIII's 1634 order restricting them.[26] They railed against Protestant funerals and lack of respect for Catholic ceremonies. They held that Protestants should not mix with Catholics in the charitable hospitals, especially as the Protestants brought sweets, fresh linen, and money to their own sick and poor, and this often encouraged Catholic invalids to consider conversion.[27] There were various protests that Protestants had thwarted the deathbed attempts of individuals to reembrace Catholicism[28] and that Protestant ministers in general defamed Catholicism weekly in their sermons. In one case the claim was made that because of the timing of the Treaty of Munster, the Protestants of Metz had no right to protection under the Edict of Nantes.[29]

In 1654 Schomberg, responding to complaints, ordered that Protestants be barred from burying their dead in Catholic cemeteries, from proselytizing door to door, from singing Protestant psalms in public, from assembling outside their temples, and from emptying their chamber pots in the streets during Catholic processions.[30] We do not know if Protestants had indeed committed all of the acts this order forbade, but local Catholic leaders, especially the Jesuits, remained adamant that they had and would continue to do so if not constrained by law. An even more vituperative document of the same year took umbrage at the number of Huguenots still wielding power in the city. More than half of the judges of the local Hôtel de Ville professed the *religion prétendue réformée*, the author stated, as did highly placed officials at the *hôpital*, more than half of the doctors and apothecaries, two-thirds of the surgeons, "almost all" of the richest gold merchants, and half of the officers of the local bourgeois militia.[31] He added that many Protestants were guilty of acts of impiety. Among them was a Protestant woman who had publicly asserted that a certain Jesuit priest "should be fricasseed like a panful of onions."[32]

In all, Catholic clerics seethed over two general issues: the continuing presence of Protestants who simply would not act as docilely as the priests felt a minority should and the random way government officials—not to mention individual Messins—enforced restrictions against the "heretics." These concerns permeate a cohesive complaint from the late 1650s or early 1660s titled "The unpunished crimes of those of the *Religion Prétendue Réformée* in Metz."[33] This document alleged, for example, that a Protestant villager from just outside the city had defiled the Catholic cemetery in a manner "which modesty prevents one from describing." The *bailliage* had convicted the man and Parlement upheld the decision, ordering that in addition to paying fines the criminal should prostrate himself on his knees in front of the church during High Mass. But the clerk for the Parlement's prosecutor subverted these orders, the author wrote. Instead of taking the miscreant to church to serve his penance, the clerk accompanied the man to a tavern for a drink and arranged for other royal agents to testify that they had seen the sentence imposed. Another Protestant—a surgeon—the document charged, had been found copulating with a married woman in the vault of the cathedral. But despite a Jesuit priest's testimony against him, the surgeon remained unpunished, largely because Catholic soldiers in the garrison where he served continued to shield him from prosecution. In one of the more amusing cases related by the disapproving author, a Messin Protestant named Petitjean was charged with installing a picture of himself in the niche outside his home designed for an image of the Virgin. "His infamous portrait," the protestor wrote, "is still lodged in the niche . . . after a complaint made five months ago."[34]

Of course government institutions did respond to such complaints, but, as mentioned, the results varied. Both Catholics and Protestants complained that enforcement of laws respectively restricting Protestants or protecting them, was lax. According to Protestants writing in the early 1660s, local authorities rarely observed the royal order requiring that an adjunct Protestant judge sit on cases involving Protestants. And though Parlement, in 1662, registered the royal order that Protestant funerals be conducted only at dawn or sunset (so that they would gain less notice and not offend Catholics), Catholics claimed that Protestants refused to adhere to it and were not always punished for flouting it.[35] Catholics held that the restrictions on Protestant teaching were being ignored, at the same time that Protestants complained that these restrictions were being applied with unfair rigor.[36]

In some cases, carping about nonenforcement was mixed with wild accusation. Consider one Catholic claim: A young woman raised as a Protestant had decided to convert and had withstood the resulting fury of her relations, a Catholic author wrote, only to be cruelly attacked late one night by Protestants brandishing swords who robbed her, abused her (a sexual attack was implied), and tore her crucifix from her clenched hands in order to burn it. There was no independent confirmation for this story, which appears to have come to the authorities from the girl's confessor, but the author expressed indignation nonetheless that the *lieutenant criminel* had not seen fit to transmit a description of the alleged crime to Paris.[37] Catholic clergy further protested that a certain Protestant noble was never prosecuted for refusing to doff his cap in the presence of the Eucharist; that local judges, even when they did fine Protestants, refused to apportion part of the take to local Catholic conversion efforts; and that Catholic individuals in Metz in general were reluctant to testify against Protestants.[38]

In all, the picture one gets of Catholic-Protestant relations in Metz is a mixed one. Obviously the most zealous Catholic clerics engaged in an anti-Protestant campaign which gained momentum after 1660. Protestant leaders, with at least as much energy, tried to fend off the attack. The *bailliage* and Parlement generally aided the Catholic cause after 1660, but one still finds such cases as that of a Catholic couple trying unsuccessfully to remove their daughter from service in a Protestant household, presumably out of fear for her conversion. The *bailliage* dismissed their case.

The king, meanwhile, was clearly following an anti-Protestant policy. In 1659 he had ordered Protestants to decorate their homes for Catholic processions. In 1660, as noted, Protestants were required to remove their hats and kneel if a priest passed them carrying the consecrated host. The requirement that Protestant funerals be held at dawn or after dusk was a royal order for the nation at-large. In 1680 Protestants were excluded from a variety of offices and barred from serving in some high level posts within the trades and from serving as midwives. In 1681 they were finally expelled from their positions in the local magistracy. Despite these laws and others, however, the king and his ministers seemed in no hurry to enforce royal orders in Metz. In addition to the laxity that caused Messin Catholic leaders to issue the above-mentioned complaints, records also indicate that one of the Crown's most devastating blows to Protestantism—that children aged seven or older be allowed to choose to convert to Catholicism—was not truly enforced in Metz and its environs.[39] The expulsion of Protestant officeholders in Metz was not applied for five years. Most important, the notorious *dragonnades*, or forced lodging of ungovernable soldiers in Protestant homes, was not enacted in Metz until after the formal revocation, as we will presently discuss.

Individual Messin Catholics, meanwhile, expressed a range of attitudes, from hatred of Protestants to sympathy and a willingness to help them. Those who show up most frequently, at least in the Catholic clerics' protests, inclined toward aiding Protestant neighbors. There simply was no clear division in anyone's mind (as there was with regard to the Jewish community) between local interests and central government interests.

What is clear, however, is that one way or another life was getting harder for Protestants, even in Metz. Their own protests, probably from the 1670s, begin to sound increasingly desperate and fawning toward the king—their last hope for protection of even minimal rights.[40] Thus Catholic critics of the Protestants solicited royal officials and institutions for aid in their campaign, while Protestants themselves beseeched the king or his deputies for help as well. Either way, central government benefited. Among their complaints to the king, Protestants accused the Parlement of upholding local restrictions that ran contrary to the Edict of Nantes, including a requirement that those wishing to convert to Protestantism undergo a complicated and off-putting bureaucratic process. Their attempts to replace deceased Protestant magistrates with younger men of their creed were being blocked, they said. And the Maison de la Propagation de la Foi, they argued finally, was overstepping its role in aiding conversion to Catholicism, by kidnapping Protestant children for this purpose.[41]

During the course of the century, pressure also increased on Messin Protestant adults to convert, and some succumbed. Let us consider a sample of almost 400 abjurations—or statements of intention to abandon Protestantism and embrace Catholicism—gathered between the years 1660 and 1686, in order to understand this phenomenon.[42] Virtually all of these abjurations came from Protestants; only seven Jews wishing to profess the majority religion appear here—an indication that Catholic clerics pursued Protestants more vigorously; that the Jews, despite the civil penalties against them, tenaciously held on to their faith (as history might suggest); or that already by this time Judaism was evolving in the Catholic mind into a state that could not be changed, even through the most sincere change of heart. Before we consider this last issue in depth in a subsequent chapter, let us first examine the Protestants' abjurations for what they tell us of their conversion experience.

Abjuration statements were generally brief and highly formulaic. The individual in question identified himself or herself, stated an intention to become a Catholic, and signed by name or mark in the presence of official witnesses. The statement was then registered with the local *bailli*. However, even in this abbreviated form, one can glean much about the condition of the abjurers and speculate intelligently on some of their motives. For example, the number of abjurations increased dramatically in the years just prior to the revocation of the Edict of Nantes, but interestingly enough did not truly burgeon until the actual year of the act banning Protestantism, or even just afterward. Of 364 statements, 187, or just over half, were made between 1660 and 1680. One hundred seventy-seven were filed between 1680 and 1686, of which 148 were made in 1685 and 1686. This confirms the view of scholars such as Michel Pernot, that Protestants in Metz clung to their faith in large numbers until the last possible moment—until forced to choose among conversion, illegal emigration, or arrest.[43] The ages of the abjurers are also telling. In the earlier period (1660–1680) 41 percent of those choosing to convert were in their 20s; slightly fewer (34 percent) were teenagers or younger (i.e., minor children converted by virtue of their parents' conversion). A much lower percentage (20 percent) were men and women in middle age (for our purposes 30–60 years old), and a very small number (just under 5 percent) were over 60 years old, perhaps a simple reflection of seventeenth-century demography. In the later more active period, roughly the same percentage of abjurers were in their 20s, and this remained the most likely age for those wishing to convert. However, the number of converts in their teens dipped significantly, to 18 percent, and was matched inversely by a sizable jump in the percentage of middle-aged abjurers—to 35 percent in those six years (1680–1686). Those over 60 years old remained the least likely to abjure their faith, numbering about 7 percent of the total of those for whom we know their age.[44]

How can we explain this age distribution? First, the attractiveness of conversion to those in their 20s can be understood in part by the fact that one in four of these abjurers was a soldier, and this is the age at which most young men went to war. This also probably accounts for the disproportionate number of men making these statements; they outnumbered women two to one before 1680 and four to one from 1680 to 1686. But beyond this, the 20s was probably the age at which most young people gained full independence from their parents, and became free, if they chose, to convert either for practical or religious reasons. The early period also saw a large numbers of teenagers converting—probably a testament to the effectiveness of the Maison de la Propagation de la Foi. Leaving aside the practical inducements to conversion, teenagers and young adults might also simply have been more impressionable and prone to enthusiasm than their parents. In the later period, as daily pressure mounted against Protestants, we see more men and women in middle age deciding to abjure, and we may consider this the result of pragmatic consideration for their future and that of their children. Older people remained the least likely to convert, though of those that did, many did so from their deathbeds.

This brings us to the anecdotal, but no less important, information contained in these abjurations. The great temptation of course (and a temptation we have not entirely succeeded in avoiding here) is to try to determine the level of sincerity of the converts. In other words, did they renounce Protestantism out of concern for their comfort on Earth or out of concern for their spiritual comfort? Was the impetus to convert imposed wholly from the outside, by government strictures and local majority oppression, or was it born from a true inner change of heart? Our collected abjuration statements, being brief and vaguely formal, offer no certain answer. Few of the records include, as does that of a husband and wife who abjured in 1676, an explicit statement making their motives clear. In that unusual case the husband, a gardener originally from Bildeborg in Morhange, and his wife, of Chalbach in Fenestrange, frankly included in their declaration that upon arriving in Metz eight days earlier they decided to become Catholics because the curé of Morhange had told them it would aid their establishment in the city.[45] Most of the abjurations lack such a bald statement, however, and one is left to try to decipher the motives hidden between the lines. Objective details, such as age distribution, suggest that grim practical considerations generally held the most sway. Only after the revocation or, more important, after the infamous *dragonnades* reached Metz, did large numbers of Protestants convert. Even then many Messin Protestants fled the country, despite attempts to prevent emigration and stiff penalties for those caught in the attempt. The city of Berlin, according to one account, owed much of its growth during this period to Protestant refugees arriving from Metz.[46] Among our abjurants the prominence of soldier converts, especially in the later period, further indicates that practical considerations usually won out. But despite this, one cannot attribute all of these abjurations to worldly concerns. A departure from the statistics in favor of a careful reading of individual statements, demands that we consider the more emotional aspects of abjuration.

For example, a remarkable number of those abjuring mentioned the recent death of a spouse or parent, and this may have contributed to their decision. In some cases the confrontation with death may have prompted them to reconsider their own ideas of faith. In 1664 a 40-year-old woman, raised as a Protestant, nonetheless abjured that religion after the death of her husband, a soldier in the Swedish regiment. In 1668 a woman converted herself and three minor children, apparently out of respect for her Catholic father who had died.[47] A 26-year-old woman, the daughter of Protestants, seems similarly to have first considered converting after the death of her father. Her mother, she said in her 1671 statement, had wept bitterly at the thought and had pleaded with her to remain a Protestant. The young woman gave in to her mother's wishes, she said, and subsequently married a Protestant man. But when her young husband also died, three months after their marriage, she determined to make her abjuration.

These examples and others bring up another point. In many cases the death of a spouse or parent may have left the survivor free to choose his or her own creed. Male and female abjurers, for example, often converted back to the Catholicism of their birth after a Protestant spouse's death. Several abjurers explicitly mentioned that they had become Protestants in adulthood only to satisfy the desires of their husband or wife, now dead. Such cases, combined with the propensity of young adults to convert, suggest that in Metz, individuals were at least as subject to familial control or concerns as they were to the control of the state or the Church. They also suggest a certain fluidity in religion among individuals that clerics must have found distressing. In 1668, for example, a woman of unknown age described how, abandoned by Catholic parents, she had been raised a Protestant but now wished to convert after the death of her Protestant husband. Another abjuration contains the account of a 25-year-old wine grower who had recently emigrated from Germany. This man declared that he had been raised there as a Protestant by Protestant parents but had subsequently become involved with a Catholic girl. The couple married (possibly because she became pregnant), and their son was baptized in a Catholic church. Despite this, the man said, the validity of their union (and hence their son's legitimacy) was questioned because he had technically remained a Protestant. Now in Metz, he desired to erase any blot on his marriage or child by converting to Catholicism officially and he did so, his statement read, over the objections of his mother, who had since come to live with him and his Catholic wife. Other abjurers said they were following the example of an adult sibling in deciding to convert.

Of the soldiers, the vast majority were from outside of the region, being French, Scottish, Swiss, English, or German, but they were now stationed in Metz. Many presumably abjured through coercion after the revocation, or if earlier, to better their prospects within the army. Soldiers also may have been more aware than most civilians of the miseries of galley service—the punishment for stubborn Protestant holdouts in Metz after 1685. But even here one cannot assume that the decisions sprang purely from expedience. Many of the abjuring soldiers mentioned the influence of a Catholic comrade or bunk-mate on their choice. Pierre Moulin, a 19-year-old soldier who abjured in the year of Raphael Levy's execution, described his odyssey toward conversion briefly in such terms. Born and raised as a Protestant by Protestant parents in Montpellier, he joined the army, he said, and traveled with a company now stationed in Metz. Before they came to the city though, the company had spent time in the city of Peronne, and there Moulin shared lodgings with a comrade named LeFleur, a Catholic. The two quarreled, Moulin said, when he wanted to eat meat on a Saturday (Catholic fast day) and LeFleur tried to prevent him. The curé of the parish was called in to settle the squabble. He told Moulin that he could eat meat but that it would be better and more considerate if he refrained. He also told Moulin that his Protestant beliefs were erroneous. From this experience, Moulin said, he framed his decision to convert. Another soldier, originally from Languedoc and also raised as a Protestant, said he decided to convert after traveling with his regiment in Italy and observing Catholics there. Reviewing these cases, we see that soldiers stationed in Metz had several reasons for being susceptible to conversion: they were generally young men, in their first blush of independence and enthusiasm; they had occasion to confront death frequently, if not daily; they traveled and were thus exposed to various beliefs and ways of life; and they were lobbied particularly hard by Jesuits and other Catholics anxious to harvest their souls. Finally, after 1685, the pressure on soldiers to convert was probably the most intense for any segment of Protestant society, drawing from the obvious assumptions about threats to Catholic security.

Combining statistics from these abjurations with the brief stories hidden within them we sense that Messin Protestants generally clung to their faith in large numbers until the end, but that certain individuals among them—the bereaved, the ambitious, the newly independent—were always more likely to consider conversion, for reasons either pragmatic or philosophical.

After 1685, those pragmatic considerations became urgent, and Protestant standing in Metz was at last effectively destroyed, at least for the next century.

By the time the revocation was enforced, Protestants made up only one-fifth of the total Messin population, and all of the community's churches and schools were torn down. Its pastors fled, in many cases to Germany. And the *dragonnades*, when they came to Metz in 1686, proved brutal. Protestant families who refused to convert (and who did not attempt illegal emigration) were forced to house soldiers chosen specifically as "the most difficult and insolent" of their troublesome class. Directions were given that short of murder these soldiers were to be allowed to do as they pleased in Protestant homes, until the inhabitants would relent and embrace Catholicism. We do not have access to many personal accounts by Messin Protestants of their experiences with the *dragonnades*, but there is reason to believe that their oppression by these soldiers was at least as pronounced as that suffered by Protestants in other parts of France. According to one man's account from the northwest, "The dragoons ravaged and pillaged without mercy, resembling in their progress a lawless and victorious army taking possession of their enemy's country. They were not accountable to any one for their acts; each dragoon was a solemn judge and executioner; he who had ingenuity enough to invent any new species of torture was sure of applause and even reward for his discovery."[48] Such tactics were apparently effective. By the eighteenth century, less than 10 percent of Metz's residents still practiced a secret Protestantism in their homes.[49]

Metz's Protestant community was vastly different, then, at the end of the seventeenth century, than it had been at the time of Parlement's founding. However, in reviewing its role during the 1600s, one might argue, as Pernot has, that the large number of Protestants in Metz who waited until after the revocation to abjure, indicates that Messin Protestants were particularly devoted to their faith. This was undoubtedly true. Despite its ultimate decline, the community was cohesive, powerful, and rich through much of the century, when other Protestant communities had already begun to splinter and succumb. But was this continuing Protestant strength in Metz simply a fact, an accident of fate, or a testament to these individuals' faith? Or was it also a situation useful to and thus promoted, or at least not impeded, by the Crown? For the ambiguous royal policy toward Protestants in Metz until the latter part of the century, and the seeming willingness of Catholic laymen to abide Protestants meant that the Counter-Reformation moved more slowly here than throughout the rest of France. The pressure on Protestants to convert was not necessarily very great in Metz before 1685. What pressure there was, in any case, came from the outside—from the Jesuits or other Catholic orders bent on eradicating the Protestant heresy, and from the Crown when, but not before, it suited the royal purpose. The combination of royal officials' foot dragging and Catholic bourgeois' sympathy for Protestants, bitterly frustrated the Catholic clerical class in their desire to eject the minority. And this created a climate in which the king's larger interests regarding Metz could flourish.

The relatively slow, inconsistent buildup to the anti-Protestant crackdown in Metz solidified the king's position in the city and helped to empower his national institutions so that they might ultimately supplant local bodies. When the king supported his Protestant subjects, Catholic clerics could do little to thwart them, beyond petty harassment. Only when the king was willing to enact restrictions against the Huguenots, and to have them enforced, could real containment of the minority begin. The Protestants of Metz were simply too numerous and too influential through much of the century to be controlled by the Catholic clerics alone. Thus, time and again, local members of the clergy went to the French military governor, to the *bailliage*, to the Parlement or the king, and pleaded for help against the Protestants. The fact that they sometimes got that help—and that sometimes they did not—only left them more beholden to the Crown. Unsure of the king's sympathy for their cause, or at least unsure that he would always take their side, the clerics were kept off-balance and in need of royal assistance and a strong royal presence. As we have noted throughout our study, supplicants make bad revolutionaries.[50]

Anti-Protestantism in Metz, like anti-Semitism, thus worked to the king's advantage. It helped him impose a national state over a previously autonomous and culturally diverse region. It represented—as did anti-Semitism—a weakness in the society that made it vulnerable to centralization. In short, local Catholic leaders accepted a king and a national government in the hope that it would succeed—where local bodies had failed—in purging the town of Protestants. The middle class (merchants, tradesmen, and others), as we have said, held out similar hopes with regard to the Jews, the difference being that at least for this century the Crown had reason to reject the Protestants and did so as much to meet its own needs as to please any local constituency. Just as anti-Semitism, then, had helped the king neutralize one potential source of opposition to his takeover of Metz (the bourgeois and secular governmental class) anti-Protestantism helped to neutralize a second possibly hostile faction—the Catholic clergy. For it was only after the clerical forces opposing Protestantism in Metz had been at work for decades that we hear any concerted voice against the Protestants there. When that voice did emerge, the king (who ironically had helped to nurture it) was there to listen. But his attention came at a price: Metz would be free of Protestants but only if it accepted the king and his central administration as the piper who would rid it of them.

And even beyond this, the triumph of absolutism in this area clearly fits into an even larger trend slowly but surely transforming Messin life—secularization. The general laity's lack of enthusiasm for strictures against Protestants points to this trend, just as the increasingly complex social interaction between Jews and Gentiles (though still largely distrustful) had done. New social realities, new social alliances, were taking shape, almost despite the intentions of those involved. It should perhaps not surprise us, then, that a backlash was likely to occur. In Chapter 6 we will examine a rhetorical backlash in the writing of an important Catholic cleric. First, though, we return to the case of our Jewish peddlar. The journey back to this particular event of 1670 cannot help but be uncomfortable for modern readers. But it is a highly illuminating odyssey, for what better indication can we find of the difference between our age and theirs than to note that for the Christians of seventeenth-century Metz, the ritual murder case against Raphael Levy brought its own profound comforts.

NOTES

1. François-Yves Le Moigne and Gerard Michaux, eds., *Protestants Messins et Mosellans, XVI–XXe siècles* (Metz: Editions Serpenoise, 1988), pp. 13–43, offers a concise overview of Messin Protestant life by François Duchastelle; see especially the useful table on p. 29. Another contributor to this collection of essays cited later, Michel Pernot, calculates the number of Protestants in the city in 1635 at 6,329 but does not include those in the surrounding villages. All the authors, at any rate, agree that Protestants comprised about one-third of the urban population, which, by most accounts, totaled between 20,000 and 22,000 at the time of the Parlement's establishment. I have relied on the figures of Jacques Dupaquier, in *La Population Française aux XVIIe et XVIIIe Siècles* (Paris: Presses Universitaires de France, 1979) as the most reliable and well defended. Information on Protestant tradesmen, including an extensive breakdown of their numbers, appears in an essay by Jean-Louis Calbat, "La communauté réformée de Metz. Approche démographique," also in Le Moigne and Michaux, pp.79–89.

2. See Philip Benedict's essay, "La pratique religieuse huguenote: quelques aperçus messins et comparatifs," in Le Moigne and Michaux, p. 93ff. for these and other facts regarding books owned and read by Protestants in Metz. We do not have comparative figures for Jewish book ownership, though Jews were often more literate than their neighbors in most of the areas in which they lived. This often increased Gentiles' suspicion of them.

3. These exhortations came to Messin Protestants from their ministers, via the national Protestant Synod held in Loudun in November 1659. Leaders at that meeting declared a fast for all Protestants in commemoration of peace, and deplored the abandon and excess displayed by the general population. See A.D.M., D.9, 24th document in packet.

4. Bossuet served as *grand doyen du chapitre* in Metz from 1652 until 1659. During that time he and Ferry engaged in several ongoing debates, including one over Ferry's *Catéchisme général de la Réformation* published in 1654. Bossuet responded to this work, beginning a long correspondence between the two men, on subjects central to the split between Catholics and Protestants. While Bossuet's hope was undoubtedly to encourage a reconciliation with the city's Protestants, through Ferry, relations between the two men seem to have been generally respectful. See Henri Tribout de Morembert, *Le Diocèse de Metz* (Paris: Letouzey et Ané, 1970) pp. 119–21 for a very brief discussion of Bossuet's years in Metz. See also François Gaquère, *Le Dialogue Irénique Bossuet-Paul Ferry à Metz* (Paris: Beauchesne, 1967). There are, in addition, many books on Bossuet and his views (too numerous to list here), as well as several on Ferry. See note 10 in this chapter.

5. Jean Rigault, "La Population de Metz au XVIIe siècle; quelques problemes de démographie" *Annales de L'Est*, 5e Série, 2e Année, no. 4 (1951) pp. 310–13.

6. Rigault's exact phrase employs the more expressive French idiom to describe Messin Protestants as living *"en vase clos."* Ibid., p. 314.

7. Le Moigne and Michaux, p. 35.

8. A.D.M., D.39, document 11e.

9. A.D.M., D.39, 1–4e.

10. For more on Ferry, see R. Mazauric, *Le pasteur Paul Ferry* (Metz: Marius Mutelet, 1964). Ferry also wrote on the history of Metz and engaged in international correspondence on the subject of Lutheran-Calvinist unification. His papers are collected in Paris at the Bibliotèque Nationale.

11. A.D.M., D. 39, 4e.

12. Ibid., 18e.

13. Ibid., 4e.

14. Ibid., 25e.

15. Records of payments made by Jesuits appear in A.D.M., D.39 10e (2d document bearing this number in the packet), and A.D.M., D.39, 25e. For Schomberg's order, see A.D.M., D9, 1st document in that subgroup.

16. Ferry made this complaint in 1648 and the word used in the record of his protest is *trous*, or holes, later described as windows.

17. A.D.M., D.39, 2d document marked 9e.

18. Ibid., 83, 2d document.

19. A.D.M., D. 11, 33d document. Exact date of this lettre de cachet is unclear, but its existence is mentioned even by Catholic authors lodging their complaints against the new temple, which was dedicated in 1664.

20. A.D.M., D.11, 8th document; undated but presumed by archivists to have been written sometime between 1654 and 1657.

21. Ibid.; see also D.10, 35th document; Catholic clerics wanted to particularly prevent Protestants from passing the Carmelite church when on their way to their temple.

22. A.D.M., D.11, 13th document, point no. 11.

23. According to numerous scholars (i.e., Warren Scoville, *The Persecution of the Huguenots and French Economic Development, 1680–1720* [Berkeley: University of California, 1960], and others cited by Pernot, the *dragonnades* or billeting of troops on Protestant households began at about 1681 in France at-large. Hubert Methivier in *Le siècle de Louis XIV* (Paris: Presses Universitaires de France, 1960), p. 90 (cited by Pernot), spoke of a "pure military violence" used to oppress the minority in the years preceding the revocation. But in addition to escaping the *dragonnades* until August 1686, laws against Protestants seem to have been often ignored in Metz. See pp. 130–40 in Le Moigne and Michaux.

24. A.D.M., D.9, 355th document (re: guarantees on Protestants holding benefices); and D.9, 34th document re: the preference for a Catholic *échevin* to replace the *maître-échevin* when absent.

25. A.D.M., D.9, 32d document.

26. For documents relating to this order, see A.D.M., D.9, 26th and 27th documents. In this decree Louis XIII had ordered that Protestants be allowed to teach their children only French reading and writing in their schools, not Latin grammar or any of the human sciences, and that these latter subjects be reserved for teaching by Catholic priests. In addition, the number of Protestant schoolmasters was to be limited. Catholic clerics claimed that Protestants were avoiding this rule by holding informal classes in private homes. Pernot notes that as late as 1683, Metz was still allowed to have four Protestant schools (two for boys and two for girls), when other localities with Protestant populations were allowed only one Protestant school. See Le Moigne and Michaux, p. 131.

27. A.D.M., D.11, 2d document.

28. For example, in January 1659, Parlement upheld a *bailliage* sentence against Jean Faron and his wife, Sara Vert (Protestants), for having refused entrance to a Jesuit seeking to give last rights to one of their servants, a Catholic. The sentence, which may not have been carried out until 1663 (see A.D.M., D11, 22d document) called for the Farons to pay a fine of 300 livres. Of this, 100 livres were to pay for the servant's funeral and burial, and for the saying of a mass in perpetuity; 100 livres were to go toward the decoration of the chapel of the Maison de la Propogation de la Foi, and 100 livres to administrative fees of the court—*"necessités de la palais."*

29. A.D.M., D.10, 36th document.

30. A.D.M., D.11, 19th document; April 1654.

31. See A.D.M., D.11, 5th document; also A.D.M., D.11, 21st document (re: complaints against the number of Protestants in Parlement).

32. A.D.M., D.11, 5th document; The woman is alleged to have said, *"Je voudrois que ce Jesuite fusse aussy bien fricassé que J'ay Jamais [sic] fricassé des oignons."*

33. A.D.M., D.11, 3d document, probably written between 1657 and 1665, reputedly by a Jesuit.

34. Ibid., example no. 4.

35. One case in which a Protestant was punished for this offense occurred in 1663, when David Coverlin was fined 25 livres for having had Magdelaine Guaretier buried in the open air (i.e., in daylight); see A.D.M., D.11, 22d document.

36. A.D.M., D.11, 3d document (Catholic complaints about schools); A.D.M., D.11, 47th document (Protestant complaints about their schools).

37. A.D.M., D.11, 3d document, example no. 2. The description of this alleged attack—particularly the claim that the attackers had tried to wrest the young woman's crucifix from her hands—is not dissimilar to those claims made in connection with Raphael Levy's case, that Jews had been seen enacting animal sacrifices or mock crucifixions; see Chapter 5.

38. A.D.M., D.11, 3d document.

39. Le Moigne and Michaux, p. 131.

40. David Parker in his essay, "The Huguenots in Seventeenth-century France," in A. C. Hepburn, ed., *Minorities in History* (London: Edward Arnold, 1978), pp. 11–25, argues that the Protestants' biggest handicap in France was in fact their lack of radicalism. Only if they had been willing to oppose the monarchy and exploit class tensions would they have succeeded in wielding political influence, he says. He admits, however, that even this tactic (based on the model of the English Puritans) might not have produced anything for French Protestants beyond a bit more time before their ultimate dispersal.

41. A.D.M., D.11, 47th document. Concerning Protestant complaints about replacing their deceased officeholders, Pernot has noted that in 1685 the king finally issued the order that Protestants in Metz holding offices surrender their posts, if they continued to refuse to convert. See Le Moigne and Michaux, p. 139. The Maisons de le Propagation de la Foi were convents founded in 1645 (for girls) and 1668 (for boys) which served to shelter children supposedly wishing to convert to Catholicism. Ibid., p. 139.

42. This and all other references to abjurations come from A.D.M., D.12.

43. Le Moigne and Michaux, pp. 137–45.

44. We do know the ages of the vast majority of these abjurers, though a few appear without this detail listed.

45. Though persecution of Protestants was not as intense in Metz as elsewhere in the kingdom at this time, this statement would suggest that even in Metz Protestants were known to be living at a disadvantage and that Catholicism was becoming a requisite to fulfilling ambitions in the town.

46. Morembert, p. 121. Morembert further states that Protestants fleeing eastward at this time might well have crossed paths with Jews coming from the East to Metz.

47. We do not know how this woman was raised, but it may have been as a Protestant by a Protestant mother.

48. James Fontaine, *Memoirs of a Huguenot Family*, ed. Ann Maury, (New York: Putnam's Sons, 1852), p. 99.

49. Morembert, p. 129.

50. Another example of these clerics' supplications can be found in A.D.M., D.10, 16th document, in which the king was asked to uphold a decision of church officials against an attack by the *bailliage* (undated).

Part III
A Shifting Intellectual Climate

Chapter 5
Ritual Murder as Solace:
The Case of Raphael Levy

Tracking ideas is never light work, but in the case of the ritual murder myth—
the misguided notion that Jewish worship required the sacrificing of non-Jews
—the elusiveness of the quarry is mitigated by the fact that there is no shortage
of prints in the snow. While we cannot be sure of the exact origin of this
legend, we do know that ancient writers like Democritus believed in it.[1] And
Josephus tells us of Apion's accusation that the Jews annually imprisoned a
Greek in their temple and there fattened him for slaughter.[2] Such early rumors
about Jews persisted and in fact only proliferated once medieval Christianity,
with its myriad symbols of blood and martyrdom, nourished the Gentile imagination.[3] By the thirteenth century the myth had become a standard trope of
anti-Jewish thought; it provoked riots and violent attacks on Jews, and it often
gave secular rulers the excuse they sought to eject Jews from their countries in
order to confiscate Jewish property.[4]

One of the first examples of such an accusation occurred in 1144 in the
town of Norwich in England, when Christian townspeople accused the local
Jews of murdering a 12-year-old boy, William. Historians of the Jews generally
credit this incident with reviving the ancient rumors of Jewish sacrifice and
with sculpting the medieval prototype of the ritual murder accusation and its
resultant cult of child martyrs. The stories of William of Norwich, "Little St.
Hugh of Lincoln," and other supposed victims of the Jews, spread quickly to the
continent and founded there a tradition so potent that its force could still be felt
in the early modern period in the trial of Raphael Levy—a case at once isolated
in time but also inseparably linked to those that went before.

In Levy's case we see as well, an indication of the primacy and true
establishment achieved by the Parlement of Metz. By 1670 bourgeois opposition to the high court was essentially neutralized. Local townspeople, in connection with this trial, looked to the *bailliage* and then the Parlement for a res-

olution of the explosive charges. They eagerly participated in court sessions, re-counting stories of Jewish malevolence, past and present. And they accepted Parlement's conviction of the hapless Levy with apparent satisfaction. Clearly the court had gained a general local acceptance—one even sufficient to embolden the judges of the Parlement, or *parlementaires*, to act against the king's interests. Therein lies the final peculiarity of absolutism suggested by the Levy affair. For in an augury of the future, the case hints that royally engineered centralization in this generation could breed resistance to monarchy in the next. In addition, Levy's case further illuminates our picture of changing social relations in Metz (a few individuals did try to come to his aid, out of neighborliness or pity) and strengthens our sense that these changes were happening too quickly for some. As Jews became more useful and more in-tegrated into Messin life, and as Protestants became even more unremarkable, at least to the common folk, should it surprise us at all that Christians would return to their age-old verity—that Jews, as deicides, reenacted their ancient proclivities on a regular basis? In this sense, Jews in general (and Levy in particular) served not as scapegoats for a specific misfortune (an outbreak of plague or a faltering economy) but rather as a poltice for a society uncom-fortably abraded by the secularization it was itself complicit in creating. Buf-feted by new political, social, and religious winds, Christians in Metz seem to have reached out for their own ancient truths. Levy was thus the victim of what we might well deem a Christian ritual murder, not the perpetrator of his own. The scene is more that of Shirley Jackson's "The Lottery"—a short story in which the residents of a modern town stone a woman to reassert their communal traditions—than of a Christian vision of the Crucifixion. As we con-sider Levy's plight, let us first trace the evolution of Christian myths regarding Jewish child murder.

The story of the first supposed ritual murder victim, William of Norwich, comes to us primarily from the contemporary account of Thomas of Monmouth, a Benedictine monk of Norwich who depended heavily on information supplied by another monk, Theobald, a convert from Judaism. Three days before the celebration of Passover in 1144, Monmouth wrote, a certain number of Jews in Norwich lured a boy "of unusual innocence" into their midst, and then subjected him to a series of grisly tortures. "The chiefs of the Jews ... suddenly seized hold of the boy William as he was having his dinner and in no fear of any treachery, and ill-treated him in various horrible ways. For while some of them held him behind," Monmouth related, "others opened his mouth and introduced an instrument of torture which is called a teazle [a wooden gag], and fixing it by straps through both jaws, to the back of his neck, they fastened it with a knot as tightly as it could be drawn."[5] Monmouth then wrote that the Jews fixed a complicated rope device with knots around the boy's head, and that they further stuck his head with "countless thorn points." He continued: "And thus while these enemies of the Christian name were rioting in the spirit of malignity around the boy, some of those present adjudged him to be fixed to a cross in mockery of the Lord's Passion." The Jews then, according to Monmouth, stabbed William in the side (another parallel to the crucifixion of Jesus) and poured boiling water over him.[6]

To supply a reason why Jews would enact this heinous ritual, Monmouth consulted Theobald, the Jewish apostate, who told him that the Jews were expelled from Palestine for killing Jesus and therefore now murdered a Christian child every year in revenge for their exile. According to Monmouth, Theobald added that Jewish leaders met annually in Narbonne France to draw lots and decide which of the world's Jewish communities would act out that year's crucifixion. In 1144, Monmouth reported, the job fell to the Jews of Norwich.[7]

Despite the fact that no one had seen William abducted or killed in this way, Norwich's Christian community assumed that it must have been the work of the Jews and must have occurred in the way Monmouth described. The town's Jews appealed for royal protection and because of their usefulness to the Crown they were sheltered in a local castle until the furor died down. No one was ever convicted of the boy's murder, but William's remains were nonetheless quickly enshrined in the local church and Pilgrims who traveled there for years afterward claimed to benefit from miracles they wrought.[8]

The tale of William roughly set the pattern for most subsequent ritual murder accusations, though minor variations occurred, and the results were often more dire.[9] One of the most disastrous accusations occurred in the twelfth century in Blois, France. Unlike the English incidents, the ritual murder accusation in Blois is recounted for modern historians in Jewish sources.[10] In the late spring of 1171, a Christian groom said he saw a Jew throw the body of a child into the Loire river. Though no body was ever found, the Jews of Blois were accused of a ritual murder. In vain, they offered a substantial bribe to the local authority to protect them. More than 30 were burned at the stake. Afterward, members of the Jewish community negotiated the release of the remaining captive men. Several Jewish children who had been forcibly converted to Christianity during the incident were ordered returned to their parents.[11]

From a review of such cases, we can loosely construct a "typical" ritual murder accusation: A group of Christian townspeople, during the Easter/ Passover season, charge a Jew or Jews with murdering a prepubescent boy. Surfacing at the time of year when images of the Passion abound, the charge generally claims the Jews have tortured the child in a manner mimicking Jesus' crucifixion (pricking his head with pins or thorns, tying him to a cross, stabbing him, etc.) but not necessarily limited to that act. Profound Gentile ignorance of actual Jewish ritual, combined with an obvious fascination with that unknown world, spawn wild speculations and inventions about what the Jews must have been up to behind their doors—hence the frequent "blood libels," or rumors surrounding the accusation that the Jews killed the child to procure his blood and thereby satisfy some peculiarly "Jewish" need.[12] And hence the fact that if not at Easter/Passover, the accusation generally occurs close to a Jewish holiday or celebration. The child, whose body may or may not be found, is subsequently hailed as a martyr and saint. During the furor surrounding the accusation, the townspeople, often with the tacit encouragement of their clergy, riot against the Jews, demanding expulsion. They succeed in varying degrees in seizing either an individual or a number of Jews, whom they then quickly try and convict, or simply attack, and execute. The financial records of resident Jewish moneylenders are often confiscated and destroyed by the mob which, not surprisingly, typically includes a fair number of debtors. And the Jews generally escape the crowd's worst violence only when a powerful third party—an influential noble, cleric, or monarch—intervenes in their behalf. This intervention usually comes in exchange for a payment from the Jews, or from some continuing financial interest in Jewish commerce in the area. Of course there are many deviations from this pattern, but as a crude schema it sets a standard from which to examine our particular, much later case in Metz.

It is not entirely clear how often ritual murder accusations took place in Europe. Scholars generally know only of those that resulted in significant violence or loss of life. There is also a complex question of definition: is every charge of a Jewish attack on Christians a ritual murder accusation? Using a broad definition, Cecil Roth cited 150 instances from standard works of reference on twelfth and thirteenth-century England.[13] More recently, R. Po-chia Hsia has used a fairly narrow definition to conclude that such charges reached their peak in Germany in the fifteenth century and declined dramatically throughout Europe after the sixteenth century.[14] Whatever the precise number of these claims, however, they were at least common enough to trouble the cooler heads of their times. In 1272, for example, Pope Gregory X wrote:

It sometimes happens that certain Christians lose their Christian children. The charge is then made against the Jews by their enemies that they have stolen and slain these children in secret, and have sacrificed the heart and blood. The fathers of the said children, or other Christians who are envious of the Jews, even hide their children in order to have a pretext to molest the Jews and to extort money from them.[15]

A century later, Philip the Good of Burgundy felt concerned enough by the number of accusations that he exempted the Jews of his province from "the consequences of dead children being hidden in their homes or gardens."[16] Evidence also indicates that beginning in the fourteenth century parents sometimes offered to sell their children to Jews, so widely was it believed that the Jews needed them for religious purposes. Even the enlightened but still anti-Semitic Voltaire believed that ancient Jews engaged in human sacrifice.[17]

There was, we should note, a division between official Church teachings (which denied Jewish ritual murder) and popular Christian attitudes, but as much public belief was encouraged by church art, Christian liturgy, and the exhortations of charismatic members of the lower clergy, it seems fair to class the Church's position on Jewish ritual murder with its other denials of institutional anti-Semitism—as part of what Joshua Trachtenberg described as church "sophistry."[18]

Within this context (if not entirely explained by it), we find the case of seventeenth-century Metz. The city had no history of ritual murder accusations, though one must remember that from roughly 1322 until the mid-sixteenth century no known Jews lived there. By and large, the trial of Raphael Levy ushered in an era of such charges, and it is his case that provides the first and most detailed view of this telling aspect of Jewish-Christian relations in that city. Because the case occurred in the period of French state consolidation, it also transpired in a unique way, affected by local-central competition.

The hard facts of this case are quickly recounted: On September 25, 1669, during a year of severe drought, Giles Lemoine and his wife lost their son near their home in Glatigny. On the same day, Raphael Levy traveled from Boulay to Metz to procure provisions for Rosh Hashanah, the celebration of the Jewish New Year, which began at sundown on that day. In the days that followed, the rumor circulated among Christian townspeople and peasants that Levy had kidnapped the child. Encouraged by leaders of the Jewish community, Levy voluntarily came to Metz for questioning. But despite his vehement denial of involvement in the supposed kidnapping, and his offer to produce proof of his innocence, the local *bailli* imprisoned and convicted him. In November, by which time Levy had appealed the case before Parlement, a child's corpse was found in the woods, badly mutilated and decomposed. Two local court-appointed surgeons examined it and declared that the boy had been attacked and partially devoured by wild animals at least one month before. The Lemoines identified the remains as those of their son, but persisted in their conviction that Levy and the Jews had killed him. They filed a civil suit against Levy demanding damages. A number of townspeople then testified, including those who had found the child's remains; those who claimed to have seen Levy in the woods on the September day in question; and those who said they knew of various atrocities enacted by Messin Jews, either in connection with Levy's case or years earlier. Records of Parlement do not indicate that any of Levy's witnesses were ever questioned or that his alibi was investigated. In December, letters written between Levy and members of the Jewish community were intercepted, confiscated, and translated by court-chosen individuals. These letters were then used against Levy, though he rejected the translations, solicited from a Jewish apostate. In January, Levy was condemned to die, and on the 17th he was burned alive and his ashes cast to the wind.[19]

With this synopsis in mind we can look more closely at individual testimony, which largely revolved around three topics: Levy's whereabouts on the day in question; the case of another man, Mayeur Chuaube, and an incident supposed to have taken place years earlier; and the alleged involvement of other members of the Jewish community in the Levy affair, particularly with regard to the child's corpse. In all three areas the judges' receptiveness to hearsay and third-person evidence is striking, and the inconsistency of the testimony cannot but startle modern sensibilities. Further, the potency of the ritual murder myth, even at this relatively late date, is indisputable. Economic self-interest, it will be shown, played some part in the testimony, but even beyond this Christian townspeople simply *believed* that Jews kidnapped Christian children and enacted strange blood sacrifices. For the most limited and minute speculations in the Levy case clearly served as the sole catalysts that called up traditional anti-Semitic lore. Christians hostile to Jews did not need to hear from an eye witness to believe a wild tale of Jewish treachery. Suspicion was preexistent, and it ran deep. What may be more surprising is that the Parlement—a relatively "modern" institution—approved that suspicion with its decision. A pernicious rumor, a few suppositions, and the translation of a single Yiddish word sufficed to make Raphael Levy the victim of a lethal ritual murder accusation, and one of the few such victims known in the early modern period.

We will begin with Levy's account of his movements on the day in question. From his first testimony until his execution, Levy held as follows: At about 7 A.M. on September 25 he, his son, and a miller of Boulay left their home on horseback to travel to Metz. The Levys' purpose was to procure food, wine, and a shofar for the holiday.[20] The trip normally took about three hours, and they arrived in Metz accordingly at about 10 A.M. or a bit later, Levy having had to stop en route at the village of Les Estangs to repair two of his horse's shoes. At one point in their ride, Levy met with a cavalier, in this case a mounted soldier; both walked their horses alongside each other for a few minutes. Levy, who was not wearing a coat remarked that it was a chilly day and spoke a few other such pleasantries, then remounted and rode on. In Metz, he said, he and his son made their purchases and strapped them to the son's horse. Levy then sent his son to find the miller (who may have had other business in the city) and instructed him to start for home. Levy would join them on the road. According to his testimony of October 14, Levy left Metz himself at about 1 P.M.; he met his son and the miller on the road between Les Estangs and Glatigny where he stopped (without dismounting) just long enough to pay for the shoeing of his horse that morning. And the three travelers arrived in Boulay at 4 P.M., one hour before the start of Rosh Hashanah.

During several interrogation sessions in October, authorities repeatedly questioned Levy's account. Had he not met a small child along the road, and had he not seized that child and taken him back to Metz? Levy, in turn, repeatedly denied any such experience. Hadn't he concealed the child under his coat and delivered him to Metz and hadn't he lied about the horse he was riding in order to mislead the authorities? officials asked. No, Levy replied, he hadn't even worn a coat on the day in question, and he had shown the authorities the horse he had ridden. The interrogation continued in the same vein.

"While passing near Glatigny, didn't you find a child in the main road, and didn't you take that child?"

"I didn't see any child at all; I didn't take any child."

"Having taken the child and having put it in front of you on your horse, didn't you bring it to Metz and leave it there?"

"No."

"Why do you deny this when one is convinced of it by someone who saw you enter the city with a child in front of you on your horse?"

"The woman who has said this is a false witness. I understand she was in bed, in childbirth, on the night of the Monday of that week. How could she have been up and at her door by Wednesday? Also, in her deposition she said that the person she saw had on a gray-brown coat, but I didn't have on a coat, and I've never worn one of such a color . . . Talk to my neighbors; they will tell you that they have never seen me wear a coat of that color."

The questioners showed particular suspicion that Levy had in some way tampered with the witnesses against him.

"On the day you were arrested and imprisoned, didn't someone write to you that you were accused of kidnapping a child, and that it was a cavalier of the Troupes Lorraine who had charged this?"

"Monsieur de la Rogadre [21] told a clerk of the Jewish community that I was accused of having taken a child, and that I should come in to clear myself, and the clerk came to me and told me to do that as soon as possible. So I came to Metz and found Seigneur de la Rogadre and he told me that there were three people who had accused me, and that among them was a cavalier Lorraine, whom he brought in to confront me with the charge."

"After you returned to Boulay, didn't you solicit this cavalier to change his testimony?"

"When I went back to Boulay I went to find the governor, and I made a complaint to him that a soldier was accusing me of having taken a child, because Monsieur de la Rogadre had told me I would have to search out witnesses to testify to my innocence."

"But hadn't you encountered the cavalier on the road on the day in question?"

"It's true I met a cavalier, but when the governor asked the cavalier you speak of if it was I whom he saw on the road, he said no."

"Didn't you give money to the cavalier, or have money given to him, to get rid of him and stop his testimony?"

"No. I didn't give him so much as one sou, nor did I arrange to have anything given to him. I never did any of the things of which I am accused."[22]

Levy spent the rest of that autumn in jail. In November the *bailli* apparently convicted him on the testimony of three original "witnesses"—the cavalier, a woman close to childbirth, and an unidentified third person—none of whom positively identified Levy as the man they claimed to have seen. We do not know the precise sentence the *bailli* imposed at that time. Regardless, the case was taken over by the Parlement during November, and at the end of the month, as mentioned, a group of pigkeepers found the remains of a child's body in the woods. The commissioner from Parlement in charge of the case ordered surgeons to examine the corpse and determine the time and cause of death. Master surgeons Jean Lucembourg (or Luxembourg) and Etienne Capusson made the examination, and on December 1, from Capusson's house (because that surgeon was then ill in bed), they made their report.

The surgeons confirmed that they examined the skull of a child, three to four years old, which was whole, without signs of lesions or other marks, but "ghastly and black because of the extreme decomposition of the brain which filled it." Various fragments of the body remained attached to the skull, though most were denuded of flesh and had long been exposed to the air, the surgeons concluded. These parts, they reported, "we estimate to have been devoured and torn apart by ravenous and carnivorous animals, such as wild dogs, wolves, swine, or other similar beasts." They continued: "As for determining the length of time during which the corpse may have been so exposed, given the extreme decomposition, together with the hardening and blackness of the ligaments remaining on the left side of the skull, we estimate that it has been about 40 days since the time of death."[23] This would have placed the time of death at about mid-October, perhaps even after Levy was imprisoned.

Despite this report, local townspeople, many of whom now offered to testify in the burgeoning case, resisted the possibility that the child had indeed fallen prey to wild animals. Dieudonné Humbert, one of the swineherds, testified that when he and his comrades found the corpse they also found the child's clothes —a small dress and a red bonnet trimmed in silk and fake silver threads. The dress, he added, "was entirely white, like a shirt just washed, without any bloodstains or other marks at all."[24] The swineherds moved the remains to a hollow tree trunk, he said, then sent at once for Lemoine, the missing boy's father. They also noticed no blood near the head or other clothes. The second swineherd, Sebastien Moreau of Glatigny echoed Humbert's report, again mentioning the lack of bloodstains on the garments or the ground. The third pigkeeper, Jean Humbert (possibly Dieudonné's brother) added on his own initiative, not in response to a specific question, that the head showed no sign of having been touched or eaten by any wild beast. And finally Fremyn Moreau (again, possibly related to the earlier witness) testified that he and D. Humbert had found the corpse about three weeks before (He testified on December 2.) They found the head, with part of the ribs attached, he said; a shock of hair lay on the ground about 20 steps away, and a white dress and red bonnet lay on the ground. This witness reported that a white shirt, clean and not bloody, was also carefully hung on a nearby bush. He also volunteered that the state of the head proved that animals had had no part in the child's death. Wild animals, he explained, "always eat the head of their prey first, and they break through the skull immediately in order to eat the brain."[25]

The judges of the Parlement were apparently swayed by such statements, despite the surgeons' report. Their suspicions come through clearly in a December 2 interrogation of Raphael Levy.

"Aren't you aware that the clothes and remains of a child were found five or six days ago?"

"No."

"Weren't these clothes and remains of the child brought to the woods by your order, so as to clear yourself of the crime of which you are accused? Didn't you tell someone to do this?"

"I never knew anything about it. I haven't spoken to anyone for about a month now."

"Would you recognize these clothes and remains if they were shown to you?"

"No. I've never seen the child or his clothes."

The child's skull and clothes were then shown to Levy; he repeated that he did not recognize them and had never seen them before.

"Aren't these clothes and these remains those of the child you abducted?"

"I never abducted anyone. Nor have I ever seen those things."

"These clothes, you know, were found largely intact. The bonnet was in one piece, and the stocking was not at all torn or mangled. These clothes were taken from the child by a man's hand."

"I do not recognize these clothes; I had no part in any such affair."

And then, directly refuting the surgeons' conclusion that the remains belonged to a child dead since mid-October, the interrogators continued.

"This head and the remains of the child still have parts of the flesh attached which still appear red and bloody. It is impossible that the flesh would still be attached after more than two months [in the woods]."

"I am innocent. I don't know what more I can say to prove that to you."

The discovery of the child's corpse, rather than clearing Levy, only complicated the case. The rest of December brought forth a torrent of testimony from Messin townspeople eager to join in the fracas. To categorize and organize their statements is somewhat artificial, for it imbues the prosecution of Levy with an illusion of logic and order it lacked in reality. Some came forward to talk about Levy, others told of being approached by Jews, and still others recounted strange tales of long-past experience with Jewish malevolence. Take, for example, the following testimony of Clemence Paquin (Closquin) [26] and other related claims.

Clemence, the 65-year-old widow of Messin tailor Antoine Closquin, told officials on December 2 that her husband had been attacked by Jews about eight or nine years before the Levy affair. Her husband, she reported, had told her that he went with a friend from Pont Iffroy (a community directly adjacent to the center of the city) to Metz to make a loan of ten ecus with the Jews of that city. To do so, she said, he was obliged to visit the home of Mayeur Chuaube, a prominent lender, during the morning of Good Friday. Entering Chuaube's home, she said, her husband had seen a group of Jewish men gathered around a table in the back room, feigning a reenactment of the death of Jesus. Once they perceived her husband in the room, she said, the Jews grabbed him by the coat and threatened him with a knife. He escaped into the street after receiving a wound to the right hand, but met another Jew named Birier in the street. Birier, Clemence reported Antoine had told her, tried to bribe him to keep quiet about the incident. The wife added that she and her husband had made a complaint at that time to the king's *lieutenant criminel* but that nothing ever came of it and her husband subsequently died of unrelated causes.

Cuny Martin, a 40-year-old master cobbler of Metz then testified that Antoine Closquin had told him the same story eight or nine years earlier, on Good Friday. Martin recalled that Closquin told him that the Jews at Chuaube's house had been assembled around a table made from planks and decorated with candles and a crucifix, and that they had worn plumed hats and carried knives. According to Martin, Closquin had said that when the Jews saw him, Chuaube's wife pushed him into a back room and cried out in Hebrew that they should kill him (Martin never explained, nor was he asked, how Closquin would have understood Hebrew, even if he had heard it).[27] Martin then related that while Closquin told him this story in the street (and showed him a wound he had supposedly received to his hand during the incident), two Jews approached them and tried to induce Closquin to accept a bribe to conceal the affair. To this, Martin said, "Closquin responded that he would never sell his blood," and insisted he would go to the authorities and file a complaint.

Others who testified about Antoine Closquin's story included Gerard Mangeot, aged 45, a gardener of Metz, who said that Closquin had described the attack to him seven or eight years earlier. According to Mangeot, Closquin said he saw about a dozen Jews at Chuaube's house, armed with weapons, but assembled around a table where they were *sacrificing an animal*. They were treating the animal, he added, "as if they wanted to represent the Passion of the son of God."[28] Mangeot's testimony was echoed—including the element of an animal sacrifice not mentioned by the previous witnesses—by a laborer who, probably not insignificantly, lived on the same street as both Mangeot and the Closquins.

The Closquin statements have all the elements of an oral tale, passed among people of a small community. Closquin, the supposed author of the account, was dead and unable to verify the details of the report, which included minor variations in each retelling. Note that the accounts, like most medieval ritual murder accusations, charged Jews with reenacting the crucifixion during the Easter/Passover season, but some hearers of Closquin's story recalled him describing a crucifix on the table, or candles, and others remembered an animal sacrifice. Martin recalled Closquin pronouncing the dramatic line that "he would never sell his blood"—a clear rhetorical allusion to Judas Iscariot's selling Jesus' blood—which served to suggest parallels between Closquin's circumstances and those of Jesus. Thus, while this story did not involve an alleged attack on a young boy (as most medieval accusations against the Jews did), it nonetheless contained many of the elements of a classic ritual murder charge. The Closquin incident was informed by the anti-Semitic myths that had long preceded it, and it, in turn, would serve to inform the Levy case, calling up for judges all of those medieval images which had proved so dangerously formative in Gentile attitudes toward Jews. While seemingly unrelated, then, the Closquin story proved an essential element in the case against Levy, convincing the judges that Levy's case was indeed one of a ritual murder. If Metz's Jews could enact the ritual that Closquin, through his survivors, said he saw eight or nine years earlier, the implication ran, they could enact such a ritual on a young child in 1669. An absurd inclusion in terms of modern judicial procedure, the Closquin tale nonetheless was one of the three legs on which the prosecution balanced its case, and it was enhanced by another fragment of testimony from a Messin woodworker.

Didier L'Egiptine, aged 32, testified that four or five years before Levy's arrest a Jesuit priest had instructed him (L'Egiptine) to transport an Avignonese Jew named Aribut to Verdun to be baptized. Aribut chose not to be baptized in Avignon, L'Egiptine recalled, because he was the nephew of a rabbi and feared the retribution of his family and of other Jews.[29] Along the road to Verdun, L'Egiptine said, Aribut told him that the Jews regularly procured young Christian girls, virgins, "to draw blood from their feet and arms and that the Jews serve themselves with this blood, for a purpose that L'Egiptine could not remember."[30] As with the testimony relating to Closquin's claims, this report was based on years-old hearsay evidence, with no direct relation to Levy's case. But in the minds of the townspeople, and the judges apparently, rumors—even old ones, even unsupported ones, even fantastical ones—added up one by one to create a case against the Jew of Boulay. The fixation with the supposed Jewish need for Christian blood was typical, and in its way part of a complex, comfortable structure for Christians. Jews had killed Jesus, they believed; they remained jealous of Christians and therefore killed them too whenever they could; they needed Christian blood (which by implication had its magical properties of purity confirmed) in ancient times, in medieval times, and even in their own times. Christians and their blood were still special, then, and the Jewish need for that blood even bolstered Christian claims to their own preeminent "election." Thus ritual murder and blood libel represented an aspect of religiosity that remained wonderfully constant and deeply reassuring for Christians. It could be returned to in times of stress or uncertainty, even belligerently so in the current shifting climate of post-*politique* France.

Other pieces of testimony heard in December, if also based on rumor, at least dealt with Levy's case specifically. Jean Bachelay, a 55-year-old master tailor of Metz, testified on December 2 that he had been at the home of an army marshal eight days before. While fitting that official for a suit of clothes, Bachelay said, he was asked what news there was of the Jew who had been imprisoned. Bachelay recalled telling the marshal that he knew nothing about the case, except that a rumor had circulated in the town that the Jews had given money to one of the marshal's cavaliers so that he would withdraw his testimony against Levy. At this point, Bachelay said, a cavalier from Prague who was also in the room (but whose name Bachelay could not remember) said that it was true that the cavalier involved had told several comrades that he had indeed seen the Jew on the road carrying a child with a red cap. Note the indirectness of this testimony. Bachelay reported hearing a cavalier of Prague say that he had heard other cavaliers say that they had heard a cavalier say he saw a Jew with a child. In other words, the information came at least fourthhand. Bachelay added that he told the marshal that he had known the imprisoned Jew for more than 15 years, and that Levy was "a malicious man and a man of bad faith who had even tried to prevent him from selling clothes." This last seems to indicate some sort of professional competition between Levy the peddler and Bachelay, a tailor, and may explain the latter's eagerness to testify.[31]

Oulry Coureur, a horse dealer, claimed that he had spoken to a Jew in the rue des Juifs[32] about the Levy affair three weeks earlier. Coureur, aged 45, said he asked the Jew, Lazare Wilestach, how the case was going. Wilestach replied that it was going badly and asked Coureur if he wanted to earn 50 pistoles. Coureur said he told Wilestach yes and that Wilestach then consulted with Abraham Spire.[33] At this point, Coureur said, the two Jewish men asked him "if he wanted to go into the woods near the village of Glatigny and search for the child whom Levy had been accused of kidnapping." They told him that the child had most assuredly been attacked by animals or taken by "Egyptians," [34] and they asked him to bring back any clothing or other evidence he might find to indicate that the boy had simply been lost in the woods, not murdered. In addition to offering him the 50 pistoles, Coureur recalled, they also assured him that "their community would assist him and his family so that they would never lack for anything."[35]

It is quite possible, of course, that Coureur's story was at least partially accurate. Knowing that any attempt to search for the child on their own would be seen as part of a Jewish conspiracy (and the finding of any corpse only more damning to their community), Jewish leaders may well have been willing to pay a sympathetic Gentile to conduct a search in the woods. However, oddly enough, Coureur's testimony seems only to have fueled the court's growing belief that the Jews knew of the corpse's whereabouts long before the swine-herds found it, and that if they knew it must be because they had put it there. Given these assumptions, the Jews had no real hope of fighting the charges against Levy and, by extension, their community. Anything beyond total passivity was regarded as "proof" of their involvement in some devilish scheme.

The conviction that the Jews had collectively hatched some plot was strengthened by the statement of Jean Gondrecourt, the 17-year-old son of an officer in the king's guards. Gondrecourt reported that in early November a Jew had approached him and offered to pay if he would search the woods for the lost child. Gondrecourt said he refused and learned only afterward that the place the Jew had asked him to look was the very spot where the child's remains were eventually found. Gondrecourt apparently did not feel compelled to relate this story to anyone until December 5, by which time the speculations of Jewish knowledge of the corpse's whereabouts were well circulated. We should add that Gondrecourt's motives for testifying would be explicitly, if unwittingly, called into question by the testimony of a subsequent witness. We will consider the statement of that witness, Nicolas Gorgonne of Hetz, later in this study.

For now we can round out the circle of those testifying against Levy directly with the statements given by two Messin women who claimed to have seen Levy enter Metz with the child on the day of the child's disappearance. Joute Charpentier, aged 50, the wife of a carter, said that after her husband told her that a villager had lost his child she suddenly remembered that she too had seen a Jew on horseback pass in front of her carrying a blond-headed child of three to four years old in a red cap and a *yellow* dress near the city gates.[36] Upon seeing them pass, she said, she had remarked to people near her (whose names she could not remember), "Look what a beautiful child; he does not look at all like the child of a Jew."[37] She recalled that the Jew had black whiskers but said she did not think she could recognize him, and she did not notice the color of his horse. Margueritte Gassin, meanwhile, said that on a Wednesday—she was unsure of the date, the time, or whether it was morning or afternoon—she too had seen a Jew pass her on a city street in Metz, carrying a blond child in a red bonnet, about three years old. She said she called to her sister, "Hey, here is a Jew with a really beautiful child." But by the time her sister arrived at the door, she said, the Jew had passed. Gassin, like Charpentier, said she was not sure she could recognize the Jew, that he had been a big man with black hair, and she believed he had been riding a white or gray horse. Given the vagueness of both these statements, and the fact that the details they mentioned were only those which had long been bruited about the city, the witnesses may well have based their recollections on rumors.

The next major circle of witnesses to come forward were those with observations or assumptions regarding the child's remains. The potency of this testimony can only be understood in the context of a society that accepted Jewish ritual murder to some extent as an irrefutable fact and that may have clung to this traditional myth for comfort in an intellectually confusing era. For the indictment of Jews beyond Levy again came entirely by way of implication and inference, suggested only by speculation. In other words, this testimony, like others in the case, merely provided plaster for the walls; the basic structure of myth had long been in place, and that structure really served as a fortress against unforeseen or unpredictable intellectual assault. One example of such testimony came on December 10 from Jean Poulain, the smith of Hetz, a village not far from Glatigny. Poulain claimed that he saw Gideon Levy (no known relation to Raphael Levy), a Jewish man of his village, carrying a hod or pail in and out of the woods several times, on two separate days. He did not speak to the Jew, he said, and did not know why he was carrying the hod, but he added that this took place at about the time the child's remains were found nearby. Poulain further informed officials that as a neighbor of Gideon Levy he had seen Jews in groups of three or four visiting the Jew "at diverse hours, sometimes as late as midnight."[38] This had only occurred during the past three weeks, he said; before that time Jews had visited G. Levy's house only during the day.

Poulain's implication here was clearly that Gideon Levy had had some hand in toting the child's remains into or out of the woods, or in doctoring the site where those remains eventually turned up, ostensibly as part of some general Jewish effort (such as a ritual killing of the child). However, his testimony was entirely speculative. He saw nothing to indicate that G. Levy was carrying body parts in his hod, or children's clothing, or anything else. In fact, Poulain's claims prove nothing at all *unless* one began with the tacit assumption (and for Christians a supremely comforting assumption) that the Jews were invariably malevolent or demonic, or at the very least, generally up to no good. Only from that starting place could Gideon Levy's actions be seen as suspect, and clearly they were, for he too was imprisoned on suspicion of involvement, even after he provided a reasonable explanation of his actions in the woods.[39] Finally, before we dismiss Poulain, we should point out that Gideon Levy was a butcher and as has been shown, the feuding between the Jewish butchers of Metz and their Gentile counterparts was intense.[40] Poulain was not a butcher, but he may have acted out of sympathy for friends of that profession, or merely from a general suspicion of any Jew whose livelihood involved constant exposure to blood and slaughter. There may also have been some problem between Poulain and Gideon Levy as neighbors. Regardless, it seems that Poulain certainly suspected G. Levy of some sort of heinous act on the Jews' behalf, and the judges must have shared that suspicion. Even if Poulain testified out of economic rivalry or personal spite, the court's embracing of his suppositions makes sense only if they too believed, or wanted to believe, that Jews did kill Christian children.

Nicolas Gorgonne, the official of Hetz mentioned earlier, then stated that Jean Gondrecourt had told him that *Gideon Levy* was the Jew who had offered him (Gondrecourt) money "to search for the child of Glatigny in the woods" and that it was G. Levy who had indicated almost the exact spot where the corpse was found. However, contrary to Gondrecourt's own testimony, Gorgonne said Gondrecourt went to Gideon Levy after the swineherds found the corpse and demanded payment himself for the discovery. Gideon Levy refused, Gorgonne reported, telling Gondrecourt that it was the Sabbath and that he had no money with him but that the Jews of Metz would pay him later. Gondrecourt returned the next day, Gorgonne said, at which time G. Levy gave him five livres worth of meat. Gorgonne's account, thus intended to further incriminate Gideon Levy, actually shattered Gondrecourt's claims, and it provides the possible reason Gondrecourt testified against the Jews in the first place. Frustrated in his own attempt to exact money from the Jews (for a discovery in the woods in which he actually had no part), did Gondrecourt decide to incriminate the Jews at large, and Gideon Levy in particular? Out of fear, did Gideon Levy try, unsuccessfully, to appease Gondrecourt's demands by giving him some meat? We cannot know the answers to these questions absolutely, but a reasonable scrutiny of the testimony suggests these as possibilities. The records show no indication that Gondrecourt's motives were explored.

When finally allowed to confront these and other witnesses against him later in the month, Gideon Levy vehemently denied any conspiracy to carry the child or its corpse into the woods. He explained to the judges that he often lodged Jews who came to his home to buy kosher meat and that he often traveled the main road with a hod of meat for sale or delivery. But, he added, he never left the main road with his wares, and he professed innocence of all charges against him. His explanation apparently did not satisfy the authorities who kept him imprisoned throughout the late winter and into the new year. In this way, Gideon Levy was locked up on "evidence" at least as spurious as that which sent Raphael Levy to his death. The two cases, or rather the rabid and somewhat desperate suspicions that spawned them, fed on each other.

The last major element of Raphael Levy's trial revolved around the interception of letters passed between Levy, his son, and members of the Jewish community throughout the late autumn. Levy's jailor apparently found several of the letters in the prisoner's straw mattress. Questioning of a prison chamber-maid revealed that she had accepted money from the Levys to spirit the letters into and out of the jail. Marguerite Houster, aged 16, was questioned about her actions, but she testified that she had delivered the letters for Levy alone and that her deed was not part of any larger plot or conspiracy by the Jewish community in general. From her description, such letters provided the only means for prisoners to communicate with relatives and friends, and though she did not say so explicitly, her answers suggest that the practice of paying the prison staff for such favors was not uncommon. After assuring the judges, upon their queries, that she was a Catholic, Houster—a resident of Boulay before beginning work in the prison—answered further questions, including the following.

"On the 8th of November, when he gave you a note [for his father] didn't the son [of Raphael Levy] tell you, 'the child has been bound?'"

"No. The Jew's son never said anything more to me than to deliver the notes, that and giving me food to take to his father."

"And didn't you then report these same words, 'the child has been bound,' to Raphael Levy in either French or German?"

"No."

"Haven't you said before that you were told these words, 'the child has been bound,' and that you then reported them to the Jew, Raphael?"

"No."

'Since your arrest and imprisonment, hasn't the Jew Raphael solicited you to conceal the truth from us, and promised you money to do so?"

"No. I haven't even spoken to him at all since Sunday the 10th of November."

"Haven't you been to the home of Jews in this city, in particular to the home of one Chuaube, on Raphael's orders, to deliver notes or other messages? When did you make these visits, and on how many occasions?"

"I have neither gone out on Raphael's orders nor delivered any such messages.

Never. However it's true that I have been sent out since this man Raphael came into the prison. I don't remember the date precisely, but it was by the order of my master, the concierge of prisons. He sent me out five or six times to the home of a man called Benediq [a Jewish man] to ask for money that he said that man owed him. The man Benediq refused to pay and [said he] didn't want to pay more."[41]

This last of Houster's answers suggests that the concierge of prisons, like Jean Gondrecourt, may have tried to profit from Levy's misfortune by extorting money from the Jews. Perhaps the concierge knew about the relaying of letters through Houster, before the day when he actually confiscated them from Levy's mattress, and he was hoping to make money from the Jewish community in exchange for keeping quiet. If so, did his demands get out of hand, and did Benediq ultimately refuse him, resulting in the concierge then turning Levy's letters over to prosecutors? As with so many of the most piquant details of this case we have no records to tell us all of what occurred. While we must refrain from committing the same sin as many of the witnesses against Levy (i.e., speculating well beyond the evidence), Houster's testimony points out that more than a mere interception of letters may well have taken place in the prison. And there was indeed a kind of secular (i.e., mercenary) self-interest at work here, from individuals not particularly scared of the individual Jews who actually lived in their midst.

By the time Houster appeared, some of the judges had clearly formed a link between Levy and Mayeur Chuaube, at least in their own minds. Witness their questions to the girl regarding possible orders sent between Levy and Chuaube, even though not even any of the earlier witnesses had suggested such a connection. Here we see the fragments of earlier testimony being sewn together into one sweeping accusation. An even more important element of Houster's examination came in the repeated questions about the phrase, "the child has been bound." This phrase and its alleged appearance in a letter from Levy to leaders of the Jewish community, was one of the most critical pieces of "evidence" used against the Boulay peddler. One might even consider it the pivot on which the ritual murder accusation hung. For this phrase, despite Levy's consistent denial that he ever spoke or wrote the words, provided judges with their own perceived bridge between Levy's supposed actions and the entire history of medieval ritual murder charges. This was, in a sense, the welcome link between the perplexing complexity of the current age (post-Reformation and pre-Enlightenment) and the desirable if idealized simplicity of the Middle Ages, when Christianity reigned supreme and intact over men's affairs in western Europe. If Closquin's posthumous tale established that the Jews of Metz regularly enacted strange sacrificial ceremonies, the translation of the phrase "the child has been bound" made Levy a part of the same continuum. From traditional delusions about Jews (reflected in such stories as L'Egiptine's) to local tales like the Closquins' to Levy—thus the chain of faulty logic ran.

However flawed this logic, it must have been, for Messin Christians high and low, reassuring in its way. Political life had changed dramatically. Local prominence had shifted to new groups of men or even to a new secular entity —the absolutist state. Like it or not, religious affiliation was more complicated. Even being a Christian was not as clear as it once was. And who was or wasn't a heretic was even murkier, as we shall see in Chapter 6. But whatever else was true or not true about seventeenth-century Metz, one thing could be counted on by Christians: the Jews were still murdering little boys and collecting their blood. At the risk of carrying this speculation too far, one might almost imagine our Messin Gentiles' relief that though God, his role in the world, or his intentions for his Church, might change, at least the Devil (in the form of the Jews) was as evil as ever. But let us return to the case at hand.

With regard to the letters, officials confiscated them in the first days of December, then solicited a local Jewish apostate to translate them from Judeo-German, probably a western variant of Yiddish, into French. He did so, but Levy objected to the translation of several passages. Louis Anne, the apostate, claimed Levy had written in one note, "I understand that the child has been bound." The crucial word, he said, came from *binden*, "to bind." Levy protested. The letter, he insisted, said "I understand the child has been *found*." The word in question came from *finden*, "to find." He had written it, he added, from the hope that locating the child's remains in the woods would clear him.[42] Investigators nonetheless accepted Louis Anne's translation, as evidenced by their interrogation of Levy on December 18, in which we see the precise elements of the previous testimonies that had made an impression on the authorities.

"Haven't the Jews of this city and the surrounding areas tampered with the witnesses and given them money to prevent them from testifying against you?"

"No. I'm innocent. And because of that there is no need to give anyone money to prevent their testifying. Every day Jews pray to God to preserve them from such false accusations."

"If the Jews were entirely innocent of such crimes they would not need to pray to God to particularly preserve then from such charges. That they do so only makes it clear that they are accustomed to committing these crimes."

"That's not true. Because we hold different beliefs from Christians, and because we are always such a small minority in the places where we are established, we are always aware of being falsely accused by evil men who want to do us ill. That is why we particularly pray to God that we not be accused of kidnapping children. Whenever any child is lost, people spread rumors that the Jews have taken it, even though we would never think of doing such a thing."

"At certain times, such as Good Friday or other days, don't the Jews hold ceremonies to commemorate the death of the son of God, in order to deride the Christian religion? And don't they hold these ceremonies in secret hidden places so as not to be found out?"

"No. I have never heard such a thing planned among us. Such things are never done."

   With regard to the letters, Levy was shown the Louis Anne translations and asked to concur that they were faithful to the originals. This he refused to do. Prosecutors asked him again and again about the phrase "the child has been bound." Levy repeatedly denied the existence of that phrase. Initially, he explained that the phrase read "the child *will be* found." Tense was crucial here, because the letter was apparently written before late November when the swineherds found the corpse in the woods. Leaving for a time the issue of "bound" versus "found," prosecutors pounced on this issue of tense and challenged Levy, noting that a second court-ordered translation of the letter, by a Jew of Nancy, generally matched Levy's account of its contents (it supported Levy's objections to the Louis Anne translations) but that even that second translation had the phrase as "the child *has been* found." Levy conceded the point. His admission seems to increase the likelihood that the Jewish community did indeed know that the child's corpse was in the woods before the swineherds found it. Afraid to tell the authorities for fear of their jumping to precisely the conclusions they did, the Jewish community may well have tried to encourage Gentiles to institute the search. But as for the issue of "binding" the child, Levy denied it to the end.

   Prosecutors also used Levy's poignant pleas to the leaders of the Jewish community against him. In one letter Levy begged for word of the progress of his case. As a defendant he was not allowed to know anything of the status of his trial.[43] Prosecutors in fact voiced suspicions over the fact that Levy had gleaned some information about the witnesses against him.[44] Levy also asked Jewish leaders for help proving his innocence, so that he could see his wife and children again, and if he were put to death, he asked that his betrothed daughter be properly married. He also asked to be given a Jewish burial "or I will never forgive you," he wrote to the Jewish leaders. This request piqued the prosecutors' interest. Why, they asked Levy, would he include such pleas for the treatment of his family after his death, and for his own burial, unless he believed that he would in fact be justly executed for the crime he had committed? Wasn't his request—like the prayers of Jews—an admission of guilt? Levy objected. By the time he had written that letter, he said, two prison officials had told him that he was going to die. Further, he had heard, or become aware in his own interrogations, of the number of false witnesses against him. Even two or three such lying witnesses, he said, "would suffice to send the most honest man in the city to his death." His instructions for after his death were intended as a precaution, he insisted, not a confession.

   Finally, the prosecutor returned to the issue of the translation of "bound" versus "found" and hedged his bets on which was more accurate.

"I must tell you that the word 'found' which you maintain appeared in the letter is no less damaging to you than the word 'bound' because if the child was in fact found at the time that that letter was written, it must have been by the Jews, who have since exposed the remains in the woods near Glatigny after having made him a martyr."

"I assure you that I and all other Jews have nothing but horror for such things, and there are prayers, as I told you earlier, to guard against such accusations."

In ultimately accepting the prosecutor's view of this issue, the judges of the Parlement seem never to have considered an obvious point here. Namely, if the Jews had found the child before the swineherds did, and if they specifically sent word to Levy that "the child has been found," then the notion that Levy had abducted the boy and delivered him to the Jews would be disproved. Why would the Jews have had to find the child, a month or more after his disappearance, if the Jews (through Levy) were the ones who had originally taken him in order to sacrifice him in some weird rite? And if the child had indeed been found by Jews in November, then the initial disappearance came about by accident and was not Levy's doing at all. The only way Levy's written phrase is truly incriminating is if the judges continued to believe that the word in question was "bound," or, if they believed Levy had taken the child to give to the Jews, the child had somehow gotten away and the Jews had then recovered him and murdered him. Obviously there was no evidence at all, even by rumor, to suggest this last. Without making the point too strenuously, the judges at some level simply wanted to convict Levy. Why? Quite possibly because religious pluralism and the resulting feuds had contributed to a general secularizing trend in Metz. This was so uncomfortable (if unconscious) a reality, that even the judges of the Parlement—agents in a way of that secularization—were relieved by a temporary return to traditional religious saws. This is difficult, if not impossible, to prove, of course, but it seems quite plausible given the rapidity of change in seventeenth-century Metz. We will return to this issue after finishing our examination of the events in the case.

Five days after his final full interrogation, on December 23, Levy was allowed to confront the witnesses against him. The procedure did not include a formal cross-examination, as in moderen-day courts. Rather, the witnesses came forward and Levy was allowed to say if he recognized them and if he had any outstanding quarrel with them. The earlier deposition of each witness was then read in turn, and he or she was allowed to add to the statement, amend it, or retract sections. And Levy was given the opportunity to respond. By and large, Levy did not know the witnesses, and he denied any knowledge of the events they described. He reiterated that he was innocent and that he had had no part in any kidnapping, and he repeatedly accused witnesses of fabricating tales and bearing false witness. In several cases, witnesses who had claimed to see a Jew on the day in question hesitated when confronted with Levy face to face, saying that on reflection they were not sure that he was the man they had seen.[45] When one witness reiterated that she could not really be sure of the day or time when she had seen a Jewish man, Levy pounced on her equivocation and asked the judges to recognize that the vagueness of her testimony proved its falsity. Would a true witness, he asked, be so unclear about the time of her observations? Would a true witness notice a man's black hair, but not his face, size, or the color of his horse? Thus confronted, the witness then said that, actually, the Jew she had seen was on foot and walking well behind his horse. She did not attempt to reconcile this with her earlier statement that the man was mounted and carrying a child before him, nor was she asked to do so.

Levy similarly questioned the testimony of those who alleged tales of long-past Jewish murder or blood rites. The testimony of Didier L'Egiptine, who had said that he heard from a Jewish convert years before that the Jews regularly killed virgins, had no bearing at all on his own case, Levy asserted. Besides, he added, "Jews never serve themselves with Christian blood, or any other human blood, or the blood of beasts. Even when the Jews want to eat meat, they soak it in water for an hour to draw off the blood. And beyond this they salt their meat for another hour so that the blood will be entirely drawn out. And after this they throw away the salt and the water in which the meat was soaked."[46]

Levy disputed the story of Clemence Paquin Closquin, that Jews had attacked her husband on Good Friday eight years before. Her testimony was a lie, he insisted, and sprang from malicious inventions against the Jews. If there had been any truth to her and her husband's claims, he said, the *lieutenant criminel* would have investigated at the time. As for Cuny Martin, the cobbler who had also testified about Closquin, Levy sharply questioned his objectivity. Martin, he explained, had once sold him some horses. But after the animals were delivered, the two quarreled about the terms, resulting in Martin threatening "to make him (Levy) pay for his actions some day." Martin admitted making the threat, but held that his testimony was accurate. After the authorities re-read Martin's deposition, Levy declared that "the man of whom this witness spoke in the deposition (Closquin) has been dead for a long time. If it were true that the said Closquin told the witness such things, the witness would have been bound by law to report them to a judge at that time. That he did not do so makes clear that this is a false report and a false testimony." Again, Levy denied that Jews engage in attacks on Christians. In defending himself, he thus repeatedly had to defend the Jewish community as a whole. Beyond the possible personal grudges against Levy, the case sprang from widespread hatred and distrust of Jews and the indictment of Levy carried with it a tacit indictment of the city's entire Jewish population.

On several occasions in late December and early January 1670, Levy or his lawyer, who then begins to appear in the records, identified only as Beausire, begged Parlement to release evidence in the case to Levy, to grant him access to the surgeons' report examining the child's remains, and to give Levy the opportunity to call his own witnesses. The discovery of the corpse in the woods, Levy's lawyer argued, "is a miraculous occurrence, which seems designed for no other purpose than to exonerate a poor accused man who has languished in jail for three months, under an assumed and false accusation." The charge against Levy, Beausire continued, dealt with a crime which "runs more thoroughly contrary to the accused's religion and belief than anything else in the world."[47] This request for information seems to have been taken into consideration by the court but generally rejected. Levy, in any case, never called his own witnesses.

On January 8, Levy's lawyer also requested that the Messin woman who had filed one of the three original charges against Levy, be recalled. The woman, now identified as Blaisette Thomas, the daughter of a butcher,[48] had told officials that she had seen Levy pass with a child on his horse, 36 hours after her lying in, the lawyer recounted. However, since Levy's conviction by the *bailli*, she had told several people that when she saw Levy she had not yet begun her labor. It could be proven, Beausire said, that she gave birth to her baby one day before "the child which was supposedly kidnapped, was mislaid." Thus, "the accused would have been seen entering the city with a child several days before the child in question was lost."[49] The lawyer strove in vain to show that hearing Levy's witnesses, and requestioning others, would show that the testimony against the Jew of Boulay was, at best, absurdly inconsistent and therefore highly dubious. He argued even more passionately later in January, as he presented Levy's defense against the Lemoines' concomitant civil charges and request for damages.[50]

In this only recorded instance of Levy's full defense, the lawyer accused the Lemoines, as well as the other witnesses against Raphael Levy, of "a blind passion," springing from "the zeal of their religion, and the hatred they bear for Jews." It was they, he said, not Levy, who were guilty of a crime, and he described in strong terms the events of the case. To explore the darker possibilities of the testimony against Levy—that is the motives or feelings influencing his accusers—we need not speculate randomly on the psychological makeup of these seventeenth-century townspeople and peasants. We need only, in fact, recount the explanation of Levy's lawyer, himself a member of the society, and his suggestions as to the emotions and desires of his fellow citizens.

On September 25, the lawyer said, Mme. Lemoine and her child were walking near the outskirts of Glatigny. "The child fell, and picked himself up. And the mother neglected to take him with her, and lost sight of him. By this occurrence, she became responsible and punishable for the loss of the child, who was in her care.[51] If she had been doing her duty she would have searched for him, and in so searching found him, and saved him from the fatal accident which befell him." If the mother had been properly zealous about looking for the child, he continued, she would have seen the cavalier who claimed to have seen a Jew on horseback with a child. "If this fable [the cavalier's story] had been true, she would have come to Metz, and in the anxiety and concern appropriate to a good mother, she would have asked the bourgeois and soldiers who guard the city gates if they had seen a Jew kidnap a child." Instead, Beausire said, "These accusers, the father and mother of the child, remained silent from the 25th of September until the 3rd of October, without complaining to the courts, praying all the while to find a means of concealing their negligence and pinning their crime on a miserable Jew, innocent of any such deed." He further pointed out that the mother had claimed she followed her child's tracks into the main road from Glatigny to Metz. But "this lie is proven untrue by the state of the ground which had been subject to such an extreme drought that it would have been impossible for a child to leave his tracks [in the dust]." These claims, the lawyer said, could not excuse the mother for her negligence. "She alone is responsible for the loss of her child, for abandoning him and letting him wander into the woods to become the quarry of wild animals, and for the misfortune which he fell to during the night, in the middle of the woods, without anyone to help him."

The parents, Levy's lawyer went on, "feeling themselves guilty and responsible before God and men for the loss of their child, strained for eight days to find a means of escaping punishment. They knew that the accused had been on the road to Glatigny that day. And they believed that they could do nothing better than to sacrifice him in order to expiate themselves." They trumped up the charge against Levy, the lawyer said, and put the cavalier, identified as Daniel Payer, up to testifying. However Payer, who had actually seen Levy on the road during the morning, denied when Levy was brought before him that this was the Jew he had seen with a child. The implication here was that Payer, while willing to claim he had seen an unnamed Jew with a child, was unwilling to send an individual Jewish man, whom he knew to be innocent, to his death.

Levy's innocence was further proved, the lawyer said, by the events that occurred after the *bailli*'s sentence against him. "The cadaver of this child was found in a state which only increases the crime and negligence of his father and mother—this cadaver, devoured and torn into shreds, serves as their trial. It is they, and no one else, who laid out their child's clothes [in the woods] in the manner in which they were found." (Remember that one of the swineherds had claimed the child's dress was so clean it seemed to have come "just out of the wash.") The parents, he continued, used "this artifice to free themselves from any legitimate hint of their crime, and to avert from themselves the black calumny of their unjust accusation." They altered the site where the child was found, he implied, "to oppress the accused, on whom they wanted, with a fiendish rage, to inflict the punishment for their own parricide."[52] To support this point the lawyer reminded officials that no one but the parents had confirmed that the clothes found in the woods were in fact the clothes the child had worn on the day he disappeared. "The father and mother alone are the parties—the criminals—who confirmed this, and they did so for no other reason than to support their own case and their own interests." Beausire questioned the actions of the swineherds and insinuated that they too may have played a part in a cover up. At the very least, they wanted to see Levy harmed. If they had not been so motivated, the lawyer said, they would not have moved the corpse; they would have gone straight to the authorities. Further, he accused officials of mismanaging the case. They should have asked the parents which clothes their child was wearing on September 25, and then, when the corpse was found, compared that description to the clothes found in the woods, not gone to the parents in late November with the clothes in hand and asked them to confirm that those clothes were the correct ones.

Levy and his lawyer (for presumably Levy made a marked contribution to his own defense—the Lemoines in their response certainly assumed the lawyer's conjectures originated with Levy) then sharply questioned the inconsistencies between the parents' original complaint to authorities and subsequent claims in the civil suit against Levy. In the second case, they argued, the parents altered their story on several key points in order to circumvent Levy's alibis. For example, in the original complaint, Beausire said, the mother claimed her son was abducted at about 1 P.M. In the civil complaint, the parents said the child was seized at about 3 P.M., after receiving an apple on the road from a carter of Waldreuange mentioned by Levy. "Thus the accusers concede that their child was not lost until three o'clock on the 25th of September," the lawyer said. "The accused offers to prove that at that same hour he joined a miller in the woods and that he met at about the same time, two bourgeois whom he has named, and that he arrived in Boulay at four o'clock. It would have been impossible to have taken this child at three o'clock near Glatigny, to have brought him to Metz, and to return by four to Boulay, where the accused was seen from that time on." The time change admitted by the parents also totally negated the testimony of the woman in childbirth, which the lawyer had already questioned. For that woman had said she saw Levy in Metz with a child at midday, between 10 A.M. and 1 P.M. The parents, the lawyer reiterated, had said the child was not even abducted until 3 P.M.

The lawyer challenged the court's translation of the purloined letters and used Marguerite Houster's testimony as proof that the word *found* had been maliciously mistranslated by the Jewish apostate to read *bound*. He further attempted to trace the origin of the information that had come to Levy through Houster—that the child had been found. Two of the swineherds, he said, had relayed the news to an oil merchant, a miller, and the court clerk of the town of Courcelles, while drinking in a tavern in nearby Les Estangs. From there it circulated around town and to Metz. If it eventually reached Levy (possibly through Jews who told the prison servant to tell him), it was in order to console him and give him hope, the lawyer said. Beausire explained Levy's instructions regarding his burial and family as entirely reasonable, not in any way incriminating. The fault, he argued, lay with the king's *procureur* for the *baillage* who, on the day the *bailli* rendered his judgment, inappropriately spoke to Levy. "And contrary to the moderation which an officer of his station should have displayed, he told [Levy] that if he appealed the sentence, he would lose, and that he would be burned alive or broken on the wheel."[53] This encounter, the lawyer added, horrified Levy "and put him in a state of such great vexation that, innocent though he was, knowing that men can make mistakes, he wrote this note. He requested to see his wife and children and spoke of settling his affairs in the manner of a man pondering death. Where is the man so steadfast that, upon hearing a *procureur* of the king tell him with authority and threats that he is going to die, he would not fall into despair and frenzy?" In effect, there was no firm evidence to convict Levy, the lawyer said in summation. The statements and testimonies made against him were merely malicious rumors. Raphael Levy, he added, "being absolutely innocent, is a criminal only in the mouths of the people." People, he concluded, "animated irrationally against him from the sole consideration that he is a Jew."[54]

Levy's defense infuriated the Lemoines, particularly the charge, which they called "ridiculous,"that they had somehow cooked the evidence. In a supplication to Parlement submitted shortly after Levy's presentation,[55] the parents spoke of Levy, and in fact of all Jews, in the harshest terms. Their statement contains several standard anti-Semitic aspersions, and reveals some interesting facets of such prejudice, at least as held by these Christians. Unlike Levy, who pointed his attack only at the parents and the other individuals who had testified against him, the Lemoines vented a polemic against Jews in general, while challenging Levy's claim. This is mentioned not so much to gain pity for Levy—presumably most observers have already found some sympathy for the beleaguered peddler—but rather to explore, however briefly, the nature of anti-Jewish thought in seventeenth-century Metz.

The Lemoines bristled at the charge that they had hidden their son's clothes in the woods next to his corpse, and they repeated that Levy had had the head and clothes carried there himself. They described Jews as people "who traffic in deicide" and who were invariably the enemies of Christians. They defended Mme. Lemoine's care of her child, saying she left him for less than a quarter hour. As for the rest of Levy's defense, their lawyer said, "the supplicants [the Lemoines] are not obligated to respond to the several claims falsely alleged and assumed by this Jew, who has no other thought than to save his synagogue." They thus refused to comment on any inconsistencies between their original complaint and their civil complaint.

Jewish ritual murder, they argued, did indeed take place, and Levy had no right "to insinuate that they [the Jews] neither massacre or sacrifice Christians, or that their law prohibits such acts. That claim is refuted by Abraham's sacrifice [of Isaac] . . . their synagogue is thus shown to always do such things." The accusations against Levy, they continued, could not be discounted, "by the Judaic allegations, drawn from the Talmud of infidels who have no other end in mind but to oppress Christians and to harbor hatred for them." They closed by insisting that they had no reason to concoct a case against Levy since "the poor supplicants have lost their only child and they would, if anything, be partially consoled if the death of this poor innocent had come about in some other way than by the hand of this new Herod, eager for the child's blood as a sacrifice to the inhumanity and barbarity of his synagogue."

As with other Christians in Metz (clerics and secular officials as well) the Lemoines, or their representative, tended here to collect all Jews into one enemy group. Individual Christians clearly had contact on a daily basis with individual Jews, but the inclination to generalize about them persisted. Indeed, the tradition of considering Jews collectively seems, like the entire case, to have served as a counterpoint to the reality of growing social contact between individual Jews and individual Christians. The reassertion of a corporate identity, for both groups in fact, resonates here as an almost desperate nostalgia for premodern forms and definitions. For example, Marguerite Houster seems to have shown the Levys some sympathy, and to have helped them to some extent. M. de la Rogadre seems to have tried to advise Levy on how best to proceed in his own defense. And business transactions clearly took place between individual Gentiles and Jews. But distrust of Jews as a group remained strong. Charpentier and Gassin, the two Messin women who claimed to have seen a Jew with a child, said they knew a Jew when they saw one (i.e., they recognized dark curly hair as a "Jewish" feature). However, their associations were entirely negative, as shown by the professions that the child they saw was far too beautiful to belong to a Jew. They also could not, or chose not to, recognize an individual Jewish man. Jews and Gentiles in Metz had daily contact, yes, but it often possessed seething adversarial elements, as with Jean Gondrecourt who appears to have particularly harbored a grudge against Jews in his community. When business dealings went sour, as they apparently did between Levy and Cuny Martin, traditional charges and anti-Semitic complaints usually surfaced. Christians seem to have wanted (with some urgency) to maintain the Jews of this area as one unified group. In the few instances in Levy's case where townspeople were forced to consider him as an individual (such as Payer and others' confrontation with him before the authorities) their hatred was at least partially mitigated and they vacillated in their claims against him.

Even more interesting, perhaps, are the persistent religious images at the center of the Messin bourgeois' anti-Jewish attitudes. Witness the Lemoines' final refutation of Levy's countercharges. As with the Closquin witnesses, allusions to the Passion abound and are far too numerous to be shrugged off as mere rhetoric. Even if such references were included by lawyers or clerics who may have advised the parents, the constant inclusion of powerful religious images clearly had a profound impact on Gentile attitudes throughout the society. Consider the almost incredible inclusion of the Abraham and Isaac story as "proof" of Jewish proclivities to human sacrifice. First of all, within that story, Abraham does not in the end sacrifice his son. God releases him from the test (which he himself had imposed on Abraham) at the last. Second, and more significant, the story of Abraham and Isaac is generally viewed as a parable about the necessary totality of devotion to God—that one must be willing even to relinquish that which is most precious in order to serve the Almighty. Abraham, if anything, is the hero of the piece—a man who showed total obedience to God. However, the Lemoines' statement suggests that these seventeenth-century Christians heard something entirely different in this Bible tale. Primed by stories of the Passion, and passively accepting of such local lore as the Closquin and L'Egiptine claims, did Gentiles see the story of the sacrifice of Isaac *primarily* as an illustration of Jewish child-murder? If so, how did they synthesize other information about Jews, such as Gideon Levy and his hod, or Messin Jews and their possible search of the woods? That Gentile thinking about Jews was in some measure warped by Christianity and its potent visceral symbols is not meant to excuse such prejudice but rather to attempt to understand its many shrouded components.[56]

It has been shown repeatedly here that the Gentiles who testified against

Levy, and the judges who ultimately sent him to his death, simply inserted Levy into an already well assembled structure of anti-Semitic ideas. They believed Jews killed children, and they believed Jews conspired to conceal such sacrifices. Testimony in the Levy case was designed only to provide a few details suggesting that these Jews, in this town, had been up to something strange. Given the deep-seated beliefs of the non-Jewish population, a suggestion was enough to convict. We may never fully know why townspeople believed the myths about Jews. At some level they believed them simply because earlier Christians had believed them. The chain, if wearing thin by the early modern period, remained unbroken. Or rather, Christians seem to have clung to the last fragments of that chain, (preserving them as their ancestors might have cherished a relic), as a source of security in anxious times. Of course some of the testimony, if not all, sprang from worldly concerns—a fight over a horse sale, competition between butchers, professional rivalry. A question we can consider, however, is why the Parlement, which had previously protected Jews (however anemically), now turned against the Jews of Metz and Levy in particular? Apparently the high court had undergone some sort of change which made it less rational, less deliberative, at least with regard to the city's Jewish residents.

The Parlement which met in Metz for the first time in 1633 comprised almost entirely non-Messin courtiers—Parisians, nobles from other areas of France, and various soldiers and bureaucrats whom the king wanted to reward. These original judges were not necessarily more enlightened or benevolent toward Jews than their descendants who had inherited their offices by 1670. But the first members of the Parlement of Metz clearly owed their allegiance entirely to the Crown. The court, as an institution, was a creature of royal government. And its individual members' fortunes depended, in part, on their loyalty to the sovereign. In 1670, the institution remained an agent of centralization, but it is reasonable to suppose that after nearly two generations in the area, the members may well have adopted and embraced local attitudes in a way their forebears had not. Still royal officials in name and deed, their zeal to defend the king's wishes, when they ran counter to that of the local populace, diminished.[57]

A careful review of local records, as mentioned in Chapter 3, indicates that anti-Semitism made Messin society in this century impotent, to some extent, against the onslaught of central control. Townspeople, hobbled by their own prejudices, failed to unite to assert their autonomy. Their local hatreds played into the king's hand. But the struggle was not entirely one-sided. The irony of this Parlement was that, while established to help speed the unification of all France under one central authority, it nonetheless showed itself—with regard to the Jews at least—increasingly susceptible to local currents and ideas as time passed. Again, we cannot say that the members of the 1670 Parlement of Metz were more anti-Semitic than the members of the 1633 court. There is no clear evidence to suggest this, but they did feel compelled, at some level, to revisit their anti-Semitism to a greater degree. After all, burning one Jew, when the local citizens and clergy cried for his blood, was hardly a blatant failure to protect the king's interests, was it?

Metz's Jewish community argued persuasively that it was. For the situation grew dramatically worse for the minority after Levy's January 17 execution. On February 5 Parlement entertained complaints that the Jews had exceeded their quota and had grown too numerous in the city, and in March the court condemned Mayeur Chuaube to pay 3,000 livres, presumably to Closquin's widow.[58] Calls for the Jews' expulsion, meanwhile, resumed, and the general atmosphere reached a state of frenzy, Jewish leaders wrote to the king in April. In that same supplication, members of the Jewish community explained to Louis XIV why they had not complained earlier, when Levy was still alive. At that time it had seemed an isolated event, and they had not intended "to take up the case of one foreign Jew . . . no matter how injurious to their community that condemnation [of Levy] might be."[59] But the events after the execution had proved too alarming for them to keep silent. Several Jewish men, they wrote, "have been imprisoned without being told the cause of their detention, and others have fled to escape similar treatment. So that in Metz today one need only be Jewish to be accused, and need only be accused to be condemned."[60] The Jewish leaders beseeched the king to extend to them, "the protection which his predecessors and he himself have never refused." They asked Louis to attest that their numbers in Metz were legal and to proclaim publicly "that these cruelties which they are accused of enacting against Christians are pure illusions, which have no basis other than the malice and envy of their enemies."[61]

The king was moved by their plea, or at least by his own interests. On April 18, 1670, he ordered Parlement to justify its decision against Levy and to release the other Jews still held in the affair. Later he exonerated the executed Levy of all guilt. But alas this did not end the Jews' troubles. We know of at least two immediate instances of copy-cat ritual murder accusations leveled against Jews in Metz. In a town that had no recorded accusations between 1633 and 1670, charges now appeared, like the aftershocks of an earthquake. On August 6 a villager complained to the lieutenant general of the *bailliage* that three or four Jews had kidnapped his 10-year-old son. On August 14 a group of Christian residents of Metz banded together to accuse the Jews of kidnapping a second child, subsequently found lost in a hayloft.[62] Neither of these accusations resulted in a full-blown trial, in part because the king had instructed all royal officials to inform him of any such charges afoot in the area and to arrest those involved in such "seditious" attacks on his Jewish subjects.[63] Still, it seems clear that the Jews' position in Metz remained precarious after the Levy affair. The central institution that should have protected them from the worst local hostility had become less anxious to do so, or marginally less accountable. Also, royal intervention could not always take place in time to save individuals. It would not be until the next century, and the violent events that produced a new, if not not intentionally, more tolerant France, that the Jews would achieve any lasting security. And in the broader sense, we might well ask ourselves if even the extension of the Rights of Man and Citizen to Jewish Frenchmen was enough to protect the descendants of Raphael Levy.

NOTES

1. Joshua Trachtenberg, *The Devil and the Jews* (New York: Harper and Row, 1966), p. 128.

2. Flavius Josephus, *The Works of Josephus*, Complete and Unabridged, trans. William Whiston. (Peabody, Mass.: Hendrickson, 1987), p. 799.

3. For more on the connection between Christianity and anti-Judaism and anti-Semitism, see William Nicholls, *Christian Antisemitism, A History of Hate* (Northvale, N.J.: Jason Aronson, 1993). The topic is also addressed in Gavin Langmuir, *History, Religion, and Antisemitism* (Berkeley: University of California Press, 1990), pp. 279ff.

With regard to ancient rumors of Jewish murder of non-Jews, Salo Baron has questioned whether the ritual murder accusation represented a seamless continuum from ancient misconceptions about Jews. See Salo Wittmayer Baron, *A Social and Religious History of the Jews*, Vol. 4 (New York: Columbia University Press, 1957), pp. 135ff. While his doubts remain valid, the repeated emergence of ideas of Jewish murder of non-Jews cannot be ignored within the very general survey presented here. Other historians have similarly seen the ancient ideas as ominous. See Cecil Roth, *History of the Jews in England*, 3d edition (Oxford: Clarendon Press, 1964), p. 9.

4. For example, the king of France, Phillip Augustus, evicted the Jews in 1182 on the pretext of their alleged abduction and murder of Christian children. See X. Malcolm Hay, *Europe and the Jews* (Boston: Beacon Press, 1950), p. 123.

5. Jacob R. Marcus, *The Jew in the Medieval World* (New York: Atheneum, 1983), p. 123.

6. Ibid., pp. 123–24.

7. Ibid., p. 125.

8. Ibid.

9. In 1168 in Gloucester, a boy named Harold was said to have been carried off by Jews in February, hidden until mid-March and then murdered. The main chronicler of that story described Harold's demise in the following way: "On that night [March 16], on the 6th day of the preceding feast, the Jews of all England coming together as if to circumcise a certain boy, pretend deceitfully that they are about to celebrate the feast appointed by law in such a case, and deceiving the citizens of Gloucester with that fraud, they tortured the lad placed before them with immense tortures. It is true no Christian was present, or saw or heard the deed, nor have we found anything was betrayed by any Jew," but the monks and citizens of Gloucester, he continued, simply assumed the Jews were responsible after finding Harold's body. "It was clear," the chronicler wrote, "that they [the Jews] had made him a glorious martyr to Christ, being slain without sin, and having bound his feet with his own girdle threw him into the river Severn. The body is taken to St. Peter's church, and there performs miracles." See Joseph Jacobs, *The Jews of Angevin England* (NewYork: Putnam, 1893), p. 46. Other celebrated accusations in England in this century resulted in the martyrdom of Robert in Edmonsbury in 1181, and of children in Bristol in 1183 and in Winchester in 1192, among others. See Jacobs, p. 75; Baron, p. 135; and Trachtenberg, p.128.

Another infamous accusation took place in England in 1255, and in fact "Little Saint Hugh of Lincoln" made his way not only into popular folklore and ballads in three languages, but also into literary tradition. Chaucer mentions Hugh by name in the

Canterbury Tales, and it was Hugh's story which served as the basis for the prioress's tale of a young Christian boy, slain by Jews, who despite a slashed throat continued after his death to sing a Latin prayer. See the Kent and Constance Hieatt edition of the *Canterbury Tales by Geoffrey Chaucer* (New York: Bantam, 1964), pp. 370ff. The story behind Hugh's martyrdom was that Jews from all over England allegedly gathered in Lincoln, stole the eight-year-old boy as a sacrifice, tried him in the style of Pontius Pilate's trial of Jesus, and then tortured him. See Hay, p.125. The real facts seem to be that a large number of English Jews met in Lincoln for the wedding of a prominent man's daughter, and during the celebration the body of a child was found floating in a cesspool. The local populace proclaimed the child a martyr. Meanwhile, a Jew named Copin, who had the misfortune to live next to the cesspool, was tortured until he "confessed" that he and his fellow Jews had killed the boy as part of a religious rite. The mob dragged Copin through the streets of Lincoln tied to a horse's tail. About 100 other Jews were arrested and taken to London for trial for their alleged part in the incident. Eighteen who asked for a mixed jury of both Jews and Gentiles were assumed, by their request, to be revealing their guilt and they were hanged immediately. All except three of the others were convicted and sentenced to prison. Only Richard of Cornwall, a businessman who managed the Jews of the kingdom and their profits for the Crown, succeeded in gaining the imprisoned Jews' release. See Roth's *History of the Jews in England,* pp. 56–57. The economic motive behind accusations of ritual murder is also discussed by James Parkes in *The Jew in the Medieval Community* (New York: Hermon Press, 1976). See particularly pp.124ff. Among other instances, Parkes cites an incident in Troyes in 1288 in which a ritual murder charge was trumped up against the richest Jew in the city in order to confiscate his moneylending records. Thirteen other Jews died at the stake in that episode.

For a recent compendium of ritual murder accusations, including many of the above examples (and an excellent bibliography on the subject), see Alan Dundes, ed., *The Blood Libel Legend; A Casebook in Anti-Semitic Folklore,* (Madison: University of Wisconsin Press, 1991). This work includes essays by Langmuir, Duker, and Roth, among others. For an excellent consideration of the case of another alledged martyr, Simon of Trent, see R. Po-chia Hsia's *Trent 1475: stories of a ritual murder trial* (New Haven: Yale University Press, 1992).

    10. Baron, p. 307.

    11. Robert Chazan, *Medieval Jewry in Northern France* (Baltimore, Md: Johns Hopkins University Press, 1973), p. 58.

    12. Among these are the notions that Jews used Christian blood to make matzoh, that they dried the blood and spread it on their neighbors' fields to induce plague, that they used it to remove a "Jewish stench," and various other wild tales of Jewish sorcery. See Trachtenberg, p. 144; and Parkes, p. 124.

    13. Cecil Roth, ed., *The Ritual Murder Libel and the Jew* (London: Woburn Press, 1935), p. 20.

    14. Hsia, it should be noted, concerns himself particularly with incidents which involve a clear allegation of ritual use of Christian blood, what I have here called "blood libels" and distinguished from charges that Jews murdered Christians for sacrificial purposes. In this way, Hsia would probably not consider the case of Raphael Levy a "ritual murder accusation" according to his criteria, because the charges that the Jews used the boy's blood for some ritual purpose is only implied, not explicitly stated. However I favor a somewhat broader definition of "ritual murder accusation," since it is

clear that charges against Jews, whether or not they supplied a reason why the Jews wanted Christian blood, revolved around the belief that Jewish worship in some way required such child murder. And while much of the charge against Levy was implied by witnesses, the implications are so clear that scholars have long considered this a true ritual murder accusation. See, for example, Bernard Blumenkrantz, dir. *Histoire des Juifs en France* (Toulouse: Commission Française des Archives Juives, 1972), as well as the anonymous *Abrégé du Proces Fait aux Juifs de Metz* (Paris: Frédéric Leonhard, 1670), the contemporary account of Levy's trial which began with a lengthy summary of earlier ritual murder charges. For our purposes at this point, the distinction between types of accusations is unimportant. It suffices to note that accusations of child murder leveled against Jews recurred from the medieval period on, and set down thick roots in Europe despite scattered appeals to reason. For Hsia's findings on such charges in Germany, see his *The Myth of Ritual Murder* (New Haven, Conn.: Yale University Press, 1988).

15. Roth, *Ritual Murder*, p. 31.

16. Trachtenberg, p. 125.

17. Ibid. For Voltaire's comments on ancient Jewish sacrifice of humans, see his *The Age of Louis XIV*, trans. J. H. Brumfitt (New York: Washington Square Press, 1963). It should be noted that Voltaire considered occasional human sacrifice as less heinous than the fomenting of civil war. See p.215. For more on Voltaire's anti-Semitism, see Jacob Katz, *From Prejudice to Destruction, Anti-Semitism, 1770–1933,* (Cambridge, Mass.: Harvard University Press, 1980).

18. Trachtenberg, p. 166.

19. In addition to the documents listed in Chapter 3, note 1, Levy's case is briefly described in Joseph Reinach, *Raphael Levy, Une Erreur Judiciaire sous Louis XIV* (Paris: Librarie Ch. Delagrave, 1898). See pp. 94–99 for the description of Levy's execution. Reinach includes a useful selection of reprinted documents. Note that this work may have been published in the aftermath of the Dreyfus affair, as a general defense of the Jews. Another brief treatment is Pierre-André Meyer's "Un cas d'accusation de meurtre rituel à Metz au XVIIe siècle," *Archives* Juives, vol. 25, no. 3–4 (1989), 62–64. The actual trial records of Levy's case, which will be used extensively here, are found in A.D.M., B. 2144, as noted. In addition, an abridged account of this trial appeared under the author's name. Sections of this chapter are there-fore reprinted from *Religion*, vol. 23, no. 1, Patricia E. Behre, "Raphael Levy: A Crim-inal in the Mouths of the People," 19–45, 1993, by permission of the publisher Aca-demic Press London.

20. The shofar is a horn, usually made from the curved horn of a ram, used in ceremonies for Rosh Hashanah, the Jewish New Year, and Yom Kippur, the Day of Atonement. Together these holidays encompass a 10-day period of spiritual self-examination and represent the holiest days of the Jewish year.

21. Exact title unknown.

22. This and all other transcripted testimony comes from A.D.M., B2144. In making the translations I have retained the original phrasing as closely as possible (resulting in a somewhat formal feel to the questions and responses) but transposed the statements from the third person ("The respondent was then asked what he . . . ") to the second and first person to enhance immediacy. Otherwise, the words are directly translated.

23. B. 2144, *pièce* no. 3.

24. Ibid., *pièce* no. 4.

25. Ibid., *pièce* no. 6.

26. Female witnesses, such as this one, were identified in the records by their birth names, without the surname of their husbands, hence the parentheses used here.

27. In the document, Martin claims the Jewish woman used the word *estrofer*, which signifies 'kill' in Hebrew." In fact, *estrofer* is suspiciously similar to *étouffer* the French word for suffocate, and bears little or no resemblance to the Hebrew words either for kill, strangle, or suffocate (*harag* or *hemit*, *chinek*, or *chanak*, respectively). Even assuming Martin was mistaken in his supposition that the woman spoke in Hebrew (Hebrew was not a language for daily use among Jews of this era), the German words for kill or suffocate are still dissimilar enough to suggest that either Martin or Closquin fabricated this detail. See A.D.M., B. 2144, *pièce* no. 5.

28 . Ibid.

29. Ibid. Again, a Jewish community had existed in Avignon dating from the fourteenth century, due largely to the special protection of the popes. See René Moulinas, *Les juifs du pape en France: Les communautes d'Avignon et du Comtat Venaissin aux 17e et 18e siècles* (Paris: Privat, 1981).

30. Ibid.

31. Certain cloth merchants and tailors, as mentioned, had longstanding feuds in Metz with Jews whom they saw as infringing on their trade. See Roger Clément, *La Condition des Juifs de Metz dans L'Ancien Régime* (Paris: Imprimerie Henri Jouve, 1903).

32. Modern-day Metz's *Jurue*, this street, once inhabited almost exclusively by Jews, lies near the rue de l'enfer—the street of Hell—undoubtedly given this derogatory title by local Christians. Jewish residence in Metz was restricted to one section of the city during the seventeenth century.

33. Abraham Spire was a prominent Jewish moneylender in Metz and an occasional spokesman for the community.

34. This is the actual word used in the document, and it referred to people known for roaming the countryside without fixed homes and later simply called gypsies. See A.D.M., B. 2144, *pièce* no. 5.

35. Ibid.

36. Charpentier's recollection that the child had worn a yellow dress casts some doubt on the swineherds' discovery of a white dress, on her story, or on both accounts.

37. Literally: *"Voila un bel enfant il ne ressemble point à un enfant de Juif."* A.D.M., B.2144, *pièce* no. 5.

38. A.D.M., B. 2144, *pièce* no. 5.

39. For G. Levy's explanation, see later in this chapter.

40. See Chapter 3.

41. A.D.M., B. 2144, *pièce* no. 7.

42. A.D.M., B. 2144, *pièce* no. 11.

43. According to French law, defendants were not allowed to know the details of the cases against them and suffered in general from a procedure that was more efficient than fair. See R. Doucet, *Les Institutions de la France au XVIe Siècle*, Vol. 2 (Paris: A. et J. Picard et Cie, 1948), pp. 534–541.

44. The fragments of information that Levy had gathered about his accusers (about the original cavalier, Daniel Payer, and about the woman, Blaisette Thomas, being in childbirth) were considered vaguely incriminating—a sign that he had had contact with other Jews who were providing him with knowledge of his case.

45. See the responses of Marguerite Gassin and Joute Charpentier in A.D.M., B. 2144, *pièce* no. 12.

46. Ibid.

47. A.D.M., B. 2144, *pièce* no. 14.

48. See Chapter 3.

49. A.D.M., B. 2144, *pièce* no. 20.

50. A.D.M., B. 2144, *pièce* no. 21.We do not know the precise outcome of this civil case.

51. The parents may have faced punishment themselves if it were proved that they had been neglectful or had purposely abandoned their child.

52. The term *parricide* here refers to the general act of killing someone one should revere or care for, in this case, a child, not the killing of one's father or mother as the term is sometimes used in modern speech.

53. There is every indication that Levy was, in fact, tortured, in an attempt to either have him "confess" or to convince him to convert to Catholicism before his death. A receipt for payment to prison surgeons for treatment of Levy after one of these torture sessions can be found in A.D.M., 17 J. See also Reinach, p. 97, in which one of these sessions is described.

54. A.D.M., B. 2144, *pièce* no. 21.

55. A.D.M., B. 2144, *pièce* no. 23.

56. For a brief, but intelligent discussion of the contributions of the Catholic Church to anti-Semitism in France, see Eugene Weber's "Reflections on the Jews in France," in Frances Malino and Bernard Wasserstein, eds., *The Jews in Modern France* (Hanover, N.H.: University Press of New England, 1985). See also Nicholls.

57. Emmanuel Michel, in his *Histoire du Parlement de Metz*, (Paris: J. Techner, 1845), tried largely to apologize for Parlement's conviction of Levy, claiming that given the witnesses' testimony, the court had little choice but to condemn the Jew of Boulay. I would contend, however, that given the nature of the testimony involved, Michel's conclusion is unsatisfying. The impetus to condemn Levy may have come from the local townspeople, their clergy, or both, but something also compelled the members of the high court to entertain the charges against Levy and to convict him, despite the fact that this decision did not reflect royal policy. A fascinating study of a similar conviction (though of a Protestant in the eighteenth century) appears in David D. Bien, *The Calas Affair, Persecution, Toleration, and Heresy in Eighteenth-Century Toulouse* (Princeton, N.J.: Princeton University Press, 1960).

58. A.D.M., 17 J, 4 (Lap 21), fol. 3 (recto).

59. Levy, who was born in a German village and lived in Boulay at the time of this incident, was apparently considered a "foreigner" by at least some members of the Jewish community in Metz. There is evidence that Boulay, in the seventeenth century was much more culturally linked to Germany than was Metz. See Jean Houdaille, "La Population de Boulay (Moselle) avant 1850." *Population*, vol. 22, no. 6 (November–December, 1967), 1068.

60. A.D.M., 17 J, 4 (Lap 21), fol. 3 (recto).

61. Ibid.

62. A.D.M., 17 J, 4 (Lap 22, Lap 23).

63. A.D.M., 17 J (Lap 26).

Chapter 6
Martin Meurisse:
A Catholic Cleric Names His Enemies

Catholic animosity toward both Protestants and Jews, it has been argued, helped to create a climate in Metz favorable to the Crown's centralizing reforms. The religious pluralism (however unwelcome) behind this animosity also bred new social alliances and was part and parcel of a new more secular orientation. Still, Catholics viewed these two minorities quite differently. In all echelons of Messin society, Catholics were far more likely to mix with Protestants than with Jews; they were far more likely to intermarry with Protestants, to do business with Protestants, and to encounter Protestants in their neighborhoods. They generally distrusted Protestants less, and some Messins, as we noted, even helped Protestants resist official oppression. For all these reasons, Protestants presented both a lesser problem and a greater one to Metz's Catholic clergy, and it is their attitude and its transmission to the larger Catholic population which we must now examine.

Admittedly, we are trying to prove by negative example (i.e., by showing the backlash against burgeoning secularization) that such secularization existed. Still, when taken together, the trial of Raphael Levy, and the urgent last-ditch anti-Protestant polemic that commands our attention in this chapter seem certainly to indicate a passionate response to the changing political, social, and religious climate in Metz and to some degree in Europe as a whole. Our examination of Catholic clerical attitudes toward Protestants also allows us to briefly compare the situation of the two minorities in Metz and to scrutinize the ideas that lay behind their respective treatment during the seventeenth century. We will concentrate on Catholic clerics' attitude toward Protestants, because it was the more explicitly expressed during this period leading to the revocation of the Edict of Nantes. But the clerical opinion of Jews, within this context, also emerges, revealing an important development. Namely, as Catholic leaders vilified Protestants in ever more strident terms as the century progressed, they helped to push the Jews to a new, even more marginal philosophical position.

For as Protestants were increasingly denounced as heretics, Jews became, to these Catholics, a species of superheretics—a people beyond the boundaries of mere devotional difference. If this idea remained hidden under the surface of daily activity, its implications are nonetheless disturbing enough to demand our acknowledgment. Let us proceed, then, to begin our examination of these issues, by first looking at just why Protestants were so troublesome to Metz's Catholic establishment.

As noted, Protestants presented a unique problem to most Catholic clerics. On the one hand, Protestants were fellow Christians, if ostensibly misguided ones. In Metz Protestant families had deep roots in the region; many descended from well-established Catholic ancestors who had converted during the upheavals of the 1500s. As we have shown, Protestants practiced many of the same professions as Catholics and shared power with them in the local government. As a result of these and other links between these two groups, Protestants could not be dismissed as "foreigners." They ate the same food as Catholics, wore roughly the same clothes, and observed many if not all of the same holidays. One should not ignore the significance of the obvious—both groups embraced Jesus as supernatural.

Of course it was this very closeness between Protestants and Catholics that also made the minority more threatening, especially in the eyes of the Catholic clergy. Because Protestants were Christians, they could not be persecuted and shut out in the same way that the Jews had been. Consequently they were freer to mix in all spheres with Catholics, at least during the first decades under the Edict of Nantes. This made them, in the short term, more dangerous than Jews. And as we pointed out in Chapter 4, there is every indication that the freer association between Catholics and Protestants resulted in a certain amount of sympathy, if not solidarity, among Catholic townspeople for their Protestant neighbors. This infuriated Catholic clerics and officials. The paramount fear of the Catholic leaders was that such casual contact would lead even further to the faithful converting to the *religion prétendue réformée*, and during the seventeenth century most of the complaints of local notables to the crown or to royal authorities fairly bristle with anxiety born of this possibility. Protestant schools should be eradicated or controlled; Protestants should not care for their sick in the presence of Catholics; and Protestant churches—if they must have churches—should remain on the outskirts of town, with access limited in such a way that Protestants would not process past Catholic sanctuaries on their way to worship. Such were the contentions of Metz's most influential clerics, as we have seen.

One might note briefly that while similar fears about contact between Catholics and Jews may have spawned the original medieval constraints on Jews (for example, that they wear distinctive hats or badges, not intermarry with Gentiles, and live and work separately), few in Metz at this time seemed concerned that contact with Jews would induce anyone to convert to Judaism. The civil penalties, not to mention the social stigma, were simply too great. Fear of the Jews was vaguer, probably more profound, but not in any case actively bound up by this time with the issue of conversion.

With regard to the Protestants, though, it was. The possibility of conversion underlay the Catholics' worst fears, and it also, particularly as the century wore on, became the source of the most intense Catholic hopes. For if contact between Catholics and Protestants could be controlled and manipulated appropriately, it might also lead to Protestants converting back to their forebears' version of Christianity. Here too we notice a difference in attitudes toward Protestants and Jews. Few in Metz may have feared Judaism attracting Christians, but the prospect of the city's Jews converting to Christianity, at least in notable numbers, seemed almost as remote. And our abjuration records support this sense among Christians. This accounts, in part, for a perceivable difference in the way the minorities were approached. In Metz, by and large, Christians were to be protected from Jews by always knowing when an individual was Jewish—by his work, his address, and his daily habits. It was even ordered that Jews keep the doors of their synagogue open during services so that nothing they did could be hidden from sight. Gideon Levy's great crime, one may recall, was having other Jews to his house late at night, when their actions could not be scrutinized.[1] Catholics were to be shielded from Protestants, at least in the first half of the century, by the opposite tactic—by those Protestants remaining as invisible as possible, their religious practices closeted away, their behavior as unremarkable to Catholics as possible. As the century wore on, this method of handling the Protestants changed to one more closely approximating that used with the Jews. This was largely the work of the Jesuits, the Capucins, and a variety of zealous Counter-Reformers who guided clerical opinion in Metz. Suspicion of Protestants among the Catholic clergy generally increased as the Counter-Reformation gained momentum, so much so that it is hard to know which impulse—distrust of Protestants, or the desire for Catholic renewal—fed which. Clearly both were linked. And as suspicion grew, the perceived need to keep Protestants under constant surveillance also grew. Still, for now we need only note that the hostility expressed toward Protestants and Jews in Metz rested on substantially different premises. Protestants were errant sheep; Jews were an entirely different species. Protestantism was an "infection" of the Christian body; Judaism was a wholly alien force. To banish a Protestant was to wrest a viper from one's own bosom; to attack a Jew was to confront an enemy who came from the outside.

It is just this philosophy that we see demonstrated over and over again in the writing of Catholic clerics in Metz. One of the most explicit works on the topic was *The History of the Birth, Progress, and Decline of Heresy in the City of Metz*, by Martin Meurisse, a Franciscan, the bishop of Madaure, and suffragant of the cathedral in Metz from 1629 to 1644. This volume, probably written in imitation of a 1605 Catholic history of the Reformation by the Bordelais magistrate Florimond de Raemond, was published in Metz in 1642—the same year in which the Jesuits took over the Protestant temple on the rue de la Chèvre.[2] Its promulgation confirmed Meurisse as one of the most ardent and outspoken of Metz's Counter-Reformers, but it also reflected many of the ideas and contradictions of its age. And in this it can be seen as roughly typical of general Messin clerical opinion—the same opinion which promoted the different treatment of Protestants and Jews already alluded to. Its style, language, and emphases also suggest a somewhat agitated effort to stem an unstemmable tide. Meurisse rails against the increasingly relaxed and even apathetic attitude of the Catholic laity toward Protestants—an attitude suggestive of secularization at work.

Meurisse was, on the one hand, solicitous of Protestants, claiming in this work only to pity them for being "isolated from the nourishing and salutary peace of the gospel."[3] He apologized to an assumed Protestant audience in the book's preface for any harsh terms he might use in the coming pages. "Please consider," he wrote, "that I am addressing [such terms] particularly to your errors, and to those [ideas] which have produced your schism and held the truth of God captive amid injustice, and not to your individual persons, which I esteem with all my heart."[4] And yet Meurisse also denounced Protestant leaders later with all the vigor, if not the comedy, of a Falstaffian curse, calling them "blasphemers, ingrates, mockers of God, incontinent slanderers, cruel and audacious traitors, puffed-up braggarts and blind men."[5] Similarly, the bishop depicted Jews as the ultimate debauchers and scoundrels (the group that he felt Protestants stood in jeopardy of approaching), while at the same time praising them as experts in biblical exegesis, sometimes revering their theology as superior even to that of the Protestants. These are not contradictions. They are actually consistent with Meurisse's (and other Catholic leaders') emerging view of these two minorities in the post-Reformation era. To generalize: Meurisse deplores Protestantism throughout his work, but despite this he makes a Herculean effort to sweetly court individual Protestants. His ideas regarding Jews are directly opposite: he either ignores Judaism or lauds it as an intellectual and spiritual antecedent to Christianity, but he absolutely rejects individual Jews.

Considered in toto, the whole work seems most explicable as a reaction against the incipient secularism furthered in part by closer contact, on the popular level, among Catholics, Protestants, and Jews. If the trial of Raphael Levy provided a comforting return to Manichean dualism for some in Metz, Meurisse's diatribe is a clerical salve of the same basic ingredients. A world of increasing religious confusion (because of pluralism and the relationships it made inevitable) required a return to basic Catholic verities: the untruth of Protestantism, the inhumanity of the Jews.

To understand attitudes like Meurisse's, we must first consider his mental outlook, if more briefly than Carlo Ginzburg entered the mental world of his Italian miller[6]. One must recognize immediately that this cleric's basic beliefs about Protestants and Jews did not spring from any precise analysis—critical or even emotional—of either minority. His views emerged instead from an overarching idea of how the world was, or should remain, ordered. Specifically, Meurisse reasserted a traditional fear and distrust of diversity of any kind, combined with an idealization of unity and an acceptance of the myth of a unified

Catholic past. From this conviction, Catholic leaders like Meurisse developed a militaristic insistence that unanimity in religion should be preserved, or reimposed, at any cost. Anything that smacked of pluralism sent Meurisse into a panic. Anything that seemed to maintain society's oneness inspired his admiration.

In his worship of unanimity, Meurisse was in step with many of his contemporaries. Even outside Messin Catholic circles, this attitude was common. Ironically, one might explore the idea particularly fruitfully in some of the newer Protestant communities of the age, for example in Geneva or the New World.[7] Yet because this concept—that diversity was always dangerous and unanimity always good—was so central to Meurisse's attitude toward religious minorities, and so central to the philosophy of the Counter-Reformation in Metz, we should explore it in some depth. This attitude is what allowed the city's most devoted Catholic enthusiasts to accept Protestant individuals as they rejected Protestantism and to excoriate Jewish people even as some admired certain elements of Judaism.

According to Meurisse, the very existence of Protestantism boded ill, and the schism of Christianity into two camps brought discernible evils into a previously peaceful world. He blamed the emergence of Protestantism for, among other things, the concubinage of priests in Metz; the falling off of confession; usury; debauchery in general; jealousy among Catholics; ambition; lying; and flattery. "Good God!" he asked rhetorically, "What reform! What religion! What gospel!" Even the plague that ravaged Metz in the mid-sixteenth century, Meurisse explained, was sent by God to punish the city for its growing acceptance of Protestantism.[8]

By and large, Meurisse held the leaders of Protestantism in Metz responsible for all these evils, not the individuals who had followed them. Luther and Calvin were described as a wolf and a fox, respectively, or as similar wild beasts[9] and he deemed Messin ministers "the true ministers of Satan and henchmen of the anti-Christ. For the Lord," Meurisse explained, "breathed only sweetness, humanity, good will and humility, while these ministers, in a violent and seditious tone, and with arrogant countenance, preach nothing but iron, fire and flames. The Lord," he wrote, "sent the apostles to be sheep among the wolves. While these [ministers], without any mission or charge, come on their own commission, like tigers, lions, and leopards to make quarry and prey of the poor innocent lambs of our sacred and sovereign Lord's flock."[10]

Being innocent, in the Catholic mind, individual Protestants were ever welcome to rejoin the Catholic Church—a point stressed not only by Meurisse but also by other Messin clerics of this period. Consider the urging of Jacques Benigne Bossuet to Protestants in Metz to quit "the path of darkness" and return to the Catholic Church.[11] Like Meurisse, Bossuet also emphasized his love for Protestants, despite their waywardness. "Certainly I can say of them, with sincerity, that which the Apostle said to the Jews—that my most heartfelt desire, and the most ardent prayer I make to God daily, is for their health. It is only with extreme sadness that I can see the very viscera of the most Holy Church torn to pieces."[12] Bossuet lived in Metz and served as *grand doyen du chapitre* there from 1652 until 1659. Not yet known as one of absolutism's main defenders, he gained a reputation in Metz for conciliation toward the Protestants, at the same time that he held firmly to the hope of converting them. Like Meurisse and others, Bossuet maintained that a policy of mildness wedded to firm action was necessary in dealing with Protestants. He pursued the latter tenet of this policy himself by promoting the sometimes questionable efforts of the Maison de la Propagation de la Foi and urging girls living there to resist any temptation to return to the homes of their Protestant parents.[13] Bossuet himself, we might add, echoed the call to unity issued by clerics such as François de Sales and Vincent de Paul. Meurisse convinced the latter of these two men to dispense alms in Metz.[14]

Protestantism, then, was unholy to all these clerics because they claimed, however inaccurately, that it alone had brought division into the Christian Church. Meurisse went even further and railed against the potential of Protestantism to divide society continuously into ever smaller factions. He pointedly recounted, in his *Histoire*, a sixteenth-century complaint that even among themselves "these *prétendues réformées* do not agree on the same belief. They are divided into Lutherans, Anabaptists, Calvinists and even atheists, and it would be necessary to establish each group in its turn."[15] In other words, once the fabric of unity was torn, nothing would stop each group from splintering into other groups; and if the first new sect were allowed to have a separate church, others would soon apply for the privilege. In this point Meurisse showed remarkable lucidity. Schism did indeed breed further pluralism in Europe as well as in the New World. But in France, at least during this period, diversity had not put down deep enough roots to resist containment when the time came. If de facto pluralism in the American colonies would demand the grudging acceptance of freedom of religion, in Europe the ability of clerics like Meurisse to trumpet their calls for uniformity—and the existence of a central absolutist monarch whose interests dictated a relative conformity—arrested any full-fledged religious pluralism for at least another century. In Metz, however, pluralism was somewhat harder to deracinate.

Among the troubling melange of Protestants whom Meurisse saw entering the city in the sixteenth century were former monks and nuns ("the excrement of ecclesiastic or religious houses"), large numbers of refugees, presumably from the religious wars, and various foreigners and "unknown persons" whose allegiance he questioned.[16] He continually associated Protestants with Germany or Geneva, and he impugned their political motives as anarchistic. In some instances his criticism was explicit. Ever since the Protestants arrived, he wrote in one section, the only threat to Metz remaining French came "from their cabals, their factions, and their communication with the princes of Germany, which I have seen myself."[17] Here, as in our earlier examples, the attack on Protestants was increasingly couched in chauvinistic terms of sycophancy, which, intentionally or not, promoted the preeminence of the French monarch.

In other instances, Meurisse sniped at Protestants and questioned their loyalty in roundabout ways. For example, in reprinting (for historical reasons, his book being ostensibly a history) an early seventeenth-century petition of Protestants to the local magistrates, Meurisse added his own critique of their views in the margins. The petition began with a title devised by the Protestants: "Remonstrance of the bourgeois of this city who follow the word of God." Here Meurisse added in the margin, "the depraved word of God." Later in the petition, when the Protestant authors complained of being deprived of rights that they had enjoyed when Metz was controlled by the empire, Meurisse added the label: "Affection of the Huguenots for the empire." Virtually every Protestant document that Meurisse includes in his work is cluttered with such annotations, and his attempt to damn the Protestants as anti-French shows just how far local leaders had acquiesced to French dominion in their land.

Beyond seeing Protestants as secretly loyal to Germany,[18] Meurisse also saw them as fomenters of discord and anarchy in general. In their preaching in Metz, he claimed, Protestants spoke against monarchy, and had thus committed *lèse-majesté*.[19] "To speak truly," he wrote, "it is in the spirit of this party of revolutionaries . . . to be unable to suffer the Monarchy, to reduce every sort of government into a republic, and to aspire to a civil libertinage under the pretext of evangelical liberty."[20] The Protestant consistory in Metz, he complained, "is like a miniature cell of anarchy and a gathering holding neither title nor character, which assembles whenever it pleases, without authorization and without the approval of the [royal] governors."[21] Meurisse argued that the German peasants involved in uprisings there in the sixteenth century had taken up arms with the design of invading France,[22] and that Protestants would always refuse to obey kings of any but their own religion. He also directly accused them of attempting to dethrone any king they were powerful enough to oust. "Witness the felony which your party is committing today in England," he wrote.[23] Meurisse, we see, was thus willing to fawn on the Bourbons, and to over-emphasize the rectitude of monarchy as a system, and of loyalty to France as an ideology. He was so willing because he believed he could paint the Protestants of Metz as chief among the disloyal and thereby gain their expulsion.

The criticism of Protestants as anarchists went hand in hand with a belief in an idealized Catholic past in Metz and, even more important, defensiveness about the Messin Catholic present.[24] Meurisse, for one, repeatedly chastised Protestants for their pride and for presuming to be more devout than Catholics. But his scoldings imply a certain insecurity about Catholic orthodoxy and a need to proclaim Catholics as more devout than they, in fact, may have been. In one section of his *Histoire* Meurisse praised at length the beliefs and practices of the ancient Catholic church, including clerical celibacy, the veneration of saints, and transubstantiation. He particularly praised the Catholic Eucharist ceremony (at rather greater length than would have seemed necessary for one truly confident that this interpretation of the rite was preeminent) and he contrasted it sharply with the Protestant view of the ritual which, he claimed, was open to "eighty-three or four interpretations of subtlety."[25] Meurisse clearly smarted under the Protestant claim of a closer adherence to the Bible. If they wanted to take the word of God literally, he said of the Protestants, they should not celebrate the sabbath on Sunday. "In order not to lie [about following God's word literally], and in order to hold absolutely to their avowed principles," he wrote, "it would be better for them to keep Sabbath with the Jews, than to observe Sunday with the Catholics."[26]

Note here Meurisse's association of Protestants with Jews and his cutting, derogatory tone. In another passage he went even further. For despite their preaching, Meurisse wrote defensively, Protestants do not keep to "the true word of God" in their daily manner of living. He exhorted Protestants to "Make your speeches about the Bible, the scripture, the pure word of God, and your glorious reform to those who do not know you and who have no dealings with you. For even the Jews—with whom you associate so much—considering the difference between your customs and those of Catholics, judge well who are the ones who live closest to the Bible, and know well that if you read the Bible, you practice the Koran."[27] In this one passage Meurisse again pairs Protestants with Jews, in order to defame the Protestants, even as he gives the Jews some credit for knowledge of the Bible. Also, note his trotting out of the Koran, of all things, as a blueprint for depravity.

This brings us to a more specific discussion of Meurisse's attitude toward Jews in Metz, as expressed in his *Histoire*. For while the book primarily considers Protestantism in the city, ideas about Jews also come through clearly, either in explicit references to the smaller minority, or implied in statements referring to Protestants, such as the above example. To recall our earlier generalization, Meurisse utterly rejected Jews as individuals even as he acknowledged Judaism's importance for Christianity and Judaic scholarship as admirable. Meurisse and his Catholic colleagues clearly felt less threatened in the short term by Judaism (at least at this point in Metz's history) than they did by Protestantism. Their attitude, of course, had a basis in their theology. For whatever the Jews' sins might be, they at least were part of biblical tradition. The Jews appeared, after all, in the Bible, and as such they were part of the Catholic heritage. Protestants had no such claim to legitimacy. Their religion was, from the point of view of Scripture, an aberration. And the early seventeenth century, we should note, was a time when Catholic tradition was being increasingly explored and stressed, not only by Meurisse in Metz, but also by a range of outspoken clerical leaders. This fervent reassertion of Catholic tradition was even carried to an extreme, it might be said, by the Jansenists and their immediate precursors. Though Metz did not truly become a center of Jansenism in the seventeenth century, there are many indications that this one aspect of Jansenism—the insistence on the importance of Catholic tradition—was tremendously attractive there, particularly among the Messin clergy.[28]

Overall, this Catholic zeal was certainly a Counter-Reformation response to Protestantism, but it may also be seen as a reaction against an even more formidable foe—secularization (a foe that ironically enough operated in tacit alliance with the Catholic kings of France). That this alliance was unacknowledged, or even unknown to either the clerical establishment or the king himself, made it no less potent or successful.

The impression that Messin Catholic leaders were more concerned in our period with Protestants than with Jews is further reinforced by their complaints (recounted in detail by Meurisse) about Protestant schools and Protestant churches in the city. The very existence of the physical structures of Protestantism unnerved Catholic clerics (recall the intense controversy over Protestant buildings recorded in Chapter 4) in ways that Jewish buildings, admittedly fewer and more isolated, did not. By the seventeenth century, we might say, the physical presence of the synagogue, while not welcome, did not seem as immediately threatening to Catholic religious leaders as did the presence of Protestant schools and houses of worship. Jewish schools and the synagogue, after all, could not be seen really as houses of conversion. In addition, of course, the Jews were much fewer in number than Protestants in Metz.

The Protestants themselves, in connection with the issue of schools, alluded to this disparity. In one of the few examples from this period they compared themselves with the Jews. Of course they did so only insofar as they wished to make the point that even the Jews were being treated better than they. Meurisse's largely successful attempt to contain Protestant teaching in 1634, they wrote, had resulted in the supreme outrage, "that in the city of Metz the Jews can freely instruct their children in religion and foreign languages, taught by teachers whom they choose from among themselves, while the supplicants [the Protestants] have become frustrated by prohibitions."[29] Meurisse responded to this Protestant complaint by explaining that the Jews were not teaching their children humane letters or the liberal arts, but only their own religious observances and literacy in Hebrew scripture, and that there was no one in the city, besides other Jews, who could impart this knowledge. (Note that despite himself, Meurisse is unconsciously bowing to secular pluralism to some degree here.) Protestants on the other hand, he argued, had innumerable Catholic schools at their disposal which could teach their children to read and write in Latin, among other skills.[30]

This is not, of course, to say that Jews had an overall easier time of it in Metz than Protestants did, or to suggest that Meurisse and other Catholic clerics in any way approved of Jews. Many of the negative references he made to 'heretics" in Metz included the Jews, even if every reference to Jews did not embrace all non-Catholics. In those instances where Catholic references to "heretics" in Metz meant Protestants only, not Jews, the Jews' position became if anything, philosophically more precarious. We have hinted that this precarious position was bound up with a more "racial" characterization of Jews—that they were coming to be seen in Metz as heretics beyond redemption, because they were seen as a different breed of men. Of course anti-Semitic depictions of Jews as inhuman predate Meurisse and occurred in places well beyond Messin clerical circles. One could not argue that a nonreligious definition of Jews originated in Metz or that it was limited to Catholics. We have intentionally ignored, for example, the existence of such an idea in Protestant societies. Nonetheless, despite occasional lip service paid to the merits of Jewish theology, one does see in Metz a component of the notorious notion that Jews did not merely practice an alternative or even heretical religion but that they were a separate and lesser people.[31]

One small way Meurisse furthered this idea was by continuously stressing the ancestral links between Catholics and Protestants, emphasizing the blood ties that bound them together, and excluded the Jews. Pleading with Protestants to return to the Church, Meurisse wrote, "We are still preserving your places in our temples. And the epitaphs of your ancestors invite you to come and engrave your names under theirs, so that just as flesh and blood unite you, belief will no longer keep you apart."[32]

Thus the rejection of Protestants in Counter-Reformation Metz was not total, nor did it in any way cause a true embracing of Jews. At most, the heat may have been off the Jews for a short span, at least on the official level, while the immediate threat of Protestant influence occupied the clergy and Crown.

Meurisse, for his part, did not neglect to mention the Jews directly in his *Histoire*. In addition to the references already cited, he dutifully recorded the complaints of the clergy against the smaller minority which, "multiplies excessively with each passing day and practices a usury which ruins the people and corrupts the hearts of Christians who let themselves be carried away by the example of these marranos, so that they ruin each other and smother in their souls all the charity which is so particularly recommended in the Gospel."[33] While Meurisse may have used Jewish theology as a cudgel against Protestant theology, he did not shy from recounting earlier clerical descriptions of the Jews as "marranos, *gens incognu*, without law or religion, blasphemers of God and of his son our Lord."[34] These same clerics complained of the "fantastical religion" these Jews practiced and of their "usury" which Christians were too quick to copy. They urged the royal governor to evict the Jews, along with "Bohemians" and "Egyptians."[35]

Still, despite such anti-Jewish statements, the overall views expressed so vividly by Meurisse—a fear of Protestants as natural schismatics and anarchists, resentment of their claims of greater piety, defensiveness about the devotion of Catholics—led to harsher immediate treatment of the Protestants in Metz. They were the more proximate foe; they were the greater danger. Reflecting this attitude, we have said, the Counter-Reformation gained a harder philosophical edge in Metz after the midpoint of our period, and Catholic reformers became more aggressive. This occurred even when the royal policy against Protestants in Metz was still ambiguous. For before 1668 Catholic clerics' efforts had been concentrated within their own segment of Christianity—increasing pastoral visits to the region's many parishes, reemphasizing preaching, and reforming religious houses. Even Meurisse, who clearly thought and wrote about Protestants in a combative way, was best known for his reform of Catholic worship and the conversions he effected through renewing Catholic discipline, tradition, and commitment.[36] It was only after the installation of Georges d'Aubusson de la Feuillade as bishop of Metz in 1668 that we see the most coercive measures against Protestants urged and enacted. Along with the Jesuits and Capucins,

Feuillade promoted a far more intrusive posture by Catholics in order to win, by any means, the conversion of the Protestants.[37] It is in this later period that we begin to see tactics used with the Protestants that formerly had been used only with Jews—essentially, a more total scrutiny of all their actions. While it is somewhat artificial to assign a clear date to this transformation—the Jesuits, for example, had been closely monitoring Protestant activity for years by 1668—it is fair to say that after 1668 Feuillade actively promoted a more thoroughgoing suspicion of Protestants among Catholics. As noted, this pushed the Jews into an even more distant niche. This conclusion is the most important point for our study, and we therefore leave the complete review of the Counter-Reformation in Metz to those scholars who have already considered that issue in depth.[38]

Was there a deeper hidden source for suspicion of Protestants in Metz? Or for the suspicions of Jews for that matter? Negative ideas about both minorities have been repeatedly discussed in this chapter and earlier ones, but still we must ask what it was that transformed the ideas of Meurisse and others like him into actual calls for action and into calls that, as we have seen, sent Messin notables invariably to the Crown. Why did Catholic clerics in Metz step up their efforts against Protestants even before the king did? Why did a ritual murder accusation occur in Metz at this time, so many years after ritual murder charges had begun to ebb elsewhere in Europe? It is time now to review our findings and to attempt at least a hypothesis on these last far-reaching questions.

NOTES

1. See Chapter 4.
2. This reference, and all subsequent references to Meurisse's work are found in A.D.M., 21598, *L'Histoire de la Naissance, du progrès et de la décadence de l'hérésie dans la ville de Metz et dans le pays Messin*, by *le R.P. Meurisse Docteur et naguière [sic.] Professeur en Théologie à Paris, Evêsque de Madaure et Suffragan de l'Evêsché de Metz* (Metz: Jean Antoine, 1642; original spellings and capitalization retained in citation). Reference to Florimond de Raemond's work can be found in Bernard Dompnier, *Le venin de l'hérésie* (Paris: Centurion, 1985), pp. 34–37.
3. A.D.M., 21598, 1st page of unpaginated introductory epistle.
4. Ibid., 2d page of epistle.
5. Ibid., p. 385.
6. Carlo Ginzburg, *The Cheese and the Worms: The cosmos of a Sixteenth-Century Miller*, trans. John and Anne Tedeschi (from *Formaggio e i vermi*) (Baltimore, Md.: Johns Hopkins University Press,1980).
7. There are innumerable studies of American Puritanism which address the issue of tolerance, or a lack of tolerance, among the early colonists there. See particularly Sidney E. Mead, *The Lively Experiment* (New York: Harper and Row, 1963); the essay by Perry Miller, "The Location of American Religious Freedom" in P. Miller, ed. *Religion and Freedom of Thought* (Garden City, N.Y.: Doubleday, 1954); and Anson Phelps Stokes, *Church and State in the United States* (New York: Harper, 1950).
8. A.D.M., 21598, p. 42.
9. Ibid., p. 128.
10. Ibid., p. 385.

11. François Gaquère, *Le Dialogue Irenique Bossuet-Paul Ferry à Metz* (Paris: Beauchesne, 1967).

12. Ibid.

13. To girls living in the Maison de la Propagation de la Foi in 1654, Bossuet said: "Persevere, my dear sisters; listen to neither the tears nor the reproaches of your parents; God will give you the grace to test how much sweeter is his holy House than any paternal house." See Ibid., p. 23.

14. Henri Tribout de Morembert, *Le Diocèse de Metz*, (Paris: Letouzey et Ané, 1970), p. 116.

15. A.D.M., 21598, p. 400.

16. Ibid., p. 225.

17. Ibid., p. 98.

18. This argument was not unlike those leveled against the Jews throughout Europe well into the eighteenth century—that they represented and would always represent a nation within a nation. This idea was particularly prominent in the debate over Jewish emancipation in France at the end of the eighteenth century.

19. A.D.M., 21598, p. 53.

20. Ibid., p. 54.

21. Ibid., p. 506.

22. Ibid., p. 25.

23. Ibid., 4th page of epistle.

24. According to Meurisse, Metz had remained impervious to heresy of any kind from 47 C.E. until the Protestants' arrival in 1528. "During this period of fifteen hundred years," he wrote, "one spoke of nothing in Metz except the building of churches, the founding of monasteries, and the endowing of hospitals." The people of Metz, as a result, lived "in a grand harmony and profound union." See pp.1–2. However once the "contagion" of Protestantism entered the city, he claimed, this long tranquil phase of Metz's history ended. The city, he wrote, "like a young virgin, or like a rich and marriageable maiden, was then ardently sought after and solicited. Two importunate cads, Lorraine and the Heretic [Protestantism] made love to her . . . both wanting to take her away from France—Lorraine in order to join her to his duchy and make her the capital of his estates, and the heretic to make of her a republic." See pp. 464–65. In this way Meurisse displayed his belief that Protestants were natural republicans or radicals; he gave his view of an idealized Catholic past in Metz, and he emphasized the links between Catholic Metz and the French kings.

25. A.D.M., 21598, pp. 199–200.

26. Ibid., p. 202. See also William Nicholls's discussion of Christian insecurity in *Christian Anti-Semitism, A History of Hate* (Northvale, N.J.: Jason Aronson, 1993).

27. Ibid., p. 203. As a cleric of some learning, Meurisse might have known something of Islam and the Koran, though in this passage he displayed little more than a knowledge that it was a crucial scripture for an even more exotic religion than Protestantism or Judaism, and one which he considered heretical.

28. Morembert, in *Le Diocèse de Metz*, discusses Meurisse's admiration for the Jansenists' moral rigor and their return to tradition, as well as other clerics' interest in such ideas in Metz. See pp. 117ff. See also R. Taveneaux, *Le jansenisme en Lorraine, 1640–1789* (Paris: Librarie Philosophique J. Vrin, 1960).

29. A.D.M., 21598, p. 535.

30. Ibid., p. 536.

31. Of course the virulent anti-Jewish writings of Luther come immediately to mind. For a brief reprinted translation see Jacob R. Marcus, *The Jew in the Medieval World: A*

Source Book (New York: Atheneum, 1983), pp. 165–69. Also, see Heiko Oberman, The *Roots of Anti-Semitism in the Age of Renaissance and Reformation* (Philadelphia: Fortress Press, 1984).

32. See the end of the introductory epistle.

33. Note that Meurisse uses the word *marranos (maranes)* here, a term usually meant to refer to Jews of Portuguese or Spanish descent in the south of France or in Spain, Portugal, or the Netherlands. Meurisse uses the word here as a derogatory term.

34. A.D.M., 21598, p. 425.

35. As in the example from the Raphael Levy trial (see Chapter 5, note 34), "Egyptian" here is probably used as an all-purpose term for wanderers or, as in modern usage, "gypsies."

36. For more on Meurisse and his reforms see Morembert, *Le Diocèse de Metz* pp. 116ff., and François-Yves Le Moigne and Gérald Michaux, eds., *Protestants Messins et Mosellans XVIe – XXe siècles* (Metz: Editions Serpenoise, 1988), pp. 49ff. For a fuller treatment, see J. B. Kaiser, "Martin Meurisse O.F.M., évêque de Madaure, suffragant de Metz (1584–1644)," *Annuaire de la Société d'Histoire et d'Archéologie de la Lorraine*, vol. 32, no. 1 (1923), pp. 1–119.

37. For more on Feuillade, particularly his opposition to hermetism and his centralizing reforms within the Church, see R. Taveneaux, *Le Catholicisme dans La France Classique, 1610–1715* (Paris: Société d'Edition d'Enseignement Superieur, 1980), pp. 93ff.

38. See works mentioned in earlier notes, especially Le Moigne and Michaux, and Morembert.

Conclusion:
Of Victims and Perpetrators;
A Community Sculpts Its Future

Politics is the art of manipulating hatreds, or so a modern adage goes. But is this purely a modern idea, and does it require a modern democratic state as its laboratory? Our attempt throughout has been to show that even in an absolutist state of the seventeenth century, the relations among members of a given society determined the rate and nature of political change. Even in a state that hardly revered public opinion, social realities profoundly affected governmental change, and even in a centralizing monarchy, royal plans required local acceptance. In short, there were hatreds to be manipulated, and manipulated they were. In Metz friction between Catholics and Protestants and between Christians and Jews helped the Crown to enact its centralizing reforms. This friction did not entirely guarantee the imposition of centrally designed institutions or the triumph of a concept of centralized authority. But it did help both to entrench royal institutions significantly and to develop a language that justified royal absolutism. This absolutism, we have argued, was part of a broader and deeper trend that included new social realities and a general, if still somewhat latent, secularization. Thus a fractious cohabitation, and the feuds that naturally emerged from it, produced a new political landscape, new social relations, and a new intellectual climate that would color all subsequent political and social developments. Let us review, briefly, how this occurred.

Catholics in Metz, themselves not a homogeneous or wholly unified group, saw in the Parlement, and to a lesser extent the *bailliage*, a new opportunity to constrain or eject the religious minorities whom, they felt, complicated their commercial and religious lives. Merchants and tradesmen especially wanted to remove Jewish competition. Educated Catholic clerics and lay leaders wanted to restore a mythical Catholic unity and uniformity by ridding the town of Protestants. Even local magistrates and bureaucrats approved of plans that would increase Catholic dominance and control. Despite their fears of royal oppression and loss of their autonomy, they welcomed royal help with regard to controlling minorities. They did not see that courting the king's assistance in one sphere would ensure royal interference in all spheres.

Of course the minorities themselves were, if anything, even more accepting of royal authority, which they rightly saw as their only hope for even minimal survival. The Jews, we might note, probably because of their vulnerability to exploitation (they could be and were made to pay extraordinary fees to the royal fisc), had greater short-term success in gaining royal protection. Protestants also had virtually nowhere else to turn for help than to the inheritors of the crown of Henri IV. Hence Messins of every rank went to the royal courts, petitioned royal agents, and sent flattering delegations to the kings themselves, vowing loyalty and asking for royal intervention. They did so particularly in small daily matters of self-interest, which individually seemed trivial but which also collectively furthered a new balance of power in Metz, with the Crown's heavy hand on the scale. The desire to defend one's office space, the need to knock down a Protestant minister's homemade garden trellises, the opportunity to harass a Jew—all seemed to make an appeal to the royal courts worthwhile.

The seventeenth-century success of French absolutism, the incremental but ongoing reconfiguration of local society, and the even more subtle process of secularization, were all foreshadowed in Metz, we have seen, by events in the sixteenth century. For even the first entrance of French troops in 1552 owed much to internal Messin conflict, born of religious strain. In the later period, which has been our primary focus, that strain continued but became even more tangled and complex.

We learned that Catholics had daily contact with both Jews and Protestants in Metz and that they sometimes helped individuals of both groups, when it served their interests to do so. Thus a cloth maker might sign a pledge that the Jewish merchants had helped his business, or a government functionary might take a Protestant detainee out for a drink in a tavern. Local magistrates might advance the interests of Jewish butchers temporarily, in order to punish price-gouging Gentile competitors. A Catholic cleric might advocate mildness and conciliation in order to gain Protestant converts.

Protestants generally elicited more sympathy from Catholic Messins, and their integration into Messin society was in every way more extensive than that of the Jews. So neither of these hatreds—for Jews or for Protestants—was total. They erupted or subsided among different individuals and groups at different times, according to events immediately at hand. Hopes to convert Protestants at the end of the century, and a certain under-the-surface desperation in the face of a burgeoning secular reality, fueled a period of more pointed and repressive attacks on that group. Underlying suspicion and distrust of Jews permeated this society in a more fundamental way and emerged violently toward the end of the century as well in a revival of the ritual murder myth. Returning to the comforting verities, or at least assumed verities, of the more religio-centric past, most Messins were dragged reluctantly, nonetheless, into a future many shuddered to embrace. Our main contribution has been to explore the ways the Messins themselves drew the general outlines of that future.

Assuming that the reader is persuaded that tension among Catholics, Protestants, and Jews in Metz aided the central government's plan for consolidation, shifted social allegiances, and contributed to the pluralism that ensured slow but steady secularization, we must now address several lingering questions. Did the Crown *knowingly* play upon that tension? Did the kings of France consciously use confessional conflict in Metz as a weapon with which to force local submission to their overall agenda, or did an already present hostility between different religious groups there simply coincidentally work to the Crown's advantage?

In the case of hatred of the Jews, royal government seems simply to have benefited from a long extant condition. The king and his agents did nothing to inflame anti-Jewish prejudices or, really, to quiet them either. The Crown followed roughly the same policy in the seventeenth century that it had followed in the sixteenth—namely, to extort as much as it could from the Jews without truly raising their civil status; to protect them for financial reasons from local annihilation; but beyond that to leave them subject to the local biases, which, at root, the Christian kings and their Christian ministers shared. Royal policy toward the Jews, and toward Gentiles in their dealings with Jews, was predicated only on reaping the rewards possible from allowing Jews to live in the kingdom. That policy did not seek to affect non-Jewish behavior per se. That it did so—primarily by ensuring that non-Jews would go to royal courts and to Paris for help containing Jewish commerce—was merely, from the king's point of view, a happy accident.

However royal policy toward Metz's Protestants was quite different. While far more lenient at the beginning of the seventeenth century, it was also far more ambiguous. Orders from Paris sometimes forbade Catholics from calling Protestants names in the street and at other times reduced the number of Protestant schools. The king and his agents allowed the building of new Protestant churches, and they encouraged the Catholic clergy aggressively to seek new converts, especially among Protestant children. Most important, the Crown was slower to impose its anti-Protestant measures in Metz than elsewhere in the kingdom. This arose in part from security concerns, but it also suggests that at some level and for some reason royal agents chose to allow Protestants to retain more power in Metz than elsewhere, and for a longer period. Could it have been because the continued Protestant presence there was helpful to the king's larger plan? Our research strongly suggests this. Certainly the Crown proved itself highly devious in other ways that advanced absolutism, by manipulating language and ceremony and incrementally changing courts' jurisdictions, for example, in order to install its Parlement and *bailliage* with minimal local protest.

In the end a definitive knowledge of whether or not the Crown's exploitation of local hatreds in Metz was deliberate is not even necessary. One way or another, those hatreds did help to aid Louis XIII and Louis XIV's centralization and absorption of provincial government. Whether knowing opportunists or inadvertent ones, the kings of France benefited from the fissures in Messin society, and as with all opportunists and all opportunities this involved an element of luck.

Royal good fortune was not, however, the only force at work in seventeenth-century Metz. There remains a nagging issue of timing for the most explosive displays of hatred in the city. Why did Messin prejudices erupt at this point in time particularly? Why were these hostilities intense enough at this moment to send local leaders and bourgeois to institutions that they were clearly not sure they wanted to support? Were they just obtusely oblivious, as the non-Messins of their day might have supposed if they had applied their overall view of the backward Messins to historical and political analysis? Did the Messins simply not see the connection between accepting the decision of a royal court of law and accepting the authority of its creator, or was there also some imperative need under the surface of life in Metz, a need even more urgent than that of preserving local determinism, even more far-reaching than the petty complaints against religious minorities would themselves suggest?

In the seventeenth century, Metz was a place undergoing profound changes and profound travails. Familiar troubles arose from epidemic, warfare, periodic food shortages, taxes, marauding soldiers, immigrants, emigrants, and the general vagaries of life. New concerns included changes in local government, reconsideration of national allegiance, and the determination of where exactly authority over Metz's political future lay. We have not dwelled on these general troubles in Metz, but they have come through clearly enough in the course of this discussion. By any measure, it was a volatile time in a volatile land. Looking beyond Metz to France or even Europe, one must acknowledge critical changes taking place in this era. Prominent among these was the ongoing transformation of cultural icons—crudely simplified, the gradual replacement of religious idylls with the worship of the secular state and of secular power. Such a transformation did not take place on a single day or in a single year or even in a single century. It was a process whose beginning can be traced well back into the medieval world and whose culmination, arguably, is not at all clear in our own. Still, scholars of early modern Europe almost invariably find evidence that this process of secularization gained momentum during the sixteenth and seventeenth centuries and that it became undeniably evident in the eighteenth century.[1]

How was daily life in Metz affected by such an extensive and abstract development? Did the crisis of definition that accompanied the middle period of this process contribute to greater daily tension, even in one small city on the Moselle? I would insist that it did, for in all the feuds between Messins recounted in the previous pages, one senses a frustration and a yearning for a return to the clearer religious definitions and divisions of another age. There appears among Messins of all classes, not just among its Catholic clergy, a resentment of the ambiguity that prevailed in a state vigorously promoting its secular needs, while still attached to its religious justification. Catholics in Metz strove to reassert their bonds with one another, in a world where those bonds were becoming less important than the bonds of nationality. The Counter-Reformation, like the Protestant Reformation before it, was an urgent attempt to restore religious definition and reinvigorate failing religious icons. Perhaps in their small way daily feuds with religious minorities marked for Catholics in Metz a similar unconscious attempt.

Readers will recognize in this line of analysis an echo of studies that explore the scapegoating of minority groups, especially the Jews, in other societies in other ages. What is peculiar to Metz is that the Catholic majority faced a general unspecified crisis—a crisis of definition or a crisis of *belonging* —and responded by developing a very specific conspiracy charge against the Jews, in the case of Raphael Levy. Beyond the case of Levy, Catholic leaders in Metz also confronted secularization with daily complaints against both Jews and Protestants—complaints that to them seemed pressing enough to supersede any consideration of political autonomy. They struck out ardently, almost recklessly, to define who properly did and did not belong in Metz. A Messin should, by definition, be a Catholic, these local notables maintained. He should live and work in the city and raise his family there, but within the confines of a single unified Church. Others who might reside in Metz were at best only appendages. They were not, according to these leaders, true Messins. Of course in the end the violent exclusivity of Catholic notables only ensured one real, unintended, definition of the Messin. Ignoring twentieth-century developments, from the seventeenth century forward the Messin would be a Frenchman and part of a centralized French state. This was the true immediate legacy of these religious struggles.

Raphael Levy and the incident involving him marked only the most visible and dramatic example of Catholic backlash. Our other incidents—from the assertion by Gentile butchers that Jews' hands were unfit to touch meat to charges that the Protestants were making their new temple into a fortress—emerge as similar expressions of frustration, reflecting similar desires. The king was head of the Gallican Church and hence the natural audience for complaints against religious minorities. But what the Messins did not fully realize was that he was also an agent of the very change which they sought to arrest—the replacement of religious icons with a new icon: the centralized, absolutist (and primarily secular) state.

Let us end with the example of Levy, since it is the most remarkable of our period. It demonstrates to us, in a phenomenon reminiscent of Orwell, that the Catholic majority in this society was never superficially stronger or more united than when it believed itself under attack and could collectively identify the foe. In the Levy affair, individual Messins came forward as "witnesses" and told stories, traditional and contemporary, of Jewish threats to Christianity. Local judges furthered the prosecution of the case by investigating a range of wild charges against other Jews besides the unfortunate Levy. Far more closely than in cases involving Protestants, the Catholic clergy and its laity stood together to brand Levy a threat. Finally, Parlement, the royal institution whose place in the local community had been questioned, came forward to support local prejudices and to confirm local fears. The entire process thus reconciled the city to a new political, social, and intellectual reality.

In this way, early modern Metz enacted its own true ritual murder. It is well worth repeating as we close: Raphael Levy, rather than a perpetrator, was actually the sacrifice. For like other more mundane disputes which Catholics had with Jews and with Protestants, Levy was offered up, in a struggle between religious unity and secular cohesion. It is perhaps the ultimate irony of life in seventeenth-century Metz that to the extent to which executing Raphael Levy helped to reattach Catholics to one another, it also blinded them, temporarily, to the triumph of secular authority which their collective action had abetted.

NOTE

1. The literature on secularization is obviously far too vast to explore here. However, for a particularly cogent brief discussion of the trend, in the context of religious tension in a local community, see David D. Bien, *The Calas Affair, Persecution, Toleration, and Heresy in Eighteenth-Century Toulouse* (Princeton, N.J.: Princeton University Press, 1960).

Selected Bibliography

SOURCES

Archives Départementales de la Moselle, Metz (A.D.M.)

A.D.M., 1Mi 191 (Bl), microfilm, *Rôle des habitants de la paroisse St.-Ferroy, 1621, 1637; Etat des logements (vers 1630)*.

B.H. 20585, microfilm, *(Protestants)*.

Series B (*Cours et Juridictions*): Vols. 1–13 (*Parlement de Metz*); Vols. 221–225 (*Recueil des édits, déclarations, lettres patentes et arrêts du Conseil enregistrés au Parlement de Metz*); Vol. 226 (*Table Chronologique des édits, déclarations, lettres patents et arrêts du Conseil enregistrés au Parlement de Metz*); Vols. 227, 228 (*déliberations du Parlement*); Vols. 514, 517 (*minutes des arrêts d'audience, justice civile, Parlement de Metz); Vol. 2144 (*Procédures criminelles contre les Juifs. Affaire Raphael Levy, 1669–1670*); Vols. 2564, 2565 (*bailliage de Metz*); Vol. 2572 (*jugements du bailliage*); Vol. 3031 (*minutes de l'Hôtel de Ville*).

Series D: Vols. 5, 9–11, 12 (Abjurations), 39, 66.

Series G (Clergé séculier): vols. 1263–1268 (*Maison de la Propagation de la Foi— Hommes); Vols. 1279–1281 (*Maison de la Propagation de la Foi—Femmes*); Vols. 1286, 1287 (*Abjurations*); Vols. 2081, 2089 (*Paroisse Sainte-Croix*); Vol. 2183 (Paroisse Saint–Livier); Vol. 2362 (*Paroisse Saint–Simplice*).

Series H (Clergé régulier): Vols. 4059, 4066, 4067 (*Abbaye de Sainte-Glossinde*); Vols. 4680, 4681 (*Hôpital Saint-Nicolas*).

Series J and Subseries 17J (*Documents entrés par voies extraordinaire*): 17J *Archives du Consistoire Israélite de la Moselle*, I. *Fonds de l'ancienne communauté juive de Metz, XVIe siécle–1791*. Vols. 2–5, 8, 9, 15, 17, 18, 21, 23–25, 31–33, 38.

Archives Nationales, Paris (A.N.).

Arréts du Conseil du Roi (Louis XIV): E1688, E1689, E1694, E1695, E1697, E1691, E1700.

Bibliotéque Nationale, Paris (B.N.)

Documents divers la plupart originaux, relatifs a l'histoire de la ville de Metz et du pays messin provenant des ancienne archives municipales de Metz, recueillis par Paul Ferry et par le comte Emmery, et classés chronologiquement de 410 à 1794 (Collection Emmery; Nouvelles Acquisitions Françaises [N.A.F.]):
> Vols. 22668–22671 (*ville de Metz, 1625–1700*); Vol. 22680 (*Evêché de Metz*, vol. 2); 22687 (*Diocèse de Metz*); Vols. 22700–22703 (*Protestants de Metz, 1525–1844*); Vol. 22705 (Juifs, vol. 1; 1574–1744); Vols. 22707–22709 (*sur l'establissement du Parlement de Metz*); vol. 22711 (*Ordonnances du bailliage de Metz, 1640–1758; copies manuscrites et placards imprimés*).

Manuscrits Divers annexés de la Collection August Prost (N.A.F.). Vols. 4916, 6693, 6734.

Pièces originales relatives à L'Histoire de Metz et du Pays Messin (N.A.F.). Vols. 6725–6733.

PRINTED PRIMARY SOURCES

Abrégé du Procès Fait aux Juifs de Metz. Paris: Frédéric Leonhard, 1670.

Bouteiller, E. de and Eugène Hepp, eds. *Correspondence Politique addressée au magistrat de Strasbourg par ses agents à Metz, 1594–1683*. Paris: Berger-Levrault et Cie, 1882.

Bouteiller, E. de, ed. *Journal de Jean LeCoullon*. Paris: Librairie de D. Dumoulin, 1881.

Chabert, F.-M., ed. *Recueil Journalier de ce qui s'est passé de plus mémorable dans la Cité de Metz, pays Messin et aux environs, de 1656–1674 par Joseph Ancillon*. Metz: Rousseau–Pallez, 1860.

Fontaine, James. *Memoirs of a Huguenot Family*. Ed. Ann Maury. New York: Putnam's Sons, 1852.

Josephus, Flavius. *The Works of Flavius Josephus, Complete and Unabridged*. Trans. William Whiston. Peabody, Mass.: Hendrickson, 1987.

Lowenthal, Marvin, trans. *The Memoirs of Gluckel of Hameln.* New York: Schocken Books, 1977.

Marcus, Jacob R. *The Jew in the Medieval World: A Source Book.* New York: Atheneum, 1983.

Meurisse, Martin. *L'Histoire de la Naissance, du progrès et de la décadence de l'hérésie dans la ville de Metz et dans le pays Messin.* Metz: Jean Antoine, 1642.

Tassin, Nicolas. *Les Plans et Profils de Toutes Les Principales Villes et Lieux Considerables de France.* Paris: Melchoir Tavernier, 1638.

Turgot (Intendant). *Mémoire de la généraliée de Metz, Toul et Verdun,* 1698. [For Extract concerning the Jews of Metz, see A.D.M., 8213]

Voltaire, François Marie Arouet de. *The Age of Louis XIV.* Trans. J.H. Brumfitt. New York: Washington Square Press, 1963.

Zeller, Gaston. "Documents d'Histoire Messine (XVIe Siècle)." Extrait de l'Annuaire de la Société lorraine d'histoire et d'archéologie, 1926.

SECONDARY WORKS CONSULTED

Aimond, Mgr. Charles. *Histoire des Lorrains.* Bar–le–Duc: Syndicat d'Initiative, 1960.

Anchel, Robert. *Les Juifs de France.* Paris: J.B. Janin, 1946.

Antoine, Michel et al. *Guide des Recherches dans les Fonds Judiciaires de L'Ancien Régime.* Paris: Imprimerie Nationale, 1958.

Ariès, Philippe. *Centuries of Childhood: A Social History of Family Life.* Trans. Robert Baldick. New York: Vintage Books, 1962.

Baron, Salo Wittmayer. *A Social and Religious History of the Jews.* 14 vols. New York: Columbia University Press, 1952–69.

Beik, William. *Absolutism and Society in Seventeenth-Century France.* Cambridge: Cambridge University Press, 1985.

Benedict, Philip. *Rouen during the Wars of Religion.* Cambridge: Cambridge University Press, 1981.
———."La pratique religieuse huguenote: quelques aperçus messins et comparatifs." *Protestants Messins et Mosellans, XVIe–Xxe siècles.* Eds. F.–Y. Le Moigne and Gérard Michaux. Metz: Editions Serpenoise, 1988.

Berg, Roger. "Les Grands Communautés Juives de France: Metz." *Amities France-Israel,* no. 264 (1979), 49–51.

Bien, David D. *The Calas Affair, Persecution, Toleration, and Heresy in Eighteenth-Century Toulouse.* Princeton, N.J.: Princeton University Press, 1960.

Blumenkranz, Bernhard, dir. *Histoire des Juifs en France.* Toulouse: Commission Française des Archives Juives,1972.

Bonney, Richard. *Society and Government in France under Richelieu and Mazarin, 1624–61.* Basingstoke: Macmillan, 1988.

Boswell, John. *The Kindness of Strangers.* New York: Pantheon Books, 1988.

Braudel, Fernand. *The Identity of France.* Trans. Siân Reynolds. New York: Harper and Row, 1988.

Cabourdin, Guy. "Démographie et registres de Catholicité dans une paroisse messine." *Annales de L'Est,* vol. 17, no. 4 (1965), 365–89.

———. *Terre et Hommes en Lorraine* (1550–1635). Nancy: Université de Nancy, 1977.

Cahen, Abraham. "Réglements Somptuaires de la Communauté Juive de Metz à la fin du XVIIe siècle." *Annuaire de la Société des études juives,* 1e année (1881), 77–121.

Cahen, Gilbert. "La Region Lorraine." *Histoire des Juifs en France.* Dir., Bernard Blumenkranz. Toulouse: Commission Française des Archives Juives, 1972.

Calbat, Jean–Louis. "La communauté réformée de Metz. Approche démographique." *Protestants Messins et Mosellans, XVIe–XXe siécles.* Eds. F.–Y. Le Moigne and Gérard Michaux. Metz: Editions Serpenoise, 1988.

Chartier, Roger. *A History of Private Life,* Vol. 3 *Passions of the Renaissance.* Trans. Arthur Goldhammer. Cambridge, Mass.: Belknap Press/Harvard University Press, 1989.

Chassant, Alph. *Dictionnaire des Abreviations Latine et Françaises.* Paris: Jules Martin, 1884.

———. *Paléographie des Chartes et des Manuscrits.* Paris: Auguste Aubry, 1867.

Chassin, C.–L. *La Préparation de la Guerre de Vendée 1789–1793.* 3 vols. Paris: P. DuPont, 1892.

Chazan, Robert. *Church, State, and Jew in the Middle Ages.* New York: Behrman House, 1980.

———. *Medieval Jewry in Northern France.* Baltimore, Md.: Johns Hopkins University Press, 1973.

Clément, Roger. *La Condition des Juifs de Metz dans L'Ancien Régime*. Paris: Imprimerie Henri Jouve, 1903.

Cole, C. W. *Colbert and a Century of French Mercantilism*. 1939; rpt. Hamden, Conn.: Archon Books, 1964.

Davis, Natalie Zemon. *Women on the Margins: Three Seventeenth-Century Lives*. Cambridge, Mass.: Harvard University Press, 1995.

Delcambre, E. *Le concept de la sorcellerie dans le duché de Lorraine au XVIe et au XVIIe siècles*. 3 vols. Nancy: Société d'archéologie lorraine, 1948–51.

Delumeau, Jean. *Catholicism between Luther and Voltaire*. London: Burns and Oates, 1977.

Dompnier, Bernard. *Le venin de l'hérésie: Image du protestantisme et combat catholique au XVIIe siècle*. Paris: Centurion, 1985.

Donin, Hayim Halevy. *To Be a Jew*. New York: Basic Books, 1972.

Doucet, R. *Les institutions de la France au XVIe Siècle*. 2 vols. Paris: Editions A. et J.Picard et Cie, 1948.

Dupaquier, Jacques. *La Population Française aux XVIIe et XVIIIe Siècles*. Paris: Presses Universitaires de France, 1979.

Elman, P. "The Economic Causes of the Expulsion of the Jews in 1290." *Economic History Review*, vol. 7, no. 2, 1st series (1936–37), 145–54.

Etat Général des Fonds, Les Archives Nationales. Vol. 1, *L'Ancien Régime*. Jean Favier, dir. Paris: Archives Nationales, 1978.

Gaquère, François. *Le Dialogue Irénique Bossuet-Paul Ferry à Metz*. Paris: Beauchesne, 1967.

Garrison, Janine. *L'Edit de Nantes et sa révocation*. Paris: Editions du Seuil, 1985.

Ginsburger, M. "Les Anciens Cimetières Israélites de Metz." *Revue des Etudes Juives*, vol. 52 (1906), 272–81.

———. "Les Juifs de Metz sous l'ancien régime." *Revue des Etudes juives*, vol. 50 (1905), 110–28, 237–60.

Ginzburg, Carlo. *Formaggio e i vermi*, [The cheese and the worms: The cosmos of a sixteenth–century miller]. Trans. John and Anne Tedeschi. Baltimore, Md.: Johns Hopkins Unversity Press, 1980.

Goubert, Pierre. *Beauvais et le Beauvaisis de 1600 à 1730.* Paris: Imprimerie nationale, 1960.

Harding, Robert. *Anatomy of a Power Elite.* New Haven, Conn.: Yale University Press, 1978

Hay, X. Malcolm. *Europe and the Jews.* Boston, Mass.: Beacon Press, 1950.

Hoffman, Philip T. *Church and Community in the Diocese of Lyon.* New Haven, Conn.: Yale University Press, 1984.

Houdaille, Jean. "La Population de Boulay (Moselle) avant 1850." *Population*, vol. 22, no. 6 (November to December 1967), 1055–84.

Hsia, R. Po–chia. *The Myth of Ritual Murder.* New Haven, Conn.: Yale University Press, 1988.
———. *Trent 1475: stories of a ritual murder trial.* New Haven, Conn.: Yale University Press, 1992.

Hyman, Paula, and Steven M. Cohen, eds. *The Jewish Family: Myths and Reality.*New York: Holmes and Meier, 1986.

Jacobs, Joseph. *The Jews of Angevin England.* New York: Putnam, 1893.

Jordan, William C. "Problems of the Meat Market of Béziers, 1240–1247." *Revue des Etudes juives*, vol. 135 (1976), 31–49.

Kahn, Daniel. "Bossuet et les Juifs de Metz." *La Revue Juive de Lorraine*, vol. 7, no. 77 (1931), 239–45.

Kaiser, J. B. "Martin Meurisse O.F.M., évêque de Madaure, suffragant de Metz (1584–1644)." *Annuaire de la Société d'Histoire et d'Archéologle de la Lorraine*, vol. 32, no. 1, (1923), 1–119.

Kaufmann, David. "Extraits de l'ancien livre de la communauté (israélite) de Metz (XVIIe–XVIIIe S)." *Revue des Etudes juives*, vol. 19 (1889).

———. "R. Joseph Aschkenaz, premier rabbin de Metz." *Revue des Etudes juives*, vol. 22 (1891), 93–103.

Kelly, Donald R. *The Beginning of Ideology.* London: Cambridge University Press, 1981.

Kettering, Sharon. *Judicial Politics and Urban Revolt in Seventeenth-Century France.* Princeton, N.J.: Princeton University Press, 1978.

Ladurie, Emmanuel LeRoy. *The Peasants of Languedoc.* Chicago: University of Illinois

Press, 1974.

Langmuir, Gavin. *History, Religion and Antisemitism*. Berkeley: University of California Press, 1990.

―――. *Toward a Definition of Antisemitism*. Berkeley: University of California Press, 1990.

Laperche-Fournel, Marie-José. *La Population du Duché de Lorraine de 1580 à 1720*. Nancy: Presses Universitaires de Nancy, 1985.

Le Moigne, François-Yves, dir. *Histoire de Metz*. Toulouse: Privat, 1986.

Le Moigne, François-Yves, and Gérard Michaux, eds. *Protestants Messins et Mosellans, XVIe–XXe siècles*. Metz: Editions Serpenoise, 1988.

Lévi, I. "Les Juifs d'Alsace au XVIIe siècle." *Revue des Etudes juives*, vol. 38, no. 76 (1899), 312-14.

Livet, Georges. *L'Intendance d'Alsace sous Louis XIV*. Paris: Société d'Edition Les Belles Lettres, 1956.

―――. "Louis XIV et les Provinces conquises." *Seventeenth Century*, vol. 22 (1952), 481–507.

Lublinskaya, A. D. *French Absolutism the crucial phase, 1620–1629*. Trans. Brian Pearce. Cambridge: Cambridge University Press, 1968.

Malino, Frances. *The Sephardic Jews of Bordeaux*. Tuscaloosa: University of Alabama Press, 1978.

Malvezin, Théophile. *Histoire des Juifs à Bordeaux*. Marseille: Lafitte, 1976.

Martin, Jean-Clément. *La Vendée et la France*. Paris, 1987.

Mazauric, R. *Le pasteur Paul Ferry*. Metz: Marius Mutelet, 1964.

Mead, Sidney E. *The Lively Experiment*. New York: Harper and Row, 1963.

Meyer, Pierre–André. *La communauté juive de Metz au XVIIIe siècle, histoire et démographie*. Nancy: Presses Universitaires de Nancy, 1993.

―――. "Un cas d'accusation de meutre rituel à Metz au XVIIe siècle." *Archives Juives*, vol. 25, nos. 3-4 (1989), 62-64.

Michel, Emmanuel. *Biographie du Parlement de Metz*. Metz: Chez Nouvian, 1853.

———. *Histoire du Parlement de Metz*. Paris: J. Techener, 1845.

Miller, Perry. "The Location of American Religious Freedom." *Religion and Freedom of Thought*. Ed. P. Miller. Garden City, N.Y.: Doubleday, 1954.

Morembert, Henri Tribout de. *La Réforme à Metz*. 2 vols. Nancy: Annales de L'Est (Université de Nancy), 1969–71.

Morembert, Henri Tribout de., dir./ed., *Le Diocèse de Metz*. Paris: Letouzey et Ané, 1970.

———. "Les Médecins de la Communauté Juive de Metz, 1610–1789." *Rencontre Chrétiens et Juifs*, [vol. no. not available], no. 33, (1973), 188–98.

Mousnier, Roland. *The Institutions of France under the Absolute Monarchy, 1598– 1789*. Trans. Brian Pearce. Chicago: University of Chicago Press, 1979.

———. *Social Hierarchies, 1450 to the Present*. London: Croom Helm, 1973.

Muchembled, Robert. "Lay Judges and the Acculturation of the Masses." *Religion and Society in Early Modern Europe, 1500–1800*. Ed. Kaspar von Greyertz. London: George Allen and Unwin, 1984.

———. *Popular Culture and Elite Culture in France, 1400–1750*. Trans. Lydia Cochrane. Baton Rouge: Louisiana State University Press, 1985.

Netter, Nathan. *Vingt Siècles d'Histoire d'une Communauté juive*. Paris: Librairie Lipschutz, 1938.

Oberman, Heiko. *The Roots of Anti–Semitism in the Age of Renaissance and Reformation*. Trans. James I. Porter. Philadelphia: Fortress Press, 1981.

Ozment, Steven. *Flesh and Spirit: Private Life in Early Modern Germany*. New York: Viking, 1999.

———. *When Fathers Ruled: Family Life in Reformation Europe*. Cambridge, Mass.: Harvard University Press, 1983.

Parker, David. "The Huguenots in seventeenth–century France." *Minorities in History*. Ed. A.C. Hepburn. London: Edward Arnold, 1978.

Parker, Geoffrey and Lesley M. Smith, eds. *The General Crisis of the Seventeenth Century*. London: Routledge and Kegan Paul, 1978.

Parkes, James. *The Jew in the Medieval Community*. New York: Hermon Press, 1976.

Pierson, Michel. "Les Juifs en Lorraine dans les deux siècles precedant la Révolution."

Mémoire pour le D.E.S. de Droit Romain: 20 mai 1953; Université de Nancy, Faculté de Droit.

Poliakov, L. *Histoire de l'antisémitisme*. Paris: Calmann Lévy, 1955–77.

Prost, Auguste. *Les Institutions Judiciaires dans la Cité de Metz*. Nancy: Berger-Levrault et Cie,1893.

Reinach, Joseph. *Raphael Levy, Une Erreur Judiciaire sous Louis XIV*. Paris: Librairie Ch. Delagrave, 1898.

Rigault, Jean. "La fortune d'un protestant messin du XVIIe siècle; Philippe de Vigneulles(vers 1560–1634)." *Annales de L'Est*, 5e Série, 2e Année, no. 2 (1951), 79–88.

———. "La Population de Metz au XVIIe siècle; quelques problèmes de démographie." *Annales de L 'Est*, 5e Série, 2e Année, no.4 (1951), 307–15.

Roth, Cecil. *A History of the Jews in England*. 3d ed. Oxford: Clarendon Press, 1964.

———. *A History of the Marranos*. New York: Jewish Publication Society of America, 1959.

Roth, Cecil. ed. *The Ritual Murder Libel and the Jew*. London: Woburn Press, 1935.

Sahlins, Peter. "Natural Frontiers Revisited: France's Boundaries since the Seventeenth Century." *American Historical Review* vol. 95, no. 5 (1990), 1423–51.

Schama, Simon. *Citizens*. New York: Knopf, 1989.

Schneider, Jean. *Histoire de Lorraine*. Paris: Presses Universitaires de France, 1951.

Schwarzfuchs, Simon, ed. *Les Juifs de France*. Paris: A. Michel, 1975.

Scoville, W. *The Persecution of the Huguenots and French Economic Development, 1680–1720*. Berkeley: University of California Press, 1960.

Sedgewick, A. *Jansenism in Seventeenth-Century France: Voices from the Wilderness*. Charlottesville: University Press of Virginia, 1977.

Stokes, Anson Phelps. *Church and State in the United States*. New York: Harper, 1950.

Stone, Lawrence. *The Family, Sex, and Marriage in England, 1500–1800*. New York: Harper and Row, 1977.

Tabouillot, Dom Nicolas, and Jean François. *Histoire générale de Metz par des religieux benedictins*. 6 vols. Metz: C. Lamort, 1767–90.

Tapié, Victor-L. *France in the Age of Louis XIII and Richelieu*. Trans. D. McN. Lockie. Cambridge: Cambridge University Press, 1974.

Taveneaux, R. *Le Catholicisme dans La France Classique, 1610–1715*. Paris: Société d'Edition d'Enseignement Supérieur, 1980.

———. *Le jansénisme en Lorraine, 1640–1789*. Paris: Librairie Philosophique J. Vrin, 1960.

Thirion, Maurice. *Etude sur l'Histoire du Protestantisme à Metz et dans le pays messin*. Nancy: Imprimerie F. Collin, 1884.

Tilly, Charles. *The Vendée*. Cambridge, Mass.: Harvard University Press, 1976.

Trachtenberg, Joshua. *The Devil and the Jews*. New York: Harper and Row, 1966.

Vanson, L. "Imposition sur les juifs en Lorraine dans l'Ancien Régime." *Revue juive de Lorraine*, [vol. no. not available], (1933), 195–207, 229–41.

Weber, Eugene. "Reflections on the Jews in France." *The Jews in Modern France*. Ed. Frances Malino and Bernard Wasserstein. Hanover,N.H.: University Press of New England, 1985.

Wedgewood, C. V. *The Thirty Years War*. London: J. Cape, 1938.

Wirth, Jean. "Against the Acculturation Thesis." *Religion and Society in Early Modern Europe, 1500–1800*. Ed. Kaspar von Greyertz. London: George Allen and Unwin, 1984.

Yerushalmi, Yosef Hayim. *Assimilation and Racial anti–Semitism: The Iberian and the German models*. New York: Leo Baeck Institute, 1982.

———. *The re-education of Marranos in the Seventeenth Century*. Cincinnati, Ohio: University of Cincinnati, 1980.

Zeller, Gaston. *La Réunion de Metz à la France*. 2 vols. Paris: Société d'Edition: Les Belles Lettres, 1926.

Index

About the Author

PATRICIA BEHRE MISKIMIN is Associate Professor of History at Fairfield University in Fairfield, Connecticut, and a Visiting Research Fellow at Yale University. Her research in early modern French history has appeared in journals and a collection of essays.

Recent Titles in
Contributions to the Study of World History